THE LAST AMERICAN IN DAMASCUS

AN AUTOBIOGRAPHY

THOMAS L WEBBER

INDIA · SINGAPORE · MALAYSIA

Notion Press

Old No. 38, New No. 6
McNichols Road, Chetpet
Chennai - 600 031

First Published by Notion Press 2020
Copyright © Thomas L Webber 2020
All Rights Reserved.

ISBN
Domestic 978-1-64760-655-8
International 978-1-64850-676-5

Thomas L Webber has written two previous books while living in California. He moved to Damascus in 1975, and while residing in Damascus for part of those 44 years, he has experienced many interesting, exciting, and unusual incidents.

Throughout his life, he has been a teacher, teaching a variety of subjects and grade levels. However, his main professional love has been in the field of business development, which took him to many countries. He has traveled, not only for business but also for pleasure and has gained many friends and experiences throughout the world.

At present, he lives with his Palestinian/Syrian wife in Damascus, Syria.

For my wife Salma…and my sister Anita
Both of whom had never lost faith in my abilities to succeed
Plus my many Friends and Students…over the years.

Contents

Prologue

As the famous writer and lecturer, Helen Keller once wrote: *"Life is a daring adventure or it is nothing at all."*

In one's lifetime, one may experience a number of: "Life-Changing Experiences or Adventures." In my own lifetime, I have experienced a profuse number and many were truly amazing life-changing experiences; in fact, so many, that I have decided to share them with the world by writing this book.

In my humble opinion, my greatest life-changing adventure was my decision to move from California to Damascus, Syria in 1975. This choice altered my life to the tenth degree and is well-documented within the chapters of this book.

Other very important life-changing experiences took place when I decided to leave dental school and pursue other completely different fields of work. Other events and adventures included being shot at while visiting Beirut during the country's civil war; to my encountering several car bombs while living and working in Damascus. There was also a harrowing experience in Syria while I outmaneuvered and outraced the then Syrian President's brother and his team of security guards in a long-distance car drama. Another major life-altering experience was when I tried living in America and found that American was no longer the country that I could work and live in peace and harmony.

Within this book, I will try to give you, the reader, a glimpse of the other important life-changing encounters.

I first thought about writing my memoirs during the summer of 2008 on my annual holiday to America. I was visiting my sister, and one evening, Diana showed me her short story about her life with her husband for 53 years. It was titled: *Our Journey Together.*

We talked well past midnight about her short story that she had just completed. She had given me a copy, and then that night, I lay in bed with her short story. I found myself fixated and completely engulfed with all their memories that she had related to within those pages.

The next morning I asked her for a copy to take with me. Her story has been with me ever since, and that is when I began thinking about writing my book.

Once I completed the general outline of my book, I soon realized that I did indeed live a very diverse and interesting life that most people would only dream of or had seen in an action movie. Since a young child, I have always loved traveling, and this-in-itself has opened my eyes to the many extremely fascinating countries which I have visited. Domestically, I have traveled to every state in our glorious country. Many of my travel adventures have been harrowing yet extremely interesting.

I soon realized that I needed a title for my original manuscript. Many titles came to mind, but the one that made sense to me was simply: Tommy, Tom, and Thomas. I felt that it would reflect my childhood as I was always called Tommy! In high school and college that changed to Tom and much later on in life as I became older and wiser, my name was gradually replaced by Thomas! I worked on and off with this draft copy, sometimes adding a few pages at one sitting and often not working on it for months on end. That title and my work continued for almost eight full years.

Then soon after my "final retirement" in the spring of 2010 from Qatar, I moved back to Damascus. Prior to my retirement, our house in Damascus was always a place for me to stay only for short periods of time as I was always working in another Middle Eastern country, and

I simply considered myself a tourist in this great city of Damascus. In 2010 I quickly rediscovered the Damascus of old. I immediately began touring the Syrian countryside and I discovered many small towns and villages in my six months of travels and once again, these travels reinforced my love and commitment for this beautiful country, but more importantly, I rediscovered the warmth; kindness and friendly nature of the Syrian people.

Unfortunately, this initial winery project was placed on hold as the Syrian Civil War commenced a short while later in the small Syrian city called Dara. In my humble opinion, this dreadful war had only one personal and positive outcome, and that was simply the fact that many western news agencies were told about this 'American living in Damascus' throughout the civil war and they wanted to conduct multiple interviews with this 'crazy' American. I still recall the first international news agency interview, it was with two AP (Associated Press) correspondents based in Beirut and they were the ones that originated the term: "The Last American in Damascus."

Once that interview was produced and syndicated to over 230 TV stations around the world, I quickly found out that I was not the only 'true' American citizen living in Damascus at this time. A girl living in Iowa had seen my AP TV interview titled: 'The Last American in Damascus' and she contacted the local TV station and told them that her grandmother was indeed a true American born citizen and living in Damascus! The stateside TV station management contacted the AP affiliate in Beirut and they, in turn, sent me the contact information for "Elaine." A short time later, I met with Elaine in Damascus and found out that in addition to her, there were two other American women living in Damascus! Since that time, I immediately changed the title of all subsequent and future interviews to: "The Last American 'Male' in Damascus."

I then felt that I should use, as my new book title, that phrase: 'The Last American in Damascus' as it would encompass all my life's adventures much more closely and completely than the original title: Tommy; Tom and Thomas.

I trust you will enjoy the many adventures of *The Last American in Damascus.*

I Never Knew My Life Would Change Forever By Knocking on That Door

I never thought by knocking on the door and entering that interview, my life would change forever!

I kept putting off this interview for months and months because: I was extremely happy as I had just completed my first book; I was in the middle of writing my second book; I was also living on a houseboat on San Francisco Bay and was enjoying my new found freedoms as a free-spirited and unrestrained bachelor. Why in the world would I want to change that?

To complete the editing of my first book for the San Diego County School System, I would drive from San Francisco down to Rancho Bernardo to meet with my editor. He was retired from the San Diego County School District but was doing some freelance work for the district. We would usually meet for an hour or so to basically go over my manuscript and then we would simply relax and enjoy a nice bottle or two of a discerning California wine. He had an extensive collection of great wines in his large wine cellar in his home and was quite the connoisseur of fine wines. I too enjoyed wine, but I was not the expert that he was. We would both wind up sitting and drinking a sizable quantity of great tasting wines. During these wine consuming sessions, he asked me about my teaching experience and if I would ever entertain the idea of returning back to the classroom after my current sabbatical. I kept insisting on telling him that I was quite happy living and writing on my houseboat and that I could not foresee my return to the classroom in the near or distant future. Plus, I was also 60% completed with my second book and that subject was about the bicycle trails of San Diego County. So why would I entertain the idea of returning to a classroom of sometimes rowdy and unruly teenagers?

He then told me that he had a very good friend that was looking for a science teacher in some international school. "Thomas, you were a science teacher, right?" Yes, I told him, but only for one year, and that first year was when I was voted: Teacher of the Year. It was also the time that the San Diego County Schools approached me to write about my teaching experiences and with special emphasis on my forty plus student field trips, which were completed in that first year of teaching! They saw a link between a student's experience of going on interesting field trips to their selection of his or her future job or occupation.

A couple of weeks later, on one of my last trips down to Rancho Bernardo, he came back to the subject of me teaching in this international school, but now his friend was desperate in finding a science teacher as he was leaving San Diego in a matter of weeks.

So finally, after months of prodding by my first books' editor, I finally agreed to meet with his friend! He told me only three things about this friend: first, his name was: Bob McGetchin; second, he was an ex-lifeguard from Mission Beach and third, he was currently the principal of some international school.

I also knew he was looking for a Science Instructor in some far away school to teach science and to help set up that school's science Department! I discovered that I would be competing against nine other more experienced Science Teachers and a few unemployed engineers. Nevertheless, I said, "What the heck I will meet him." I never seriously considered that I would land that job, as I only had one year of teaching experience and was up against many more qualified candidates than me.

So out of pure curiosity and inquisitiveness, I made an appointment to meet Mr. Bob!

I found the temporary office he was using inside the main building of the San Diego County School District and slowly approached the door. I knocked on the door and then entered and introduced myself. Immediately, I liked this guy, I don't know why or what it was, but there was a certain connection between us. The interview continued and went extremely well, yet I sensed he knew that I really did not want to change my current situation nor lifestyle as I was quite aloof in my answers and in my attitude. He started to describe the city of Damascus as well as the country and I became more and more interested. I guess he sensed my latent interest and after about an hour, we concluded the interview and he told me: "Thomas, I really want you to be my Science Instructor at the Damascus Community School." You will really enjoy the school, the students and especially the city of Damascus. I was really taken aback, surprised and quite bewildered. How could I have been selected over all the more qualified candidates? Nevertheless, I told him that I would need one or two days to decide, but then he became emphatic that I should make my decision on the spot, as he was leaving San Diego and going back to Damascus in the next few days!

Without further hesitation, I said: "Yes!" To this day, I do not know why I accepted on the spot as up until then I thought I had always been a very rational person and I was one to sit and contemplate any major decision!

We shook hands, and he said my contract would be ready to sign the next morning. He then asked if I had a valid US passport, and I said yes, but I must check to see when it expires. He asked me to please bring it with me in the morning so he would arrange my Syrian Visa. I remembered that my passport was at my bank in my safe deposit box here in San Diego. He said that in the morning he would also let me know about the airline tickets, the visa requirements, any required vaccinations, the housing accommodations in Damascus, etc.

From his temporary office within the San Diego Country School District offices when I was leaving the building, I must admit I was quite 'light-headed'...and thought to myself: "What have I done? What did I get myself into?"

I slowly walked out of the building and got into my car and very leisurely drove out of the parking lot. "What was I to do? Had I made a decision in haste that I would regret for the rest of my life?"

While driving, I remembered the time I received my Lifetime California Teaching Certification, and then the only thought that crossed my mind was about teaching and working in a California school. It never ever entered my mind that I would be teaching in a school somewhere overseas!

Why would I want to change my current lifestyle to go to some godforsaken country called Syria? And where was this Damascus, the capital of Syria?

As I slowly drove up to Park Boulevard towards El Cajon Boulevard, I decided to stop by a San Diego Public Library. I still remember this very small library, I found a parking space and I gradually got out of my old red, now pink, 1959 Volvo PV-544. I slowly entered the main door of this library and asked the librarian for the location of the libraries' maps or World Atlas. She pointed over to one corner. I found a very large World Atlas and started looking...first the Middle East; then: Syria and then: Damascus. Humm not too bad as Damascus was near the Mediterranean Sea between some country called Lebanon. That's nice...

Let's see now, I had traveled a few years ago to that region, and that was when I was free camping in a VW Camper in Istanbul. We also crossed the Bosphorus Strait on a car ferry as there were no bridges connecting Istanbul Europe to Istanbul Asia. We did spend a few days on the Asian side and that was only to say and lay claim that I had been to Asia!

Now this city called Damascus was in a large country called Syria directly below Turkey, and to the East, it was Iraq. Let's see directly below Syria was Jordan. Wait a minute...what was this? Near the southern border of Syria was...Israel! Really? Wasn't there recently a major war between these countries? I thought that Israel is America's closest 'friend' a strong ally and they are the 'only democracy' in the entire Middle East? Aren't these Arab countries both Americas and Israel's sworn 'enemies'? What have I gotten myself into?

Nevertheless, I agreed with Mr. Bob that I would teach science in this small school in Damascus, and my word is my word and there was no turning back.

I then left the public library, and I thought it would be best to inform my ex-wife and my son Thomas II of my major and foremost decision. It would, of course, affect both of them! Their apartment was very close, so I simply stopped by to announce my decision. I was lucky as they were both at home and when I mentioned Syria, my ex-wife was in a momentary state of shock! Her first thoughts were that it was not fair to Thomas to be without his father for such a long period as we both understood that my only chance of seeing Thomas would be during the summer holiday months. I then promised that I would find time to be with Thomas before I flew off to the Middle East.

Of course, the next person I wanted to see was my sister, Anita, who was living up in Costa Mesa in Orange County. So I decided to drive up there to talk with Anita and her family in a calm and composed manner and to spend the night with them. By the time I arrived at their house, it was time for dinner. So around the dinner table was when I opened the subject of my new job in an unknown and foreign country! My sister Anita took the news very well as she knew that I was the most adventurists in the family, and this would simply be another chapter in my life story. Bill, my brother-in-law, was very well-informed about current events and had his concerns that it may not be that safe for an American working and living in a potentially hostile environment. I remember him saying: "Tom, don't forget that America has always been backing the state of Israel so there may be some antagonistic feelings and negative sentiments against Americans in Syria." I told Bill that the principal had mentioned the school was supported by the US Embassy in Damascus and this afforded us many advantages with this association with the US State Department.

After dinner, Anita suggested that we call my mom and dad to inform them of my surprising and startling news. We called and of course, my mom was out that night playing BINGO, so I told my dad of my decision. He asked me when I was planning to start work and the only point he made was to ask me to make sure I stop by in Western New York and see my mom. I promised I would.

Later that evening, Anita and I were talking, and she mentioned that they had arranged to go to the June Lake Camping grounds to camp during their summer vacation and asked if I would like to join them! At first, I said I don't think I would have the time and then I remembered my talk earlier with Diana and Thomas. I then thought I must arrange the time as this would be a great way to spend quality time together prior to my departure and a really good way to say goodbye to my son.

I spent that night at my sister's home, and I couldn't believe that I slept amazingly well. The next morning, I drove back down to San Diego to accomplish five important items that day in San Diego.

First, I needed to collect my US passport from my bank's safe deposit box to make sure that it was still valid.

Second: I wanted to sign and finalize my contract. Plus, I wanted to tell Mr. Bob that concerning the flight tickets to let me purchase them and then simply have the school reimburse me once I arrived in Damascus. Like last night, I started thinking about the airline tickets and whether I would be able to see my mom and dad. Plus, on my way to the Middle East, I could stop in Europe and do some touring as well.

Third, to see Thomas and Diana and to make sure she would accept the idea that I would be taking Thomas camping in the High Sierra Nevada Mountains that next week.

Fourth, to see Jerry Johnson, a very good friend, and to tell him of my future work plans and see if he would be able to store many of my personal effects in his garage that I would not be taking to Damascus.

And finally to see the editor of my book and inform him of my acceptance of this teaching job that he had originally told me about, and to see how much more time may be needed to complete the editing of the final manuscript.

I must admit that I successfully accomplished all five items, commencing with the retrieval of my US passport. It was my second passport and was issued at the US Embassy in London in February of 1972. I was living in Europe at the time during which my first US passport had expired. So this second large green tourist passport was valid till February 1977. Enough time, I thought, to teach for one year in Damascus and return back to the States using this same passport.

When I arrived at the San Diego County Schools building to see the principal Mr. Bob, he had everything ready for me. This was really encouraging for me as he appeared to be very organized and well prepared. I signed the contract, and he actually had a secretary take a photo of the two of us. I gave him my valid passport, and he said that they will mail it to Washington and asked me where I wanted it returned. I felt the best address would not be my houseboat in San Francisco but to my sister's home in Orange Country. We discussed my one-way air ticket to Damascus and he agreed that if I paid for the tickets, I should save the receipts so I could be reimbursed once I arrived in Damascus. He fully understood my desire to see my parents and family in Western New York. He said that there were no vaccinations required to enter Syria which was a blessing as I did not want to add that to my list of things to complete prior to my eventual departure. Finally, he told me that I would be sharing a large three-bedroom apartment, walking distance to school, with the Social Studies teacher. His name was Steve; he was from Texas and I would like him because Steve really enjoyed his first year of teaching at the school and loved living in Syria. Finally, he asked me to send him a letter to the school with the flight details of my arrival, so they would have someone there to pick me up and to take me directly to the apartment. It was neat as all mail would be sent first to the State Department in Washington and would be delivered via the State Departments Diplomatic Pouch. I would later find out that this special mail service was a great advantage in receiving and sending mail; letters and packages. When I finally completed all tasks, Bob and I simply shook hands and he said: "I will see you next in Damascus." These events all took place in July 1975.

My next stop on this very important day was to see Thomas and his mom. I really wanted Thomas to join me on this special camping expedition to June Lake in the Sierra Nevada Mountains of North-Eastern California. Luckily, they were both at home and they greeted me warmly. I explained my morning meeting with the principal and that our communication would be very easy because of the affiliation of the school with the US State Department and our embassy in Damascus. I would send them all the mailing details once I arrived in Damascus. Then I mentioned about the camping trip with Anita and Bill that next week and Thomas was, of course, very, very excited about the idea as well as his mother. She agreed that this would be a great way to spend some precious time together prior to my final departure. Little did we know then about the forthcoming bizarre and strange encounter that Thomas and I would experience during this five-day camping trip.

That afternoon we all went out to lunch, and then we went to a sports store and bought Thomas a great pair of hiking boots and other hiking equipment. We had also arranged that Diane would drive Thomas to my sister's house on the morning of our travel to the campsite.

I then drove over to La Mesa to visit Jerry Johnson and to update him on my camping plans. He was very helpful and said to feel free and bring whatever I wanted, and they will find room in his already overcrowded garage. Jerry was always very optimistic even with the decision that would take me out of California for a year or so. At that time, we never knew or thought that I would never reside in sunny California.

I had one last stop to make before my return to San Francisco and that was to consult with the editor of my first book and thank him for suggesting that I meet with his friend, Bob. Rancho Bernardo was just 32 km north of downtown San Diego, so it was a short drive. When he came to the door, I knew immediately that he and Bob McGetchin had been talking as he had a smile from ear-to-ear. I found out that Bob had called him and thanked him for sending me to the interview.

We had a very productive meeting in which he told me that he had completed the editing. All that was needed is for him to send the full manuscript to the San Diego County School District; they would approve the book and then forward the final payment to my bank. He wanted me to stay and enjoy one more bottle of his precious wine, but I declined as I wanted to head back to my houseboat in the San Francisco area. He bid me a warm farewell and wished me a successful year teaching at the Damascus Community School. Unfortunately, I never saw him again, which I deeply regret, as if it wasn't for his perseverance and tenacity I would have never known or traveled to this beautiful country called: Syria.

My ride home to San Francisco seemed to take forever, as it was very late by the time I left San Diego County. During the drive, my mind was setting "action items" to complete prior to my departure from the States. At this time, the most important action was: what I was going to do with my houseboat?

Chapter Two

From a Houseboat in San Francisco to a New Life in Damascus

I arrived home to my houseboat in the San Francisco Bay Area from the most life-altering three days of my entire life.

I entered the marina well after 3:00 a.m., and Ginger, my girlfriend, was sound asleep. I was trying to make as little noise as possible, but my arrival woke her from her sleep. She sat up in bed and I could tell immediately that she was very, very upset. Ginger had always been a very calm and relaxed person, but unexpectantly being woken at three in the morning, she was very disturbed. "Why didn't you call me? I was worried sick that something had happened to you!"

I tried to calm her by saying that I did try to call her twice at her work with no luck. We must remember that in 1975 there were no mobile phones or the internet, so all communications were completed by 'landlines'. I had unsuccessfully called her office number twice while I was in San Diego.

I told Ginger that a lot of things happened while I was in San Diego, and I would tell her about them in the morning. She wanted to talk right away, but I wanted to sleep as it was getting close to four! She saw that I was exhausted and so she reluctantly agreed and didn't push the subject any longer. I then simply brushed my teeth and went to bed, and I slept within seconds on my head touching my pillow.

Ginger and I had met while I was earning my California Lifetime Teaching Certification from San Diego State University at the beginning of September 1972. I had to complete certain courses, and one elective was to teach in a San Diego school as a student-teacher.

She was a special education instructor for hearing impaired students and I was to teach General Science to her 6th grade students for a full semester. I was just divorced and Ginger and I began dating and soon thereafter became romantically involved. Ginger was also instrumental in my writing of what was going to become my second book. We both enjoyed bike riding and had a mutual interest in riding each weekend to a new and interesting San Diego County destination. She knew that I enjoyed these one, two or three-day excursions around San Diego and she insisted that I should take notes and photos to document each journey. These notes became very useful as a year and a half later, I had completed my first book and then started my second book, which was titled: '*Bicycle Trails of San Diego County*'.

Upon completing my one year of student teaching and taking other teacher training classes, I received my Lifetime California Teaching Certification from San Diego State University in May of 1973. I then went searching for a suitable and well-paying teaching position, while Ginger wanted me to teach in a San Diego school. Unfortunately for her, I had secured my first teaching job at Rancho San Joaquin Middle School in Irvine, California.

It was very difficult for us to see each as I was living in Orange County, which was about an hour and a half drive north from her apartment in San Diego. In addition, I was working part-time as a waiter each weekend in a five-star restaurant in Newport Beach. So invariably, we began drifted apart during my first year of teaching. We did stay in sporadic contact, but our relationship was not as strong as when I was living in San Diego.

After successfully completing my first year at Rancho San Joaquin Middle School in 1974, I had decided to take a one-year sabbatical, but most importantly, I needed time to complete the two books that I began writing earlier and to leave Orange County to get a new vision of life.

Ginger had informed me that she had left her special education teaching position in San Diego and was now working and living in

Redwood City, a city south of San Francisco at Marine World/Africa USA as the director of student tours. After I had just completed my first year of teaching in Irvine, I talked to Ginger, and she suggested that I came up to the Bay Area to scout for a potential location to work on my two books. I never forgot how helpful Ginger was in persuading me to take photos and notes during our many weekend biking excursions around San Diego County. I also knew that she could be a major contributor to my second book.

Plus, I had always loved San Francisco on my many previous trips yet, I had never lived there. So why not travel up there for a long weekend, first to see Ginger and then to investigate if that area would be more conducive in order for me to complete my books.

Shortly thereafter, I decided to drive up to the Bay Area for a long weekend to meet Ginger and to explore the possibility of relocating to the area.

From Orange County, you had two options in driving to San Francisco. If you were in a hurry, you would take Interstate 5, which wasn't the most scenic, but the fastest. The other choice was to take California Highway One along the beautiful seacoast of Central California. My choice was simple: being a well-seasoned traveler, I selected the slower, more scenic Pacific Coast Highway! I truly felt that this highway may be the most beautiful highway in all of America. It is simply breathtaking and offers one a view of nature at its fullest!

I located Ginger's apartment with ease, and we enjoyed a nice late dinner in the area. Our relationship was rekindled and we discovered that it was as strong as it used to be in those great days and nights in San Diego.

The next morning we decided that we would become: 'tourists' and discover San Francisco as a sightseer. Our goal, during this first long weekend, was to discover the city of San Francisco and the surrounding Bay Area. After our first morning of touring the city, we drove to a small city called Sausalito across the Golden Gate Bridge to have lunch at one of their famous seafood restaurants along their main marina and corniche. We had a great window table, and during lunch, I was observing the many people going in and out of the houseboats docked in the marina. After lunch, I asked Ginger if she'd like to go for a walk along the docks and look at those houseboats. I was intrigued as these houseboats were considered 'the world's largest waterbeds' and maybe great to experience and possibly to live in. We talked to a couple of owners and they were very positive about their experiences. I thought that living on a houseboat would really be a different experience which I may never have the opportunity to enjoy again. There were one or two houseboats that had a *for sale* sign so we wrote down the phone numbers and had planned to call them later that evening. Once we left the marina, we drove a bit further north and spotted two additional marinas that had an even larger number of houseboats. We decided to continue our search the next morning as it was getting late and I was a bit tired from my drive a day before from Orange County. That evening at Ginger's apartment we only talked about one thing and that was the idea of living on a houseboat, both the positives and the negatives. I then constructed my renowned "Benjamin Franklin Table" and we soon found that there were many more positive reasons than negative. I decided that we should both 'sleep-on-the-subject' and discuss all the options the next morning. When I woke up the next morning, I looked at Ginger and said: "Let's do it!" It should be a very new and relaxing way to live and a tranquil environment for me to begin completing my two books. We had a light breakfast and then we headed back across the Golden Gate Bridge to Sausalito in the Northern Bay Area of San Francisco. I decided that we should start at the first marina we had visited the day before after lunch. The previous night I tried calling the two numbers to no avail. I felt that it would be best to go first to the marina's management office and get all the details as to which houseboats were for sale if they knew the selling price and if they could give us an idea of the facilities, services, and the monthly berthing fees. Unfortunately, both the owners of the houseboats for sale were traveling, and the management office did not know their asking prices. He gave us a detailed list of the marina monthly fees and the charges for a typical length houseboat in Sausalito Marina. We were taken back as it was very, very expensive in our humble opinions. We thanked him and decided to go to the next marina that was less opulent and hopefully less expensive.

In the next two marinas, we found four houseboats for sale, and we really liked two of the four. Ginger and I went back and forth between the two and then I finally decided on the smaller one of the two. I asked for his price and then we negotiated and agreed on a reasonable price. I gave the owner a deposit and said to hold the houseboat until we found another marina which was less costly. These two marinas were less expensive for their monthly fees than the first in Sausalito, but still, they were too expensive. The owner tried to explain the reasons for their high rentals and suggested that we look at the marinas east and south of San Francisco Bay as they had a totally different pricing system mainly due to their different city municipality rules and regulations.

It was early, and we were not discouraged so we decided to search the east side of San Francisco Bay for another marina to berth my new home. We drove back over the Golden Gate Bridge into the city to take the Oakland Bay Bridge on to Oakland and the eastern suburbs. There we checked the available facilities and services rendered in two different marinas in Oakland and Alameda and we did find the prices much lower than the three northern marinas. However, we found that we did not like the mediocre environment of these marinas and the fact of the great distance from Ginger's workplace.

We then drove down the east shore of the San Francisco Bay to the San Mateo-Hayward Bridge, which connected the eastern shore communities to the western shore communities. This was also the area where Ginger was currently living and working and was called Redwood Shores of Redwood City.

We were then told about a
funky marina just south of the San
Francisco International Airport in
Redwood City called Pete's Harbor.
It was getting late yet, we said to
each other: let's try to find this
cool and trendy place! There was
a very small exit just off California

Pete's Harbor in Redwood City

Highway #101 in Redwood City,
and we took that dirt road towards the South San Francisco Bay. This
road was called: Uccelli Boulevard, which we found out later, was named
after Pete Uccelli the owner of Pete's Harbor. This guy Pete had placed
a large sign along the side of this dirt road stating: "You are now leaving
the United States of America and entering Pete's Harbor, Italy." Is this
guy for real? Is this place for real? We parked the car and asked the
first person we saw if either the owner or the manager was around. He
replied in a strong Italian accent: Yes, my name is Pete and I am the
owner of Pete's Harbor. I explained what had happened in the past two
days and how my only missing link was for me to find a new berthing
for my houseboat. He walked us around his marina and then showed us
a boat slip at the end of an old pier that he thought would be great for
my houseboat. It was fantastic as it was at the very end of a long pier so
we would have a lot of privacy and less marina noise.

Then we asked him for the 'bad news', how much were his monthly
fees? We found his berthing fees were much, much lower than any of the
other marinas that we had visited that day in the entire San Francisco
Bay Area! Actually, they were a quarter of the monthly cost of the
Sausalito Marina. Of course, the Sausalito Marina was much fancier
and much more upscale yet, Pete's Harbor had full facilities on the dock,
such as a freshwater supply, an electricity cable plus a small sewage line.
He did explain that they had shower facilities within the clubhouse if
we wanted to use them, but there would be at an extra charge. We did

not require that as my thirty-five-foot houseboat had a shower within the small bathroom!

Finally, I asked him if he knew of a towing or tug boat company that could pull my houseboat from the North Bay Marina to his marina? He asked me to come back in a couple of days, and he would introduce me to his boat handler. Two days later, I stopped by and met his contact and we agreed on his price and date which was either nine to ten days from then. That was no problem as I had a great deal of work to do before the houseboat could be towed down to Pete's Harbor.

I remember Ginger, and I enjoyed talking to Mr. Pete as he was a very interesting person whom we were going to get to know over the coming year.

I consummated the purchase of the houseboat in the North Bay Marina and informed the owner that I had arranged for 'my new home' to be towed down to Redwood City and to Pete's Harbor.

This San Francisco trip was simply amazing as in only five days I was able to find and purchase a houseboat; arrange delivery for my new home to a groovy and hip marina; pay the yearly rental charges on a boat slip and have a new place to live and for me to write.

I left Ginger after this productive and positive long weekend and drove back down to Santa Ana in order to pack my things and leave the house that I was sharing and renting for the past year.

When I arrived at my sister's house, and when I explained what had just transpired, she was shocked. Firstly, she wasn't happy that I took a year's sabbatical from my first and successful teaching job in Irvine; I had just purchased a houseboat and now that I was planning to move to San Francisco. Still, to this day, I am not sure why she

U HAUL Trailer 5 x 8

was upset. Perhaps, she was unhappy to see me move so far away.

Well, it took me about five or six days to consolidate all my earthly possessions, and then I rented and packed a small U Haul trailer.

The car that I had been driving was an old 1959 Volvo PV 544 that I had purchased during my last semester at Rancho San Joaquin Middle School. I paid only $75 for this car, and it remains today one of the least expensive cars I have ever owned. Originally it must have been bright red, but when I bought it, it

1959 Volvo PV-544

was a faded pale pink color. This Volvo had a small four-cylinder engine that I believe was a tractor engine and was extremely slow yet reliable. I believe that I had changed the oil only once or twice and never had a lube-job in the two years of ownership. Now I was going to drive it back to San Francisco hauling a U Haul trailer! To exasperate the challenge this was now the month of June so the daytime temperatures were in the low to mid 90's. I decided to leave Orange County around 10:00 p.m. and head to San Francisco, first to avoid the notorious L.A. traffic and second to have cooler weather all the way.

I stopped by my sister's home and said goodbye to everyone and drove slowly to the San Francisco area and my new home. I made it with no problems what-so-ever. I left the trailer for a couple of days in Ginger's garage as the houseboat hadn't been delivered to Pete's Harbor.

The day they'd promised to begin, the towing process was too windy so they had to postpone to the next day. The next morning, I went to the marina to make sure everything was set for my houseboat's arrival. Yes, Pete's friend had collected the houseboat early that morning and all I needed to do was to wait and pray that they would not encounter any problems or difficulties along the way.

I had decided to go back to Ginger's apartment and do a little bit of writing and organizing on my two books. Around two in the afternoon,

I went back to Pete's Harbor to make sure I was there to welcome my houseboat to the marina. Three, four and then five hours had passed, of course, I became worried. Ok, there were no stiff winds; no white caps and the waves were minimal. Why were they taking so long? I went into the Waterfront Restaurant to have a quick drink, and it turned out to be 'Happy Hour' so I had more than one drink. Waiting for one's arrival can be a nerve-racking experience, especially knowing that this was the new home that you were waiting for and expecting! Then around seven p.m., I saw my new home coming up the Redwood Creek. The tug boat was traveling very slowly so I immediately realized why this trip had taken the captain over ten hours to complete. It took quite an effort to steer my houseboat around and move it into its slip. We had two people on each dock and another at the head of the pier helping to pull the houseboat into my slip. Once we successfully moored the houseboat to the dock, I invited everyone that helped into the Waterfront Restaurant for drinks on me. Ginger joined us a short time later and was extremely happy to see and witness this happy bar scene.

After most of our friends had left the bar, Ginger and I went to inspect my new arrival. Everything was what we expected, and it was really clean and surprisingly dry for a ten-hour tug boat haul. I was expecting that the flooring would have accumulated a great deal of water on its maiden voyage, but it remained dry through its first trip. Then we heard some tinkering sounds outside on the deck and low-and-behold it was Pete connecting the main water supply as well as the electrical connections. He said that the sewage connections would be made in the morning. We invited him inside to inspect the interior, and he was very impressed with the furniture and general layout of the houseboat.

I moved in the next day, and Ginger joined me one month later. We had a very satisfying and fulfilling living arrangement over the full duration of our stay.

During my fourteen month habitation onboard this magnificent houseboat, I was able to complete my first book: Educational Awareness

Through Field Trips and got a very solid start on my second book originally titled: 'Bicycle Trails of San Diego County' and later co-published as: 'Bicycle Trails of Southern California'. In addition, I enlarged the houseboat to include a full second floor, thus doubling the living space. The upstairs now was our master bedroom, a second bathroom, my modest office, and the new sitting room facing a very small balcony. Ginger had continued to work at Marine World/Africa/USA, and in addition to writing, I had a part-time job bartending at a local bar/restaurant. That simple job developed into a great and interesting work as so many people would come in and would need someone to talk to or better still someone to listen to them. Many times I wished that I was more attentive during my Psychology 101 class as the interaction between one's bar customers was great. A bartender learns a lot about his customers as many of them are very stimulating talkers and give thought-provoking messages. I quickly learned that successful bartenders develop into great listeners.

This houseboat was my home for only fourteen months, yet I loved it more than any home I had ever lived in during my entire life.

During those fourteen months, I had completed my first book and almost completed my second.

For some reason, I felt that I was ready to intuitively search for another adventure even though I was extremely happy and content living in this magical bedroom and office. That adventure arrived, most unexpectantly, during the editing process on my first book in San Diego.

In late July, when I drove back to the houseboat that early morning from Orange County, Ginger never expected to hear the news that I was about to deliver: *I have taken a job to teach science in an international school in Damascus Syria.* Those words still resonate in my ears today. One can only imagine the shock and disbelief from Ginger...she was shaken, saddened, bewildered, and in a state of total confusion. *What would make you leave your life here in the Bay Area?*

Eventually... after many long talks, she began to understand my position and was quite encouraging about my next international adventure. Ginger also enjoyed living on the houseboat as much as I had, so I told her that I would sign the ownership papers for the boat over to her before my departure. She really appreciated my gesture and generosity and I believe she lived on the houseboat for a few more years. Unfortunately, we lost track of each other and my only wish was that she enjoyed her time on her houseboat.

Ginger and Thomas, my son, had got along very well during the trips he made to see me on the houseboat. Ginger also understood that by me taking my son camping would create a strong and long-lasting bond between the two of us for many years to come. No one had expected or foreseen that Thomas and I would experience such a strange and extraordinary experience during this "camping trip."

I prepared my camping items with Ginger's help, and I drove back down to Orange County to meet with Thomas, my sister, and her family. In actuality, it would have been faster and closer for me to drive due east from San Francisco to the camping area instead of me first driving down to Orange County and then driving back up north to June Lake. But, with this way of travel, I would be able to see Thomas's mom and update her on my upcoming travel plans to the Middle East. She was planning to drive Thomas up to Orange County the afternoon prior to our morning departure.

Once I arrived at my sister's house from San Francisco, I was amazed and astonished on how well prepared they were for this five-day camping adventure. There was food ready for each meal for the entire five days plus light snacks for our drive to the resort the next day. Bill, my brother-in-law, had also prepared the camping equipment from lights and candles to firewood and matches. They had rented a medium-sized camper so they would all be sleeping together and Thomas and I would be sleeping in a tent a short distance away from their camper.

After dinner, Thomas's mother, Diane, drove back to San Diego, and we went to bed fairly early as the plans were to leave at five the next morning.

The drive was uneventful, a bit long as their large camper was quite slow along the main highway and quite sluggish climbing the mountain highways. Nevertheless, we arrived at the campsite, and everything was in order. They had their site already reserved and they set up all their attachments for water, electricity, and sewage. Thomas and I selected a nice flat open area to pitch our tent with plenty of fresh air and a beautiful sky above.

There were many activities available for us to enjoy: discovering, canoeing to hiking. Unfortunately, the water at this time in June Lake was a bit too cold for Thomas and me, so we did not swim, but we did enjoy sunbathing on the shore of the lake. Thomas had met a boy of his age, and they had become good friends as they discovered that they a great deal in common and enjoyed the same things. I was happy that Thomas had found a friend while on this trip as I felt that he was developing into a 'loner'.

After our daily activities and upon completing our usually early dinner, we would simply enjoy sitting outside the camper and looking at the night sky and discussing many things. The night sky was dazzling that we had spent many evenings simply star gazing and dreaming of many beautiful things. For me, it was dreaming of what lay ahead of me.

Those five days passed by very, very fast and we found ourselves on the last night, getting everything ready for our departure the next morning. Once again, we had a great dinner, and we then all sat outside our camper. We would reminisce and recollect our thoughts and feelings over the past five days. This was a great time for my son and me to be together and also for Anita: her family and us to be together for one last time before my departure to "parts unknown."

That last night we were all very tired due to many great activities over the past five days. We decided to conclude the night early so we said good night and that we would see each other in the morning.

Thomas and I walked back to our small tent site and talked a bit before we both agreed that it would be best to get a solid night's rest before our trip back home in the morning. I know that Thomas and I went to sleep quite quickly as we didn't talk very much before sleeping.

It must have been just around midnight or just thereafter that I was awakened by a very, very bright white light above our tent. I got up and opened the zipper to scrutinize the entire area outside our tent. The complete field was flooded by this extremely bright white light. I still remember the light casting a dazzling shadow upon a large oak tree near my sister's camper. It was incredible…so much that I woke up Thomas to see this extremely bright light. He reluctantly woke up and immediately noticed the bright light within the tent, and I convinced him to look outside our tent. The entire meadow was drenched in this bright white light. To this day, he remembers the bright white light. Amazingly, that night we did not remember or recall any sound associated with this unbelievably brilliant white light. Within a minute or so, it was gone. No sound, no trace, no light, nothing except the eerier darkness. It was so dark that we couldn't see that tall tree near my sister's camper. There was no moon that night so everything was completely and unequivocally black. One must also note that due to the extremely bright light for only a few minutes, our eyes were adjusting and our pupils must have been very small and then after the light disappeared, we perceived everything in a much more limited manner so everything appeared darker.

The next morning Thomas and I tried to explain what we had experienced; unfortunately, no one, including my sister and her family, would believe what we saw. They thought that we had a bad dream or a nightmare.

To this day, Thomas and I believe that this was an extraterrestrial or interstellar meeting that was very real and genuine. Even now, by simply thinking and writing about this experience, I still get a very eerie and spooky feeling!

What convinced me that it wasn't simply me that remembered this uncanny event but also my son Thomas. Later on, Thomas had joined the US Air Force after high school, and regrettably, he and I had lost contact for a number of years. We reconnected in England, some eight years later and in my first letter to him, I asked him if he remembered this unexplained camping experience and if he thought it was an extraterrestrial encounter. His reply letter was very specific and to the point: "Yes indeed dad, I remember you waking me up and the entire tent was lit from above by a very bright white light and then we both looked outside and we saw this very intense white light making a strange silhouette on a big tree near Auntie Anita's camper." Every time I would meet with Thomas, our conversation usually turned to our joint comments on our extraterrestrial experience and our recollection of that strange and galactic experience that we both had encountered.

After breakfast, we began breaking down our campsite and repacking the camper. While driving away from the campsite Thomas and I experienced a sense of sadness. We were gloomy because the camping trip was too short and we had great fun and partook in many activities. More importantly, we both knew that I would be leaving to the Middle East in the next few weeks. Even though my first wife and I were divorced in 1972, I always made it a point to see Thomas in San Diego or have him fly up to San Francisco to stay with me on the houseboat. Now, for the first time, I would not be there for Thomas for a very long time.

I drove Thomas home to San Diego and dropped him off at his mother's apartment and told her that I was planning to leave California to the Middle East within the next two weeks.

I then drove to Costa Mesa to see Anita and Bill and to hopefully collect my US passport. When I arrived at their house, they were still busy emptying out their camper and I asked about their mail. Anita had collected the mail and said there was a postal receipt in my name. Their mailman could not leave the registered letter without a signature, so I decided to spend the night with them and go to the post office first thing in the morning. We decided to eat out as everyone was too tired. That night we talked a great deal about my upcoming trip to the Middle East and that my first stop must be to West Seneca to see my mom and dad. That discussion had triggered my mind to come up with other stops along the way and a few more people I wanted to see before my departure.

Early the next morning, I'd collected from the post office the registered envelope containing my passport with the Syrian Visa and drove immediately north to San Francisco. For the past month, many of my trips to and from San Francisco were along Interstate 5, as it was much faster than taking the more scenic California Highway One. This trip I decided to take the more picturesque Pacific Coast Highway as it may be my last opportunity to enjoy this beautiful drive.

It was great seeing Ginger and I told her about the camping trip and our bizarre extraterrestrial experience. She was more understanding than my sister and her family and asked many questions about this alien's visit. It remained a 'hot topic' over the next few days.

We also talked about my trip to the Middle East, and she agreed that seeing my mom and dad would be paramount. That evening I also started planning my travel itinerary so that I could purchase my tickets the next day. We felt the best airport to leave California would be Los Angeles International Airport as it offered more flights than the smaller San Francisco International Airport. To get to Buffalo, New York, would require a stop in Chicago and then on to Buffalo. I found Los Angeles International Airport had many more daily flights to Chicago. I planned to stay for two days with my parents. There were no European flights from the very small Buffalo Airport so I then thought I would fly out of Boston Logan International Airport directly to Europe. A stop in Boston would also give me a chance to see my college roommate and his wife as they were living and working in the Boston Area. Where should I fly into from Boston in Europe? I had traveled to Europe on two different trips the first in the summer of 1967 and the second a much longer journey of almost one full year from 1971 to early 1972.

I pondered a while and felt that London would be great to see once again since we had lived there for three months in early 1972. I still had a few additional days, so I decided to fly from London to Madrid as again I had always enjoyed that city and we also lived there from late 1971 to early 1972. Now my time table was closing in on my travel plans as I was required to be in Damascus by the end of August. I did calculate that I had two or three extra days for touring. I had a crazy thought: *why not see an Arab Capital before arriving in Damascus*. I had no idea about the flight schedules from Madrid into the Middle East so I left that decision up to my travel agent. My final leg was, of course, Damascus and there again I would listen to the advice of my travel agent to decide that final leg of my travels.

That morning I went to my favorite Travel Agency in Redwood City to make all my bookings and to pay for this important one-way ticket. She had always been my agent to purchase all my airline tickets for Thomas from San Diego to San Francisco. She was very knowledgeable and extremely polite. She was quite shocked when I told her as I walked into her office that morning that I was planning to travel to the Middle East.

I still recall that I was in the travel agency for well over four hours, making the necessary airline bookings. Remember there was no internet in 1975, so each airline booking was made with a very large 'Airline Directory' and then directly with that specific airline. I had three domestic flights to book and an additional three or four international tickets to find and reserve.

I told her my tentative travel itinerary, which I put together the night before and I said that I would like to spend two days in each city. Finally, I wanted to arrive in Damascus towards the end of August.

For my domestic three flights, she selected United as they had the most flights to select from, and they served both Buffalo and Boston Airports. Now internationally was a totally different story as I'd insisted on seeing both London and Madrid. We selected a Pan American flight from Boston to London and then I think it was a British Airways flight to Madrid. When we finally came to the last two stops, she suggested without hesitation that I fly from Madrid to Cairo, Egypt. Cairo, little did I realize, would be a near catastrophe and potential disaster. Now from Cairo to Damascus, she suggested that I take Syrian Arab Airlines as their schedule was good. She had never heard of this airline but said that it can't be all that bad.

I left her office and had only a skeleton itinerary, as she needed to contact the international airlines, and that was going to take some time. She told me to come back tomorrow at noontime.

Ginger and I talked a lot that night, especially about my travel itinerary. I hadn't realized that she had never traveled to Europe and just talking about London and Madrid made her a bit sad, but I talked to her about the idea that in the near future we could plan a joint European trip with her flying in from California and me flying in from Syria.

The next afternoon all my reservations were in order, and the tickets paid and confirmed. After the travel agency, I remembered that I must call my parents plus Gary in Boston in order for them to know my travel plans and receive me at the two airports.

The next item on my hit lists was to legally turn over the ownership of the houseboat to Ginger's name. We saved a great deal of time and money by using one of the corporate lawyers at Ginger's work. It was a very simple process as he was also a Notary, so both signatures were legalized at the same time.

Now my next decision proved to be the most time-consuming and more than I anticipated. I wanted to find another author to purchase my second book manuscript and all copyrights. I had completed almost 75% of this "The Bicycle Trails of San Diego County" and Ginger, and I felt that it would be a complete waste to simply discard the many months of work, toil, and effort. I spent the next two days reorganizing and downsizing all the chapters and multiple bike outings. By the time I had completed these, I had over 120 pages of typed manuscript and many, many photos of various restaurants, B&Bs, and sights of all bike trips. I simply did not have the time to search for another person to co-author my work. Ginger volunteered to find a third party after my departure. She would be in a much better position to find a new publisher or author.

One of the final items that I had to decide on was what to do with my $75 Volvo PV – 544. I put zero dollars into this vehicle over the two years that I owned it, and now what should I do with it? The interior headliner was falling off, and the car really needed an urgent paint job as it was now a light pink color. I thought that it would be crazy to sell it in Northern California as I still needed to drive down to San Diego and Orange County, and also, I was flying out of Los Angeles International Airport. So that night I called Bill, my brother-in-law, and asked if I could have him sell it after I flew out of California. He agreed and said we would split the final selling price. So that was another worry out of the way.

I had one final item to take care of, and that was I had to begin to pack my traveling clothes as well as the items I was not planning to take to Damascus. I had only two days to finalize my packing, and then I would be off to San Diego to drop off my items for storage and to be with my son for one last time. Then up to Costa Mesa to say my final goodbyes to my sister and her family and then I would be off to the Arab World for the first time in my life…

I discovered during these two days that I was a fairly organized packer as I first purchased a larger suitcase plus a new Dopp Kit/Toiletry Kit. So my travel items were all selected first and set aside. I knew that Madrid would be very hot during the month of August, and I was told that Damascus was very hot during the summer months and well into September, so I made sure I had enough short sleeve shirts, underwear,

T-shirts, socks, and shoes/sneakers, I simply visualized my body and what was required in order to be dressed in that particular environment! Believe it or not, I still use the same system today when I travel, but today I feel that I became more refined and have added such items as: shoe bags; three colors of empty dirty cloth bags; assorted electrical plugs/adaptors; a great travel alarm clock and even a small flashlight.

Also, for the past eighteen years, I have been adding to my "Travel Bear" collection, and these are eight to ten small teddy bears that go with me on every trip. Each and every night while traveling, they are always placed on the nightstand next to my hotel bed.

Then it was time to select the items that I was not planning to take to Damascus. I started by visiting each and every supermarket in Redwood City to collect clean empty cardboard boxes, and these were then be used to pack and store all my personal belongings that were not going to the Middle East. I soon discovered that there were fewer personal articles than when I originally moved up to the area some fourteen months earlier! Why? I don't know. All I know is that instead of renting a U Haul trailer, I was going to rent a car roof luggage rack. Those two days flew by very, very quickly, but I had completed my packing and now I was ready to leave the houseboat and Ginger and drive south one last time.

That morning leaving Ginger was a very difficult undertaking as we were really 'partners' and not simply friends. I kept insisting that I would be back, and we could start over again as we did fourteen months earlier. That reunion never happened as we had unfortunately lost touch with each other. That chapter of my life was never reopened; nevertheless, I still have fond memories of those great times living on the "world's largest waterbed."

I made it down to Jerry Johnson's house just outside of San Diego, and we unpacked the Volvo and then went inside to have a farewell drink. Jerry today still remains my very good friend. As a matter of fact, I had just visited him in October of 2018. We sat around his swimming pool and stayed up very late that night talking as there was so much to catch up on and the time simply flew by. We both did not realize when we finished talking it was well after two in the morning.

It was now time to see Thomas and his mom, and that visit turned into a tearful occasion. There was a great deal of emotion from both sides as we knew that I would be gone for a year or more so, it was a disconsolate departure for both of us.

I decided to drive up to Costa Mesa to spend that night with my sister; by the time I arrived, they were fast asleep. I knew precisely where they hid the spare key so I tiptoed into their house, brushed my teeth, and then fell asleep. The next morning was a Saturday so Bill was not working and we enjoyed my last full day in sunny California simply relaxing and having lunch at my favorite seafood restaurant. The last day zipped by very, very quickly as it seemed that Sunday morning was upon all of us.

I showered and had a large breakfast with my family, and then we headed to Los Angeles International Airport for my first domestic flight to Chicago O'Hare Airport and then on to Buffalo, New York. My travel agent in Redwood City was very wise and professional as she made my flight from Los Angeles on a Sunday morning, thus avoiding the massive traffic delays that the city has always encountered during a weekday. We made it to the airport in time and after parking the car we entered the airport and they followed me to the check-in and then to the boarding gate. Remember, back in 1975, we had no TSA or US Homeland Security so the entire family could walk me directly to the departure gate. We had a little time so we all had some tea and coffee while we were waiting. As we were getting closer and closer to my actual departure things became very emotional. Once they called, my flight tears were flowing like running water from everyone's eyes. I did make it to the departure desk and then I waved goodbye from the boarding bridge.

I found my window seat and immediately began thinking about the total events that had transpired over the past thirty days! I had been living and working on a houseboat in the San Francisco Bay, and now I was heading to a city I did not know and a country that was completely unknown to me!

What would be the consequences of this drastic and major change I had just made in my life?

The two domestic flights were uneventful, and I landed at Buffalo Airport a bit late, yet my parents were waiting for me at the arrival gate in the early evening, just as they had for my many flights before. They were their 'regular self' basically meaning my mom was always anxious and as overexcited as I remembered, dad was much more relaxed yet he was always twisting coins he had in his right-hand pocket. I guess this was a tension release mechanism that he had developed and used for many years. Maybe, he started this trait on that eventful day in 1933.

1930 – Ford Model A – Tudor Sedan

My mother was teaching my dad how to drive in a 1931 Model A Ford. Dad had stalled the Model A Tudor Sedan in the middle of a busy intersection and could not restart it. To make matters worse, my mom kept yelling: do this: do that thus making the entire situation worse.

Finally, my dad had enough and simply turned off the car and humbly handed my mom the key, then got out of the car and merely walked home. He never ever got behind the wheel of any car from that momentous day onward. He had simply and unknowingly added to my mother's duties and responsibilities as a wife and chauffeur!

I never remembered my dad ever sitting in the driver's seat of any car that we had ever owned, and once we were leaving the Buffalo Airport that day, things were exactly the same. Dad was sitting in the passenger seat, and mom was driving.

In addition, I remember that my mom was really not a good driver, as she frequently ran red lights, omitted slowing down, or even stopping at stop signs while driving. Plus, she was always exceeding legal speed limits. Somehow she was able to talk her way out of each policeman issuing her a ticket. Nerveless, she got us home safe and sound that night. I had two great days with my parents and at the end of my short stay, they were still confused about my reasons why I would leave California and go to this "foreign land." All the same, I tried to talk with them to explain the reasons why I was leaving the States, but I do not think that one reason ever made sense to them.

Finally, one thing I really missed doing during this last visit home was to enjoy a good old fashion Friday Night Polish Fish Fry with my mom and dad. While I was growing up in the Buffalo area, it was always a family tradition to go to a local bar/restaurant and enjoy a very special and old fashion fish fry. In those days, the fresh Perch served was actually from Lake Eire. In the late nineteen seventies and through the late nineties, there was so much pollution in the lake that the Perch population was decimated and drastically reduced.

The last time I was back in the Buffalo area was in late September 2018, and it appeared that Lake Eire Perch was now being served as the local fish for the famous Friday Fish Fries! A true tribute to the active environmentalist in that area.

My time with my parents went by so fast that I found that Wednesday came so quickly, and it was now time for my mom to drive me back to Buffalo Airport. During this last car ride to the airport, I could see that both of them could not clearly understand or fathom the thought of why I was flying off to this godforsaken place at the "end-of-the-world!" At no time in their life did they truly understand why I was traveling and living in the Middle East!

I was taking my third United flight from Buffalo on to Boston Logan International. On this flight to Boston, as on my previous two flights, I once again encountered strong remorse that I may not ever see my parents again. Dad was born in 1897, so in 1975, he had almost reached his 78th birthday. My mom was born in 1901, so she was getting close to her 74th birthday. I began to regret my decision afraid of what might happen when I was away.

I am not a superstitious person, yet on that flight, I had encountered a bizarre occurrence, as when the stewardess had served me my Bloody Mary, the lady sitting next to me accidentally knocked my drink over onto my lap. She was so sorry, but I had a very wet and well-stained set of pants. Was this an omen or premonition of worse things to come? Once again, I thought: "What was I getting myself into?"

All the same, I arrived on schedule to Boston Logan Airport, and Gary and Barb were waiting for me at the arrival gate. I hadn't seen them in over two years, and seeing them there waiting for me to disembark really made me feel positive once again. After Gary and I graduated from San Diego State University, he went his way and I went to dental school in Buffalo so we didn't see much of each other, yet we always stayed in contact by mail. They were now living in the southern part of New Hampshire, which was only an hour or two drive from Logan Airport. So we dropped off my suitcase in their apartment and we immediately went to their favorite restaurant for an early dinner or as they say an East Coast early: 'Supper'. We had the next day and a half together to catch up on old times and to discuss our futures. My future was, of course, up-in-the-air while their future had seemed well planned. Gary took that Thursday and Friday off so we could discuss a lot as we hadn't seen each other in a few years. Also, since they had moved to New Hampshire, they had very little time to be tourists, so my coming gave them a perfect opportunity to tour New England. The next day we drove to the adjacent state of Maine and did a lot of touring along the rugged Maine Coastline. It was an enjoyable trip with a great deal of fresh and fantastic seafood and some outstanding American wine.

I was leaving the next evening from Logan Airport, so they said that we would stay in New Hampshire and drive up to Mt. Washington the highest peak in the North-Eastern United States. Nearly the entire mountain is in the White Mountain National Forest and is surrounded by the Mount Washington State Park. This is a very beautiful part of New England and all of America. We decided to take the Mount Washington Cog Railway to the summit for the fantastic view it offered of the other very green mountains surrounding this great tourist site. We had a light lunch on the summit in their very small restaurant called the "Tip-Top House" and we saw their museum in the Summit House. It was getting late so we decided to descend the mountain again in the old 1869 Cog Railway. On our way to the airport, we decided to have one last and rewarding New England Lobster dinner in an old fishing village along the New Hampshire Coast. The meal was wonderful and out-of-the-world. We were not paying much attention to the time, but more important to the fact that our wine glasses were not empty.

My Pam American flight to London was scheduled to leave Boston Logan at 9:00 p.m. and Gary kept insisting not to worry and that he will get me there on time. Well, one thing he didn't anticipate was the traffic heading into downtown Boston on that Friday evening. We arrived at the airport at about 8:45 p.m. I remember grabbing my suitcase from his trunk, and Barbara and I rushing into the departure terminal while Gary went to park the car. We found the Pan American Check-in Counter and amazingly, it was empty, not one passenger; only the airline counter staff was present. I had my passport and ticket in hand and immediately went to them and asked one nice looking girl for my boarding pass and luggage check-in. I can still remember her telling: "Sir, you are very late, but let me call the gate to see if you can make it." She called and as she was talking to the person in charge, I could tell by her facial expressions that I was not going to London that night on that Pan Am flight. "I am very sorry sir, but the aircraft is about to leave and there would be no chance of your luggage making it to the aircraft." Gary just arrived and he tried to intercede but to no avail. I said: "Ok, what can you do for me?" She said that her Pan Am flight was the last departure to London from Logan that night. I asked what other flights are leaving later that evening. She telephoned her supervisor and explained the situation and then got him involved. He called back in a few minutes and said that there was only one more flight that evening to Europe and that I should rush to the Ticket Office of Aer Lingus to see if they had any seats remaining. I remember that this was August and still 'high season' for all flights to and from Europe. So the three of us hurried over the Aer Lingus Check-in Counter and then we were told that there were no seats available, but they had a few passengers that had not checked in. So I asked what I could do as I should be in Europe to connect to other European flights. She said: please let me see your Pan American Ticket. After looking at it, she said: Thanks be to God as we can use your ticket if there are any cancelations on our flight. I asked what my chances were, and she said quite good as they always had one or two 'no shows' in economy class. "Please, immediately take your ticket back to Pan American and have them directly endorse your ticket over to Aer Lingus. I will guarantee that you will have a seat on our airline." Back across the large departure area to Pan Am and then after they had endorsed it, we came back to the Aer Lingus office. The three of us were really getting a healthy workout. Our last stop was to the Aer Lingus Economy Check-in Counter and once I arrive at the desk my first question to the ticketing agent: "Where is this flight flying to?" In all the hectic running around, I never asked to which city I was going to be flying. She said in an amazed and startled manner: "To Dublin, sir!" Dublin, Ireland. Humm…I had never been there…I received my boarding pass and my suitcase was checked directly to Dublin.

Well, we had over an hour before my Aer Lingus flight's departure, so I suggested we find a bar near my departure gate and enjoy a few Irish Coffees to celebrate my new departure and airline. I told Gary and Barbara that this would be a new experience as I have already been to London several times, but never to Dublin! I felt that I was getting a little bit tipsy as along with dinner, we had a great deal of wine, and now with two or three Irish Coffees, I said we must stop. My flight was called and so I thanked Barb and Gary for the great couple of days and went directly to the boarding desk. I believe the aircraft was a Boeing 707 and I boarded and found my window seat and was set to leave America for Dublin.

What struck me as very funny when I looked around the aircraft, it appeared that well over half the passengers were either priests or nuns. I was laughing to myself and felt: if this airplane ever crashed, we would all go directly to heaven. The takeoff was smooth and shortly thereafter, the stewardess came by asking for my drink order. Well, next to me was a sister and in front and behind me were three priests and I felt a little embarrassed asking for a glass of wine with so many righteous and holy people around me. I said faintly to the stewardess that I would have a glass of white wine. Then she asked: "Sister, what will you have?" Assertively she said: "I will have a double Jameson Irish Whiskey, with no ice, please." What was this? Here I was embarrassed to ask for a glass of wine because I thought there might be a hint or trace of alcohol on my breath and BINGO the sister sitting next to me orders a double Irish Whiskey! This was going to be a great and very interesting Trans-Atlantic flight!

While I was settling in for the long flight and after our meal and a few more glasses of white wine, I thought about my last Trans-Atlantic flight that I had taken. It was a flight to Europe from the States in 1971, and my return flight was in late 1972. Both flights were on the Iceland based carrier called Icelandic Airlines, and on both flights, they were still using a DC–6 propeller aircraft. We had left from JFK with a stop in Reykjavik, Iceland and then on to Luxemburg and both flights were very, very long, uncomfortable and quite noisy.

Now I was enjoying a four-engine jet aircraft, and it was a non-stop flight in half the time it took me three years earlier! The leg space was ok; the engine noise was minimal, and the food fantastic. The opposite of my previous flight called at that time: "Hippy Airlines."

I slept very well, and I was woken up by the stewardess when we were preparing to land in Dublin. I asked the sister if she had slept well and she said no, she could not sleep on a flight... I guess she was drinking her Jameson Irish Whiskey throughout the flight!

We landed at Dublin Airport, and it was an organized disembarkation from the aircraft. No visa was required because I was carrying an American passport. I located the correct baggage carousel and saw my bag going around and around. I found an available luggage trolley and headed towards the green customs "Nothing to Declare" airport exit line. That was a very fast and professional airport arrival procedure. Little did I know that this would be one of the last easy airport arrivals! In the arrival hall area, they had an Information Desk and I immediately went up to the counter to find and secure a room for the next two nights. The young lady was extremely helpful as she found a great clean and inexpensive hotel for me plus she told me which bus to use instead of paying for a city taxi. She then gave me a great tourist map and circled all the sights that she said I must see. She was such a big help and so friendly. She helped in making my uncertainty over visiting a new city disappear.

The hotel/pension she had recommended was good, the room was a bit small, and unfortunately, the washroom and toilet were at the end of the hallway, but that's the way it was in any two or three-star European Hotel in 1975. I rested for an hour or so and then set off to see each and every place that the airport receptionist had circled on the map.

I remembered I started with the free tour and more importantly, the first free beer tasting at the famous Irish Beer company called Guinness and in their special place called the: 'Guinness Storehouse.' I soon discovered that this was a great way to introduce myself to a new city as I had a slight buzz due to the four good-sized samples of beer. So my new travel idea was to have a couple of glasses of Guinness beer and then go out to discover the rest of the city.

So for the next two days, I saw many churches, two castles and walked along numerous and most important streets within the city of

Dublin. What I especially enjoyed was walking along the Boardwalk along the River Liffey and stopping at various pubs along the way. I later discovered the best restaurants were along O'Connell Street as they were not too expensive and had a wide variety of Vegan Foods available for my budget.

Most importantly, I needed to find a professional travel office as with me missing my original Pan Am flight to London, I had to try to get Aer Lingus from Dublin to meet my ongoing London to Madrid flight. At the first travel office, they told me that my best option was to go directly to the main Aer Lingus ticketing office and have them sort out this small challenge. That advice was well given as I entered the airline's main ticketing office and left about thirty minutes later with my new one-way ticket to London.

The remaining time in Dublin was very enjoyable and well spent. On Monday morning, I caught the same bus that brought me from the airport two days earlier, and it dropped me off back at Dublin Airport. It was a very short flight of just over an hour to London Heathrow Airport. Heathrow in 1975 was nothing like Heathrow today. I think there were only two terminals at Heathrow Airport. At that time, Terminal One for all domestic and short-haul flights and Terminal Three for all long haul flights. I arrived in London on Monday, August 25th and left the same day to Madrid Barajas Airport. I have always enjoyed Madrid's IATA Airport Code…MAD.

I believe that the flight time back in 1975 between Heathrow Airport and Madrid Barajas Airport was just less than three hours, today it must be a bit faster. Once I landed in Madrid, I passed through passport control, collected my suitcase, cleared the customs checkpoint, and I was on my way by airport bus to Puerto Del Sol, an area I knew quite well. Once I arrived there, I simply walked to my favorite neighborhood in Madrid called Plaza de Santa Ana. I knew this area of Madrid because in late 1971 to early 1972, I lived in this district for three months. I had no reservations at the same pension that I stayed three years earlier yet,

I was sure that I would find a room. I found the pension or two-star 'hotel' very quickly, which surprised me a bit as I hadn't been back to this district in three long years.

I was lucky as they had one room remaining for the three-night stay as this was still 'high season' in Madrid. While I was checking in, I met another American who had checked in a couple of days earlier. We started talking, and I asked him if he wanted to join me to enjoy a cold beer? He agreed and that was the start of a solid yet brief friendship that I still recall today. The local bar was only 50 meters from our pension and was called: Cerveceria Alemana directly in Plaza de Santa Ana. It was quite famous because Ernest Hemmingway used to frequent this particular bar many years earlier. I remembered this special bar on my last trip to Madrid when I stayed at the same pension and drank the same draft beer. The Cerveceria Alemana had not changed and I guess it hadn't changed since the thirties when Hemmingway used to frequent this place during his famous stay in Madrid.

Hemmingway Statue in the Cerveceria Alemana

I believe he wrote most of his famous book: *For Whom the Bell Tolls* as well as his one and only full-length play, *The Fifth Column* while enjoying the same beer back in the late thirties and early forties. Every time I entered this bar, I really felt a certain warmth and nostalgia, knowing the simple fact that I was in the same bar as Ernest Hemingway.

That evening my friend and I went to several of the famous Tapa Bars that were in the immediate area of our pension where I had eaten three years earlier. At the first Tapa Bar, we met twin American girls who were both teaching English in Madrid. Their Spanish was much better than ours, and we connected with these two Americans for the remainder of our stay. They knew Madrid very well, and they became our 'tour guides' from then on. The word: Tapa, in Spanish means "a small portion" or as the girls said, it is also the word for a "lid" or cover that had been used in the past to keep the flies off of the food. We discovered there are many types of tapas to select from: ham; olives; Spanish omelets to a wide variety of seafood. My favorite, unquestionably, are the fresh mussels or as they are called in Spanish: '*mejillones*'. The four of us went to three different Tapa Bars that evening in Madrid and all three were famous for their mussels. They usually had three types of sauce they placed on top of the mussels and throughout the evening, we would switch between their: spicy tomato, oil and garlic and a very spicy pepper sauce. I believe there were usually six or eight mussels on each plate and when you would eat each piece, you simply throw the mussel shell on the floor. One could always recognize the best Mejillones Tapa Bars from the large number of empty shells on the floor. When you enter, you hear and feel the crushing sound that you make simply walking up to the bar. We usually started our evening with a small glass of draft beer called: '*caña*' and then after a few plates, we would switch to a small glass of their local white wine served from a label-less bottle. We discovered the only time they would sweep up the shells was after they closed.

In each Tapa Bar, we would usually order between five to six plates of mejillones and then a few plates of their other seafood selections such as their: sautéed prawns, anchovies and hot calamari's. After enjoying two or three different Tapa Bars, we never once required to eat dinner. Plus dinner was always served well past 9 p.m. These twin American girls loved seafood and they always knew the best Tapa Bars in Madrid.

In the three nights that I spent in Madrid, we had enjoyed our meal in these same Tapa Bars. I never got tired of those delicious mejillones.

During the day, we visited the Prado Museum as I felt that this is one of the greatest museums in the world. I especially enjoyed seeing the works of: Goya; Velázquez; Raphael and Rubens. We needed those two days to see, maybe, only 30% of the total works on display.

My short time in Madrid was spent visiting the Prado Museum, eating mejillones, and getting to know this very interesting American English teacher!

From Madrid, I had planned to stop in an Arab Capital before I ventured to Damascus so I could acquaint myself with the Arab World.

Chapter Three

My First Visit to An Arab City

On my final travel leg to Damascus, I had planned a two-day stopover in Cairo to simply view the Pyramids and become a bit 'acclimated' to my first Arab City. I had expected that Cairo would be better organized and orderly as it was a 'tourist mecca' for thousands of years, right? Wrong…

That August, I flew into Cairo International Airport from Madrid in the late afternoon on an Iberia Airlines flight and we landed at the 'original international' terminal in Cairo that must have been built back just after WW II.

My first: 'New Arab Experience' was when the plane landed at Cairo International Airport, just as the wheels touch down all the passengers began clapping. This was not negative in itself, and I took it as a positive and genuine gesture of happiness and relief that we had landed 'safely'. What happened next for me was sheer astonishment…just as the aircraft touched down and before the airplane left the main runway, it appeared that every passenger unbuckled their safety belts, stood up and started getting their carry-on luggage from the overhead luggage bins. What was this? The Iberia crew began making urgent announcements to the passengers: 'please sit down, and please wait until the aircraft comes to the arrival gate and the engines are turned off'… to no avail. No one listened and it appeared that no one was concerned over their own safety or the safety of the passengers. In addition to standing up and getting their carry-on luggage, they then started moving towards the front of the aircraft. I couldn't believe it…How could they be endangering their own lives and maybe injuring fellow passengers? For the stewardess's nothing worked as each standing passenger ignored all requests to sit down and they remained standing all the way to the terminal. Needless to say, the few passengers that respected the rules were the last to deplane. There were no jet-ways into the terminal back then only a few old, non-air-conditioned busses, which appeared to be again leftover from WWII. The only two ground busses were literally jammed packed with passengers like sardines. All the disembarking passengers wanted to get into the first bus as they knew they would be the first to arrive at the arrival hall. I waited in the aircraft until the first wave of passengers quickly got out of the airplane and ran to the waiting bus. This, at the time, was a wise move as by the time I left the airplane, the second bus was only half full. Unfortunately, shortly afterward, I was to find out that the passengers on the first bus were much smarter than all of us on the second bus as when our bus arrived, we entered the arrivals hall and the queues at the passport control were unbelievably long!

Cairo airport was very old, very dirty, hot, and very humid. Remember this was late August and the temperature was in the low forties degrees Celsius and any 'normal traveler' would have expected the airport to have air conditioning or at least fans, but none were to be found.

On the positive side, I found that all the passport control gates were very well marked in both English and Arabic. Unfortunately, I found the 'Foreigners Line' very long, and then I discovered that more than 90% of all the passengers were Egyptians in this special line for foreign passport holders. In addition, there was another plane that had landed and these passengers were simply cutting in front of the existing passengers waiting in line. All very unaware, unassuming or simply ignorant that there was a line at all. I soon learned to use a weapon that I never expected to use and that was my elbow as a deterrent. When the next person tried to get in front of me, I simply aimed my elbow into their chest and politely said: "Oh, I am sorry!" This tactic worked and still today I occasionally use this proven 'line defense mechanism'.

Even before I got close to the passport desk, I was overwhelmed by the odor and stench of my fellow passengers. It appeared that they hadn't showered in months and their clothes were not the cleanest! Added to this, the very high temperature plus the lack of air conditioning made my first visit to an Arab Airport quite an unpleasant experience.

I thought to myself, what was I getting into?

Things got worse as after the passport control was completed, the luggage claim area was packed, and we had to wait a long time for the bags to appear. Once the conveyor belt started, it seemed to be a small panic that broke out as everyone ran to the start of the beltway. People seemed to be taking any bag that resembled their own and when they discovered it was not theirs, they simply left it on the ground and off the belt. Somehow I managed to detect my bag coming slowly and with many inquiries and somewhat inquisitive hands looking at my luggage tag on my suitcase. Nevertheless, it did arrive and I went to the departure area for Customs Control. Again, long lines awaited me and of course, no one seemed to respect a line…I was lucky that I did not have to open my suitcase as I quickly discovered that it pays to flash your US passport while standing in an inspection line.

When I finally exited the airport, I was hit by 'true Sweltering Summer Heat of Cairo'…and I thought it was hot inside, outside felt like a hot oven blasting the heat on each and every exiting passenger. To be very honest, while I was standing in front of the terminal, I began to question my own logic of why in the world had I selected my travel agents idea of a stopover in Cairo.

I already had my hotel booking and confirmation for the Hilton Hotel, and now I only needed to find a taxi. There were plenty of taxi drivers, as a matter of fact, maybe fifty per passenger. Each taxi driver was yelling and hawking to find potential passengers. Pandemonium broke out as there were so many taxis available that each was trying his hardest to secure at least one passenger. I looked beyond this chaos and saw only a few meters away a more civilized looking taxi driver and a bit more organized as he wasn't shrieking at the fellow passengers. As I approached him, I discovered, to my luck, that he spoke very good

English and looked quite decent. I told him that I needed to get to the Hilton Hotel. Once we got to his taxi and my suitcase was packed away, he told me that he had a much better hotel at half the price of the Hilton. Humm… I insisted that he take me to the Hilton and if I did decide to change my hotel, I still needed to inform the Hilton to cancel my reservation plus I wanted to exchange some of my dollars for Egyptian Pounds. So on our way to my original hotel, he kept telling me that his hotel was far better, much cheaper, and in a better area of the city. I later discovered that he was right on only one of those three points…it was cheaper.

I began trusting my driver and had agreed that I would take his suggestion. He did stop outside the Hilton as I later found out that he was not a 'real taxi' so he was not allowed to enter the hotel grounds. I walked up the slight incline to the hotel, leaving my suitcase to my new trusted 'friend' Ahmad, my 'taxi' driver. I entered the Hilton and was immediately impressed with its' grandeur and luxury. All the same, even though I was impressed with the Hilton, I was able to cancel my reservation and I assumed that I was to save a lot of money. I found an exchange counter to get some much-needed Egyptian Pounds.

Ahmad was waiting for me, and I started feeling better about my decision to take his advice…That comfort level quickly evaporated as we entered the district of old Cairo and we approached the Cairo Metropolitan Hotel. It was far from being a 'metropolitan or cosmopolitan hotel' but the rates were very reasonable.

I had arranged with my taxi driver Mr. Ahmad that he would collect me at 10:00 a.m. the next morning to take me on a personal tour of Cairo and to see all the famous sights of the city.

I then made my first mistake, I checked into the hotel without seeing my room! I went to my room, and at first, it appeared to be 'clean' at least no odors were emanating from the room or bathroom. I then looked in the bathroom and found no toilet, only an oval hole in the floor. This was my first experience of using an Arabic Toilet. Everything then continued downhill as there was no hot water to wash; no shower in the bathroom only a very small shower head and drain; no ac only a ceiling fan and finally, my neighbors were having a lengthy argument all evening. I barely slept and the next morning I managed to take a lukewarm shower and get ready for my first Arabic Breakfast which was included in my room rate. I went down to the ground floor at 09:00 a.m. to locate the breakfast room only to find Ahmad waiting in the lobby. What was he doing there so early? He then mentioned that it was 10:00 a.m. as there was an hour difference between Madrid time and Cairo time. He suggested I forgo the hotel's breakfast as he would take me to a better local restaurant for a more 'typical Arabic Breakfast'. I quickly returned to my room to gather my camera and passport and then went on a 'sightseeing tour' like no other!

I never imagined a city could be so polluted; congested with uncontrolled and unmanageable traffic as I witnessed that first day in Cairo. All cars, but especially the taxis, had no respect for traffic signals or even the police at each intersection. Their horns were constantly blaring in a very deafening manner, and it appeared for no reason what-so-ever. It was simply an unreal experience, especially for someone coming directly from the States where rarely one blew their horn and always respected the traffic signals and traffic laws. I don't know how we made it without getting involved in a traffic accident, but we did…

Our first stop was Ahmads 'favorite restaurant' and I use the term 'restaurant' with much reservation. Finding a parking space was an endeavor that took a very long time, and finally, I don't really believe it was a legal parking space as it appeared that we blocked three cars in the process of finding 'space'. The restaurant was nothing more than a 'hole-in-the-wall' place that had a very small kitchen in the back and a couple of tables in front. He told me that I must try a local dish called: 'Fattah Hummus' or as he claimed: the "Poor Man's Breakfast." It was made with: chickpeas; something I learned was called tahini; some olive oil, lemon juice, and garlic all served on some old dried Arabic bread.

I simply loved it and finished the entire bowl! OK, I was really hungry, but actually, it was very delicious.

As James Michener once wrote: *"If you reject the food, ignore the customs, fear the religion and avoid the people, you might better stay at home."* I have always been the traveler that tried the food no matter how small and inconspicuous the restaurant appeared to be at first sight.

I really liked this new dish called Fattah Hummus since it had no meat, it was very fast to prepare; it appeared to be very healthy, and I found it was quite inexpensive. Today in Damascus, I call it: 'Fateh Samneh' and is, by far, and unquestionably my most favorite Syrian Breakfast food.

Well, after this great breakfast, it was back in Ahmads' taxi to fight the maddening traffic and to try to get to Cairo's most famous and renowned tourist attractions: The Pyramids of Giza. These were far outside the city and took us over an hour to get to them. Again, parking was a major challenge that Ahmad took in a stride. We arrived at undoubtedly the worst time for any human to tour this magnificent site...noontime in Cairo in August of 1975.

I was most impressed with the first sight, and that was of the Sphinx. It was spectacular, even with its nose almost missing. Ahmad was a great taxi driver, but he excelled at being a very professional tour guide. He had explained many things and one of the first facts that still remains in my mind today was how the Sphinx lost its nose. He explained that during Napoleon Bonaparte's time in Egypt, he had his artillerymen practice using the Sphinx as their main target. Hence the major damage to the Sphinxes nose. Of course, I believed him as I didn't know any better at the time. Well, some years later, I did my research and found that it was not Napoleon Bonaparte's army that damaged the nose of the Sphinx, but it was done at a much earlier time in history around 1378. A Sufi Muslim leader named Muhammad Sa'im al-Dahr destroyed the nose out of anger when he saw people practicing idolatry to the Sphinx.

Ahmad did ask me if I knew the answer to the famous Greek riddle about the Sphinx? It went as follows: if any traveler tried to pass by the Sphinx and didn't know the answer to his riddle, he would devour them. The Sphinx posed the following question: "What is the name of the creature that walks on four legs in the morning, two legs at noon and three in the evening?" The Greek hero Oedipus gave the Sphinx his answer: "Man." Thus causing the Sphinx's death. I did not know the answer back then, but today it makes good sense.

I was amazed at how large and sprawling the entire pyramid area was in-so-much that Ahmad convinced me to take my first camel ride. That was quite an experience from getting onto this creature to getting off. I never realized how high up off the ground you are once he gets up and starts walking…That was very nice, but the camel's odor was a little too much, especially during the very hot afternoon.

Despite the heat, the dust, mobs of tourists and the countless small shop owners hustling and hawking their souvenirs, I really enjoyed my visit to these stunning Pyramids of Giza.

After our lengthy tour, we stopped by another small café and had my first: 'Arabic Fast Food Lunch'. Ahmad convinced me that we should have another Egyptian specialty, and this time, it was in the form of a sandwich called: 'Falafel'. Some 'unknown' ingredients were simply rolled inside a piece of flatbread along with a few small pieces of falafel, which I think were originally chickpeas that were fried and smashed along with some tomatoes, this great tahini sauce, and some unknown greens. It was then heated in what appeared to be a waffle iron and served piping hot. This sandwich was outstanding and still today I have several falafel sandwiches each week in Damascus.

So Ahmad, my taxi driver/tour guide, and now food connoisseur, was 'making my short stay in Cairo a very memorable experience'. He then suggested that I must visit the Egyptian Museum as it was very close to my hotel, and I could walk back to the hotel. We once again maneuvered through the amazing Cairo congestion and finally made it to the entrance of this famous museum. Ahmad bid me a fond farewell and said he would collect me the next morning at 10:00 a.m. from my hotel.

After my numerous visits to the Prado Museum, I never thought any other museum could match the Prado I was in for a shock of my life. The Egyptian National Museum had a staggering collection of ancient artifacts that were simply out of this world. It seemed that each room displayed more amazing relics than the last, and this continued. I completely lost track of time and then there was an announcement that the museum was about to close. I was very disappointed as I made my way to the main exit as I knew that I had only seen twenty percent or less of the entire collection. All the same, I said I would return, which I did several years later.

Once outside, I found a taxi, and he took me back to my splendid Cairo Metropolitan Hotel and when I arrived that early evening back to my hotel, all I wanted to do was to find my room and go to sleep. I decided that I better have something to eat so I had a simple salad and a bowl of soup and went directly to my room and fell asleep.

Around four in the morning, I was awakened by the sound of the morning prayer call. It was so loud that I felt the 'muezzin' or the one calling for the prayer was in my room. I discovered that the mosque and its' tall minaret was just outside my window, and the minaret had a series of loudspeakers along the top. I have no idea why I woke up this morning, whereas I did not hear the call for prayer the morning before. I got out of bed and looked down at the entrance of the mosque and was surprised to see so many men entering the mosque to worship.

I was able to go back to sleep, and this time, I woke up at the true Cairo 9:00 a.m. and not one hour past my scheduled collection as the day earlier. I went down to the hotel's restaurant and had my first and typical Arabic Breakfast. I was amazed at the number of small plates that were served. Each plate had some special white cheese, olives, Foul Mdammes, Lebneh, Za'atar and Manakeesh, and of course, some very sweet hot tea. It was also the right size for starting one's day.

That same afternoon, I had my flight to Damascus so I decided to check out of the hotel that morning then to simply wait for Ahmad and to place my suitcase in the trunk of his taxi and after our second day of touring Cairo he could drive me out to the international airport.

I knew that Ahmad would show up to the hotel as I had yet to pay him for both the drop off from the airport and yesterday's full-day tour. Ahmad showed up exactly at ten sharp as I was checking out of the hotel, and we were ready to discover more of this amazing city called Cairo.

He said we would see only two tourist sites that day as he didn't want me to miss my flight late afternoon. He first wanted me to see more of the old city of Cairo, so he suggested that we go to the old Cairo Souq Quarter and then we would stay in the old city and visit an old mosque that he thought I would like to see. I said: "Let's go!"

The old market or souq was very interesting, and we walked and walked through these very narrow alleyways. We saw many shops, everything from a small stall which had a great variety of exotic spices; to a special coffee market when you could smell the fresh coffee roasting; too many shops selling typical Egyptian antiques and many souvenir shops simply selling useless trinkets and curios.

From the Souq Quarter, we drove to visit a very old mosque called Al-Azhar Mosque. This was the second time that I had entered a mosque, the first being on my vacation to Europe in 1967. I had visited the beautiful Cordoba Mosque in Cordoba, Spain.

I was impressed with Al-Azhar Mosque as it is the first and oldest mosque in Cairo completed in 972, and it had four tall ornate minarets. Ahmad told me that Cairo has been called: "The City of a Thousand Minarets" and this, in fact, was due to this Al-Azhar Mosque. We entered the Al-Azhar Mosque through the "Gate of the Barbers" or in Arabic: Bab al-Muzayinīn, so named because students would have their heads shaved outside the gate. This gate eventually became the main entrance to the mosque. We took our shoes off and stored them on a shelf just outside the entrance. I was very impressed with the main entrance as it opened into a very large white marble-paved courtyard and at the opposite end, the entrance to the main prayer hall. The large prayer hall had many columns throughout, thus making it very interesting to view. I was also very impressed by the huge dome with a massive chandelier hanging from the center. What I remember, to this day, was how quiet and relaxing it was inside Al-Azhar Mosque. It was in complete contrast to the hustle and bustle of the streets just outside this beautiful mosque.

On this second and final day, our time was passing very quickly, and Ahmad had reminded me that we must leave the old city soon in order for us to get to the airport in time for my late afternoon departure. So it was time to bid a final farewell to this very beautiful mosque in old Cairo and to face the commotion and disorder of one more drive on the crazy streets of Cairo.

Finally, on the way to the airport, I asked Ahmad how much would he like to give me an eye-opening experience in Cairo for the past two days. His comment was, "As you like sir." Still to this day, many Arabs say the same thing. I decided to pay Ahmad in US dollars, so I would have enough small Egyptian Pound notes for the airport and for the return trip. He was very happy with his payment and insisted on carrying my bag into the terminal and on showing me where to check-in and receive my boarding pass, etc.

At Cairo International Airport, the Syrian Airlines check-in process was in chaos and a total disaster. There was absolutely no organization or order at the check-in counters. There were no lines, just a vast multitude of bodies pushing towards the three small check-in counters. I finally arrived at one of the counters, and the girl took my passport and ticket and then checked a list of passenger names. Shortly after, she returned and claimed that I was not booked on this flight. She then took my ticket to the adjoining counter and that girl looked at my ticket and then looked at me and told my counter assistant: "That's OK, give him a boarding pass." Everything was disorganized as she never asked me if

I had a suitcase to check-in; if I had a Syrian Visa or which seat I would prefer. She simply handed me my boarding pass. I thanked her and then asked if I could check-in my one bag. Oh yes, I am sorry, she weighed it and placed a baggage tag on it and gave me the small receipt sticker. What was this? If the check-in process was this chaotic and disorderly, what was the flight to Damascus going to be like? And what was I to expect in Damascus?

As a bit of solace and comfort, the Egyptian Passport Control was a bit more organized as they had insisted on having everyone stand in a line or at least a semblance of a line. I got my exit stamp and then headed to my departure gate.

This first Arab City experience had stayed in my memory for many years as I had just discovered, on my first visit to an Arab Capital, that many of the Arabs I had met were very friendly, warm, helpful, and very outgoing. I then began thinking about my next Arab City…Damascus… could it be the same?

Chapter Four

Love at First Sight, Almost!

After my initial and negative impressions of Cairo's Airport, I was now hoping and praying that Damascus Airport would be a much better experience. Unfortunately, and to my horror, when I landed at Damascus Airport, I discovered it was exactly the same as my initial Cairo's Airport experience and maybe a bit worse.

My Syrian flight departed over an hour late from Cairo and mind you this was only a scheduled one hour and forty-minute flight. There were no apologies for the delay from the cockpit, but that was OK as it could have been beyond their control as Cairo Airport was very busy when I departed that Friday late afternoon.

The exact same action was taken by the preponderance of the passengers when we landed at Damascus International Airport that occurred on my Iberia flight as we touched down in Cairo a few days earlier. This time it seemed worse as the majority of the passengers simply stood up when the wheels first contacted the runway and had no regard for any of the safety of the other passengers nor their own safety. I now guessed that this must have been a 'natural' experience as on this Syrian flight, there were no announcements telling or pleading with the passengers to 'please sit down'! Again I stayed in my seat until these passengers disembarked and simply prayed that none would fall upon me or any other seated passengers. As the last freestanding passenger passed me, I simply stood up and grabbed my carry-on and proceeded to leave the aircraft. What surprised me next was that the pilot had already left the aircraft before the remaining passengers had all deplaned. I had never witnessed this behavior on any airline before this flight.

There was a passenger sky bridge to the terminal, and the airport appeared to be very new and most importantly with the air conditioning working. Once inside, I went down the escalator to discover that the passport control lines were incredibly long including the 'foreign passport holders.' I surmised that another aircraft or two or three had landed prior to our landing as there were many foreigners waiting in this single queue. Nevertheless, the line moved quite fast and before I realized it, I had already made it to the front of the line. There was no problem with my passport or entry visa as I had already obtained my Syrian Visit Visa while still in San Diego back in early August. The real problem occurred after I left the passport control line and when I was searching for the correct conveyor belt for our baggage collection. There was no clear sign indicating our flight from Cairo had landed or on which belt our bags were to be found. Finally, I did find the correct belt and shortly thereafter, my lone suitcase appeared. Then the real challenge occurred as there was only one x-ray machine used for 'customs clearance' and there wasn't much of a 'line'…it was simply mass chaos and disorder. It appeared that at least one hundred people were all simply pushing forward at the same time from all directions and of course, many people were trying to come in from each side. This 'line' took a very long time as many of the suitcases were opened for inspection as they exited the single x-ray machine. Again, I was patient and I had my American passport in my hand having just shown it to the lone inspector. Again this small trick and technique worked very well. They did not open my suitcase.

Then the next challenge occurred when I exited the departure area. There was a very small departing area for all the passengers to pass through, and hundreds of people were waiting for the arriving passengers behind a flimsy barricade. I walked slowly and finally saw a small placard with my name on it. I discovered that the American School had arranged for a US Embassy driver and car to collect me. This gesture was a real 'godsend' as I had no idea of how to find a taxi, exchange money, or locate my apartment and accommodations in the city of Damascus.

Once the driver and I had exited the airport terminal is when I was hit by a tremendous heat surge. I had never, in my entire life, ever experienced such intense and strong heat at that moment. I remembered during my time I was living on my houseboat in San Francisco, it was never as hot as this. As a matter of fact, several years earlier, I'd driven through Death Valley in California, which had some of the highest recorded temperatures in all of America and this heat that hit me that evening in Damascus was much worse than I had ever experienced anywhere!

I asked the driver if this heat was 'normal' and he simply said that this was 'common' at the end of August in Damascus. I had a very difficult time breathing, and for me, this was simply not healthy, not bearable, or endurable and I was ready to go back inside the terminal and catch the next flight out of this exceedingly hot, unorganized, and chaotic country. How could any country be this scorching and sweltering at seven in the evening? And how could any international airport be so new yet so hectic? I thought to myself: "What have I gotten into?"

We finally made it to the Embassy car in the large parking lot, and I must admit I was sweating from head-to-toe. Thank goodness that the car was a large American sedan and the air conditioning quickly cooled the inside of the car. I then had time to discover that this was no ordinary vehicle as the front and side glass were very thick and the door was very heavy. It was my first experience in a bulletproof car. I did feel 'safe', but more importantly, I felt cool and it was a great relief from the blistering heat outside.

The driver asked if I had a safe flight, and I described the confusion and disarray upon landing at the airport. He said that I should never let that bother me as the passengers are simply overjoyed on arriving safely that they feel they must move about and simply get out of the aircraft. He also informed me that nine days earlier Damascus Airport had experienced its worse air crash in history. A Czechoslovakia Airlines flight from Prague to Damascus crashed while landing some 17 km from the airport killing all 126 passengers and crew. This information did not make me feel any better about this city; instead it made me feel worse as now flying into and out of this airport may not be the safest journey for one to take.

I discovered that the airport was a long distance from the city center and with the number of cars on the roadway it appeared to be almost bumper-to-bumper traffic all the way into the city. What made this journey worse were the hundreds of cars parked along the side of this motorway. It appeared that the entire population of Damascus was either driving along this highway from the airport or simply picnicking that evening along this road. Things did not improve even as we left the divided highway and hit the city streets…it was again madness. So many cars and at each traffic light, it seems to take hours to simply pass the intersection.

So now, within the first few hours of my arrival in Damascus, I was ready to head back home to California. Was this country going to ever become endurable or manageable for me?

We finally reached a small tree-lined street and the apartment house that will house me for the conceivable future. The embassy driver parked his car, helped me with my suitcase, and we headed up to the second floor to discover what was going to be my new home.

We rang the bell, and Steve, my new roommate, opened the door. "You must be Thomas, how are you?" "Well, other than being very hot, not too bad… Is the weather always this stifling," I asked? Yes in July; August and the first part of September it is usually this hot. Do you ever get used to it? "Yes, I guess…"

Humm…that wasn't the answer I was looking for, as I thought he was going to be kind and say 'well, only today it got this hot'…'yes, I guess'…humm…

Well, weather aside, I entered, and then the embassy driver excused himself as he was not to leave his car unattended. I thanked him and said I would see him again, which I did on numerous occasions.

Steve, I learned, was from Odessa, Texas, and was just starting his second year at the American Community School. I thought to myself that Steve must have his wide-brimmed Texas '10 – gallon hat' in his room or somewhere around the apartment. As far as my knowledge of Odessa, Texas, is that it has a very strong cowboy culture. Well, Steve never produced that special hat. The first evening he told me that he was an ordained Southern Baptist Minister. Now that was a real shock, much more than never finding his 10-gallon hat. His evangelical beliefs were the mainstay for many long and extensive conversations over the next twelve months.

Steve wanted to show me the apartment, so I could select my bedroom, as our apartment had three bedrooms. The apartment was quite large, especially for two single guys as in addition to the three bedrooms, it also had a very large living room plus a dining room that was by the main entrance. The kitchen was off the dining room and was large and had a small room that was considered a maid's quarter. There was a small toilet and above the maid's room was a strange 'storage area'. This created a very low ceiling in the maid's room and part of our kitchen. But I found that this storage area was great as it gave me a place for my suitcase and any large boxes, etc.

There were three balconies in our apartment, the first between the living room and the kitchen, the second off Steve's bedroom and the other off the bedroom that I had selected. My bedroom balcony looked directly onto the garden of the Saudi Arabian Embassy, which was interesting as the Saudi Ambassador had many functions in his garden over the next couple of years. What I enjoyed was the view from my balcony of the famous and very high mountain called: Mount Qasioun. This Qasioun Mountain was very pretty, especially at night as the city seemed to have expanded almost to the very top; thus, the city lights would twinkle at night.

Steve then asked if I was hungry, and I simply said: famished. I explained that I had nothing to eat that entire day since my breakfast in Cairo. He said that he would take me out to his favorite restaurant, which was, fortunately, a walking distance from our apartment. I told him that I would like to take a quick shower and change my clothes before going. Well, Steve said the only problem we had was that there was no hot water as the water heater was electric and must be turned on and usually only in the morning. I replied that it didn't pose a problem and that he should let me at least put on some clean clothes.

We then walked over to a very small restaurant that was called: Chevalier. I immediately found the décor was very nice and inviting. The Chevalier was quite busy as it was Friday, and I discovered that they didn't work on Saturday in Syria. During our dinner, we talked about many subjects, but mainly about the school. I wanted to know so many things about where I would be teaching for the next year.

Now, this Chevalier restaurant was quite amazing as the food was exquisite, and the service was fast and professional. Today, the Chevalier is still in the same location, and believe it or not, the décor is exactly the same as it was in 1975 with the same paintings, knick-knacks, tables, etc. I continue to dine at the Chevalier, some forty-four years from my first meal. This is incredible in today's world because fast food is forever changing, international eating habits, etc. So today a meal at the Chevalier restaurant is still a pleasure and an occasion I look forward to in a very positive manner.

Steve and I walked back to our apartment. I was very surprised that there were so many people walking on the streets and many cars on the roads. Steve explained that since it was a Friday night and most of the offices didn't work the following day, many people were enjoying getting out of their apartments, going on walks, meeting friends, etc. For me, the weather was cooling down, so the walk back home was much more pleasant than when I'd left the airport terminal a few hours earlier.

I found Steve was a very positive person and when it came to discussing the heat and unpleasant weather, he would say: "Don't let the heat get you down, it will not last..." It did last until mid to late September, and he was right as it cooled considerably so that the temperature was tolerable.

Steve suggested that the next morning we go to the old city of Damascus to show me the many sights of the "World's Oldest Continually Inhabited City." All I could think about on the way home was not the next day's tour, but getting a good night's sleep and taking a much-needed shower in the morning.

My first Saturday in Damascus started out very well, as I had slept in and had taken my essential and quite crucial shower. Steve had prepared a small breakfast and then asked if I wanted to walk or take a taxi to the old city of Damascus. It would take about fifteen to twenty minutes to walk or five minutes by taxi. I suggested we take a taxi as I was still not too happy coping with the city during the hot weather.

We went out to the main street called Abu Roumaneh Street, and we flagged a very old taxi. As a matter of fact, all the cars on the streets were extremely old, especially the taxis. I couldn't believe the number of antiquated cars that were still plying the streets of this city. Yes, Damascus has always been considered the oldest inhabited city in the world, but the cars seemed to be just as old. There were 1949 Studebakers; 1950's Buicks; very old French cars such as a Citroën's 2CV; Peugeot 104's and Renaults still driving on the street. I was extremely impressed when I saw an old Jaguar in mint condition. Most of these ancient antediluvian relics appeared to be in great condition on the outside, yet it was obvious that the engines had been replaced as most sounded like noisy and polluting diesel engines.

Nowadays, you still see a few of these very old foreign cars as they are mostly parked, but presently you do see them being driven, and they all appear that the bodies are in a very good state and seem to be in solid running condition. Today, in my neighborhood, I still see the following:

a white 1939 Citroën, a cream-colored 1954 Jaguar 4-door sedan and across from my mother-in-law's house a mint condition 1952 or 1953 big black Buick sedan.

We did make it to the oldest part of the city of Damascus, and the taxi let us out at the entrance of the street called: Straight or also called Midhat Pasha Street and the souq of the same Arabic name. This Damascus street, Straight, was an old street built during the Roman period and which runs the entire length of the old city of Damascus. Steve had mentioned a passage in the Bible as the saying goes: *"And the Lord said unto him (i.e., Ananias), Arise, and go into the street which is called Straight, and enquire in the house of Judas for one called Saul of Tarsus: for, behold, he prayeth."* Later, it became known that this Saul of Tarsus converted to Christianity and became known as Apostle Paul. It is said afterward that Apostle Paul was lowered over the old Damascus city walls from a window in a basket to escape an angry Jewish crowd, as he was converting too many of the Jewish faith to Christianity. Many historians agree that Apostle Paul is one of the leaders of the first generation of Christians, often considered the most important person after Jesus in the history of early Christianity.

On my first visit to the old city, I discovered that the western entrance to the street called Straight was one of the original seven Roman Gates called: Bab al-Jabiya, and this is the main entrance on the city's western side. We immediately entered an amazing souq called: Medhat Pasha Souq. This souq is covered and very long. As I looked up at this high arched metal cover, I could see many small holes. These holes made a beautiful lighting effect upon the walkway like twinkling stars. I was very curious so I asked Steve how were these punctures made and he said that these were bullet holes as a result of the Syrian Revolution against the French just after WW I. The holes are still there even today and remind me of glimmering stars!

Over the next couple hours of walking and touring around this street called Straight made me a real believer that indeed, Damascus is one of the most beautiful and unusual cities in the world. What I discovered in this unique Middle Eastern City was really a city of exceptional and unequaled splendor. It appeared that in each meter of my walk, I discovered unparalleled and matchless sights, and still today, I am still amazed at these outstanding sights!

Off the main Medhat Pasha Souq on Straight Street, you constantly come across a labyrinth of little alleyways that lead to smaller and more unique souqs. Over the years, I have spent a great deal of time discovering these marvelous and matchless souqs.

A few meters further along on the left side of Straight Street, you come across several very old apothecaries. Lining the walls of each, are many round and old leather boxes that must contain some ancient remedy or cure for any known disease. You can talk to the pharmacist and describe your health problem or ailment, and he would readily make a concoction for any of your disorders or complaints. I had never witnessed this type of 'drug store' being so readily available to the general public as I did that day. Even today, while walking on Straight Street, I stop by my favorite apothecary and the old druggist still remembers me and we always have a nice conversation.

As you continue down the street, your nose immediately informs you that you are now coming into the fresh coffee part of the souq as you begin to smell the aroma of freshly roasted coffee beans. The roasted coffee smell immediately floods and permeates the entry of this souq. As you look in most of the shops, they are roasting their fresh coffee beans in large, oval, copper, rotating drums. This process does produce a great deal of heat so you see most of the workers wearing short sleeve shirts and they are dripping wet. We bought a kilogram of freshly roasted coffee to have the next morning with our breakfast.

At the next corner, we turned left and entered the spice souq. This souq was on our way to the famous Omayyad Mosque. These spice vendors lined both sides of this souq, and the colors of the various spices were simply amazing as you see the brightest and most brilliant colors one could imagine. Plus the unbelievable smells and aromas filled the air with such a strong and pungent Indian smell. I still remember that I had closed my eyes and felt that this spice souq could have been located in any Indian city such as Bombay or Calcutta. The brightest colored spice appeared to be something called Turmeric which was a very bright yellow/orange color. Next to it were piles and piles of Cloves, Cumin, Cinnamon, and Nutmeg. Plus something very

Damascus Spice Souq

unusual that was derived from Nutmeg and was called: Mace which was a very nice golden orange spice. The most unusual of all spices, because it simply looked like the bark of a tree, was called Cassia or Chinese Cinnamon. I was astonished to find four colors of Pepper Corns. I had only seen black peppercorns, but in this souq, I had seen: white, green, and red in addition to the common black peppercorns. Two new spices I saw were both in what looked like seed pods, but of different colors and sizes and they were called: Cardamom and Coriander and had a great smell. Finally, in a small jar tucked away on a side shelf was an unusual dark red string looking spice called Saffron. The shopkeeper told me that this was his most expensive spice and that is why he had such a small quantity and why he kept it aside from all the other more common and much less expensive spices. I did not buy a single strand of this Saffron but yet was very intrigued by its shape and high price.

I think that Steve and I must have spent an hour looking at the difference spice shops each plying for our business. Unfortunately for all the shop owners, we told them that we were only looking.

From the spice souq, Steve and I headed towards the famous Umayyad Mosque. This was a short walk, and we passed through several different souqs, and each shop owner was welcoming us in his store: "just to look." So after the ninth or tenth shop owner said this phrase, Steve felt it was time he taught me my first Arabic word as he suggested that I then answer each person with the word: "Shukraan" meaning thank you. This helped immediately as most of them simply smiled and said, "Afwan," which means "You're welcome."

As we came closer to the Umayyad Mosque, you could clearly see the tall front minaret and the high walls of this famous mosque. This was a very impressive building directly in the old city of Damascus. When we entered, we were obliged to take off our shoes, and we

Umayyad Mosque – Main Courtyard

placed them in a wooden rack near the entrance. I then noticed that all the women were putting on a black cover of sorts before they were allowed to enter the mosque.

Upon entering, the first view that takes your breath away is the sheer size of the very great courtyard of this famous mosque. It was very long and quite wide.

I found that it contained two 'dome-like' structures. The smaller one was at the far end of the courtyard and called the 'Dome of the Clock'. The much larger one and much more decorated was called the 'Dome of the Treasury' and was closer to the main entrance. In the Dome of the Clock, one expected to see a clock, hence its' name, yet no clock was found. I discovered that this clock seems to have stopped functioning in the middle of the twelfth century and was never replaced. The Dome of the Treasury definitely lived up to its name as it was very ornately decorated with gold mosaics on upper sides, and the dome was being supported by many columns.

From the courtyard, you could see the three minarets. The first minaret we had seen walking from Straight Street was called the 'Minaret of Qaitbay'. The name, I found out, came from the Mamluk Sultan of the same name that ordered the construction of this tall minaret in 1488. This is, therefore, the 'newest' of the three minarets.

The second oldest minaret, which is along the Northern Wall of the Courtyard is called the 'Minaret of the Bride'. Steve explained that the name of this minaret came from the fact that a wealthy Damascus merchant and financer at the time donated the lead material for the construction of the roof that separates the main square tower base from the spire. His daughter later married the Syrian ruler at the time.

The tallest and oldest minaret and maybe the minaret with the most interesting name is called: 'The Minaret of Jesus' or in Arabic 'Isa.' This was the original minaret and was built in 1247. It is said that in Islamic belief, it holds that Jesus will descend from heaven before the: 'Day of Judgement' to confront the Antichrist, and Jesus will reach earth via the Minaret of Jesus, hence its name.

The Umayyad Mosque

Above the main entrance of the mosques prayer hall is a very large dome that is called 'The Dome of the Eagle.' It receives its name because it is thought to resemble an eagle, with the dome itself being the eagle's head while the eastern and western flanks of the prayer halls represent the eagle's wings. Steve and I then went inside the 'haram' or main sanctuary, and I was astonished by the silence and tranquility inside. Plus it was much cooler than the very hot courtyard outside.

Steve was telling me a bit about the history of this famous Umayyad Mosque. After the Muslim conquest of Damascus in 634, the mosque was built on the site of a Christian basilica dedicated to John the Baptist, honored as a prophet by Christians and Muslims alike. Inside the main sanctuary, there is a shrine that legend holds is the shrine that contains the head of Saint John the Baptist. In Arabic, John, the Baptist, is Yahyā.

There is also a tiny mausoleum in a small garden adjoining the north wall of the mosque containing the tomb of Saladin. Saladin was one of the greatest Arabic Warriors and was the first sultan of Egypt and Syria and the founder of the Ayyubid dynasty.

Saladin led the Muslim military campaign against the Crusaders in the Levant, and at the height of his power, his sultanate included Egypt, Syria, Upper Mesopotamia, the Hejaz, Yemen and other parts of North Africa. I was told that there is a big statue of Saladin in front of the Damascus Citadel which we would see on our next trip downtown.

After our great visit to the Umayyad Mosque, we headed back to the street called Straight and headed to another of the seven Damascus Gates called: Bab Sharqi or the Roman 'Gate of the Sun.' While walking towards the end of Straight Street and to Bab Sharqi, we passed through different sections along the street which were devoted to certain dry goods and merchandize such as soap, nuts, and even the Jewish Quarter. In each of these unique areas, Steve and I would stop in almost every shop to see exactly what they were manufacturing and selling.

The soap souq was very interesting as all their soaps were either locally made or manufactured in Syria's second city Aleppo and every handcrafted bar of soap had a special fragrance. Their local names for these soaps were: 'Ghar' or 'Aleppo Soap.' Ghar is another name for Bay Leaf or Laurel Leaf and has a very strong aroma. I was told that the manufacturing process for each batch of handmade soap would take three days of boiling and then another six to seven days to dry and then aged for six months! I remember buying a great deal of different and unique bars of soap!

Next, we passed another section of Straight Street that dealt exclusively with assorted nuts. There were nuts of every description, from peanuts to pistachios and from almonds to cashews. Plus, there wasn't simply one shop, but a large number of shops all displaying their nut assortment in the same manner. Each variety of nuts was in nice organized mounds one after another, and each batch culminating into a neat and pointed apex. The specialty and more expensive nuts, such as pine nuts, macadamia, and pecans were all in jars behind these displays. I promptly discovered why these nuts were placed away from the less expensive nuts. In each store, the shop owner would always offer you a small scoop of the common nuts for a free tasting; he never offered us these more expensive nuts tucked away on the top shelf! The nuts they offered were either salted, unsalted, candied, or even smoked. After tasting several kinds, it was hard not to resist purchasing a half kilo or more. The other very interesting sight I saw while in the majority of every nut shop was a nut roaster in the back room. The predominance of them was being used. These nut roasters were very similar to the coffee roasters I had seen earlier that morning. Each had a fire on the bottom of the drum and the cylinder slowly turned by a small electric motor thus eliminating the possibility of the nuts burning or roasting unevenly. If the shop owner wanted to add a flavor to that particular batch, he would simply add the flavor or salt while the fresh nuts were roasting! Today these same drums are roasting fresh nuts on a daily basis.

Even though we just sampled many nuts and we had a bag full of nuts, Steve and I both became hungry, and we decided to have my first lunch in Damascus at a typical Syrian restaurant. It was very easy to find as this restaurant is immediately after the famous Roman Arch which dominates Straight Street. This restaurant is in the Qaymariya Quarter of Damascus and is facing the very old Mariamite Cathedral which I soon learned is the seat of the Greek Orthodox Church of Antioch, making it the home of the Eastern Orthodox Church! The Mariamite Cathedral is dominated by a tall belfry and we decided to tour the cathedral before having our lunch. The façade of the cathedral really didn't look like a real church or even a cathedral as it was quite plain and austere on the front. I discovered that this cathedral was built in the second century AD, thus making it one of the oldest Greek Orthodox churches in Damascus. Once inside, we found the main church building called: the Church of Mary and this section dates back to the late fourth century. It was quite ornate and richly decorated befitting the head of the Eastern Orthodox Church! The internal temperature was quite cool thus making the atmosphere quite serene. I guessed the walls must have been very thick thus making excellent insulation from the very hot weather we were experiencing outside the church. There were two small chapels the first called: the Chapel of Saint Tekla and the second was called: the Chapel of Catherine. Saint Tekla was an early Catholic saint and she was reported to be an eminent follower of Paul the Apostle or as we know him as Saint Paul. Also, within this Chapel, there was a chair and this was the 'official seat' of the Eastern Orthodox Church. This was a very nice and interesting tour of this famous Mariamite Cathedral.

By the time we left this interesting church tour, we were both famished, and we could not wait to find a seat in the famous restaurant. What immediately caught my attention was the interior décor of this restaurant.

Typical Arab Home

The walls were made from black and white stones, which indicated that the restaurant was quite old and I later found that many of the old palaces; hammams (old Bath Houses); Khans all used these special stone blocks and especially in the construction of each of their archways.

It has always amazed me as to the strength of these arches and is always due in part to the topmost important stone called the 'keystone' or 'capstone'. This is the final stone added during the construction of an arch, and all the other stones press against this wedge-shaped stone at the apex of each arch, giving it substantial strength.

After this first and most superb lunch in the old city of Damascus, we walked a short distance down Straight Street and discovered a very busy number of craftsmen working in very small shops within the Jewish

Quarter! Yes, the Jewish Quarter in this predominately Arab section of the old city! Each shop had one or two skilled workers making, mainly decorative copper plates and other copper handicrafts. The plates were round and made of copper and it appeared that one worker was etching and carving a beautiful design onto the surface of this copper plate. The other worker was taking small strands of silver and painstakingly hammering the silver threads into the surface of the engraving. Both workers appeared to be very skilled in their workmanship as each plate was a beautiful piece of art!

My next question was quite simple, how could you have these Jewish shop owners open and working within the old city of Damascus and all within a predominately Arab section? The answer was quite simple and straightforward: 'for thousands of years, Damascus has always had a Jewish community living, working and thriving in peace and harmony.' There were also several Jewish Synagogues in Damascus, one in the back streets just behind these copper workshops and also in a section of Damascus called: Jobar. I never got to see this magnificent and beautiful Synagogue in Jobar and I have recently learned that the Islamic State or ISIL had destroyed this stunning 2,000-year-old Synagogue in 2014.

On my first trip, while visiting these very old Jewish shops, I was amazed that: just less than two years earlier, Syria and Egypt had fought the: 'October War' with the Zionist State trying to regain the land lost in the 1967 'Six-Day War.' Yet here we were in several handicraft shops owned and operated by Jews right on the street called Straight!

Later I did my research and had found that Damascus and Aleppo both had a very large Jewish population since 970 AD. It seemed like a 'love-hate' relationship for many of those years the Jew had a large community, and they worked alongside the Syrian non-Jewish population in a very favorable and auspicious atmosphere.

I also learned that during the Roman period, around 49 AD, Paul of Tarsus, later know as: Apostle Paul had converted many Jews of Damascus to Christianity. So many Jews, in fact, that Apostle Paul was forced to hastily depart Damascus to avoid the Jewish ethnarch who wanted him arrested. Also, during the Crusader Period, many Jews from Palestine came to Damascus and Aleppo to avoid the high taxes imposed by the Crusaders in the 'Holy Land'. Finally, in 1492 many Jews were expelled from Spain, and many came to Syria, especially Damascus and Aleppo as a result. In the 1630s, there were many Shuls and several Jewish schools located in Damascus, Qameshli, and Aleppo. As a matter of fact, it was written and documented that the Jews of Aleppo were all speaking Castilian at this time. It is also believed that Jewish studies flourished in Damascus and the total population was well over 15,000 to 20,000 in the 1630s and 1640s.

Pogroms and persecutions ensued over the years, and the population slowly decreased to just 15,000 in 1947. With the formation of the Israeli State in 1948, many Jews went to Israel and the Jewish population declined even further and in 1968, it was estimated to be just 4,000 Jews living in Syria.

So in 1975, during my first journey to the Jewish Quarter along the street called Straight, there must have been a slightly lower number of Jews living and working in Syria.

The Syrian government made many changes, and the mass migration of Jews, especially young Jewish women, had taken place since 1975. Of course, today there are far fewer Jews living and working in the Jewish Quarter along Straight Street. Over the years, I had purchased many copper inlaid plates from these Jewish craftsmen; unfortunately, today none exist along Straight Street.

Steve and I continued to the very end of the street called Straight. There were many interesting and very old buildings along the street and on every side street and alleyway. This Straight Street ends at Bab Sharqi, which is one of the seven original gates found in the old city.

On that first tour and within the old city, I found that life was quite tranquil and extremely interesting. Once we passed through Bab Sharqi, we found a very different and much busier lifestyle in that part of the city. Many cars, taxis, and minibuses were plying the major street, which encircled the outside of the old city.

There was such a striking difference in these two worlds as inside the old city, you had a history around each corner, and once outside the walls, you had a modern, busy and bustling city.

One day before this first tour of the old city and during my first six hours in Damascus, I was ready to get on the next airplane and get myself out of this: scorching hot, chaotic and hectic city. I was really disappointed in this city called Damascus. Firstly, with the confused condition of the airport, then with the scorching hot weather, then with the multiple traffic jams and finally with the tumultuous honking of the car horns. Initially, I'd even found the people to be rude, bad-mannered, offensive, and disrespectful. I thought to myself about how I could last one more day or even one full year in Damascus.

There were many factors that helped to change my initial and overall negative impression of Damascus. The first two were within a very short period of time, and the other factors developed over the coming months after arriving in Damascus.

Simply put, one single trip to the old city of Damascus completely changed my attitude, perspective, and viewpoint of this city. No longer was I upset with the sizzling temperature, jumbled traffic, disorderly population, etc. I found that the old city held a stash of treasures never before seen and the great possibility for me to visit the old city on a constant and continual basis.

So within my first twenty-four hours in Damascus, I had begun to completely change my opinion, so instead of wanting to depart on the next flight, I was now looking forward to my subsequent trips back to the old city of Damascus.

I often think that Steve knew exactly what he was doing and was expecting my initial negative reaction to the city as he too experienced the exact feelings when he arrived in Damascus a year earlier. It was a brilliant idea for him to take me out of the residential part of the city and to suggest on my second day in the city that I discover the 'heartbeat' of Damascus within the old city.

I had also discovered that my entire pre-perception of Damascus had changed. I now uncovered a dynamic and vibrant inner city in which all the 'locals' were very hospitable and very pleasant. The things I had seen were fantastic and that indeed I had never seen before in my life.

I forgot who wrote the following: *"Damascus surpasses all other cities in beauty, and no description, however full, can do justice to its charms."* This sums up my own feeling of this great city called Damascus.

Now, my memories, after forty-four years in this city, are still as vivid and intense as during my first tour of the old city in August 1975. Today, I still look forward to every trip to the old city and believe it or not, I still discover new and interesting sites within the old city walls!

So the first and the most important factor that influenced my rapid change of opinion of Damascus was, of course, the old city of Damascus, which took place on only the second day after arriving in the city.

Chapter Five

How My Love of Damascus Continued to Grow

Many other positive factors did take a much longer time to develop, thus making this precipitous transformation of opinion more deeply rooted, longer-lasting, and totally engrained for the remainder of my life.

The Syrian people and other foreigners that I met upon my arrival at the airport were really not true 'Damascenes'. The true down-to-earth people of Damascus were the ones I had continually met week in and week out in the old city of Damascus. They were the original and true descendants of Damascus. They were born and raised in the beautiful old houses on the many old, small streets within the old city. They were reared and fostered with the belief that one's family must: work hard, do well, and treat all people they meet as equals. Their family name was and is today the most important part of their existence. One always respected their parents and grandparents. When the family elders were too old to look after themselves, they were never sent to an old-aged home or retirement facility, they simply stayed with the eldest son or daughter. In this regard, they would be able to instill their life's insight and wisdom to their children and their grandchildren. These Damascene Families always maintained that their family name and family's reputation would never be tarnished or tainted. To date, certain families are still well known for generations and generations for being honest, sincere business people and usually in one trade or craft.

It is still seen today within these famous families that the eldest son would eventually take over their father's trade or business. Hence the family's reputation and family's name would be well-preserved and well-maintained.

These old city Damascene people are also very outgoing and very friendly as many were descendants of trading families. They always asked me: "Where are you from?" And when I answered America, they would say: "You are most welcome to my city!" Then they regularly invite me into their small shops for coffee or tea. Today that hospitality is still very common and still quite normal in the old city of Damascus.

No other city in the world has impressed me more than Damascus has…most importantly because of its people.

I soon discovered that Syria had a very special and unique cuisine like no other that I had experienced up until that time. Not only was the food always garden-fresh, but extremely discriminating and quite flavorsome. I soon discovered that the spices that I had seen in the Spice Souq that first day was used in the various dishes served not only in restaurants but also in the kitchens of all Syrian families. Syrian cooks, regardless of their age, use a wide variety of spices and herbs such as: thyme, cumin, saffron, garlic, cardamom, and turmeric, etc.

Personally, what was especially heartwarming for me was the fact that the Syrian food had a special name for their many appetizers, and it is called: the "Mezze." Each lunch or dinner while enjoying a meal in a typical Syrian restaurant one would have to order several of the Mezze items such as: Hummus; Babaghanous; Borak; Mutabbal; Lebaneh; Yalanji; Olives; Fulmedamis. And all are served with fresh hot Arabic bread. Then you would usually have two or three Mezze Salads such as Tabbouleh, Fatoush, or a nice Season Salad. Still, today when I eat out in a restaurant or a friend's house, I normally do not have a main entrée as the Mezze dishes are more than enough.

Over ninety percent of all components of a Syrian Mezze are vegetarian, and this was extremely important to me as in 1973, while living and camping in Europe, I became a vegetarian! To this day, which is now some forty-six years on, I have never tasted a piece of red meat or chicken. And still today, I never get tired of the many small dishes made up in a typical Syrian Mezze.

The typical Syrian lunch or dinner entrée is usually a meat dish and is commonly either a grilled Kebab made from meat or chicken; or Kubbeh which is finely ground meat with bulgur and minced onion and a great deal of local spices or even Kufteh which are meatballs and sometimes Shawarma which is also either chicken or meat, thinly sliced and stacked in a cone-like shape and roasted on a slowly turning rotisserie. So still today, there is no reason to have any main dish or entrée while having my lunch or dinner.

I have never been a 'desert person' but this city had taught me to enjoy some very tempting, alluring, and famous Syrian desserts. First, I discovered the two types of Syrian Ice Cream, the local or what is commonly called: 'booza' and the traditional western style of ice cream, The local ice cream has a slightly elastic texture; it comes in rolls and is quite good. The best know local shop for booza is called; 'Bakdash'. Bakdash still has its' original shop located in the old city and is in the large Al-Hamidiyah Souq. It has been making and serving booza since 1885 and still makes its famous frozen dessert directly in front of you. They use large wooden pounders or pestles to 'beat' the ice cream into this unusual texture. Damascus has, of course, the more traditional 'western' ice cream shops and with all their ice creams that are made locally and all do not contain color or food additives. Today, I always have a kilogram or two in my freezer of both booza and the regular western ice cream!

I discovered in fact that Syria had a large capacity for multiple beverage production. Many small shops and stalls in the souqs and on many of the streets would have a wide assortment of freshly squeezed juices from Orange to Pomegranate and from Strawberry to a great 'mixed cocktail' of many fresh fruits. Even today, I love to watch these shop owners squeeze the fruits as they are still using a large metal 'squeezer' in which they place a sliced half of the fruit and proceed to squeeze the fruit through a large strainer into a large pitcher below. You can drink your fresh juice in the shop or they have it 'to go'. These freshly squeezed juices are so refreshing, especially on a hot afternoon or evening during the summer.

Something very unique to the old Hamidiyah Souq is the Erk Sous or Licorice drink vendors or the Tamarind drink vendors all found within the souq. They all have their drinks on their backs in brightly decorated brass containers, and they are all wearing old traditional Syrian clothing. They have their glasses ready to serve their drinks and water to rinse each glass. They are like a: 'self-contained beverage vendors' and are very unique to the old city of Damascus.

Street Juice Vendor

So one can see that in addition to my being very impressed in touring and visiting the old city of Damascus, I then began to enjoy the fine food that Damascus has to offer.

So it was easy, and very soon after my arrival in this city, I truly 'fell in love' with this amazing and astonishing city.

That being said, one of the other initial reasons that I fell in love with Damascus and was the main purpose that I traveled to Damascus was my new teaching job at the Damascus Community School or better known as the: American School in Damascus.

I don't remember exactly on which day the school reopened, but I did have sufficient time to familiarize and acquaint myself with the school's science curriculum and the teaching staff. I should readdress the term: 'science curriculum' as the school really had no set science program, and I was expected to develop the full science syllabus for grades kindergarten through the ninth grade. This was a daunting task as I discovered the school had many old science books available, and the new science program that I had suggested including the new science text books would not arrive until mid-November from the States. Nevertheless, I began to investigate the available textbooks starting from our ninth grade class and worked my way down to the kindergarten class. By the time the school opened, I had each class core curriculum under control and well explained to each classroom teacher within the lower levels.

I was scheduled to teach sixth to ninth grades; therefore, I needed to work with each of the lower grade classroom teachers so they could follow my science program. Knowing all the time that this was going to be a temporary stop-gap syllabus as our new science program was due to arrive in several months.

The next challenging task was to finalize the interior design of the new science building. While I was in America and discussing my new teaching position, I was not told that the school had spent that same summer building a new classroom that was to be used as the school's science lab! So when I arrived for my first school visit, I was astonished what had been constructed was only a shell of a concrete building! They had decided to wait until my arrival to complete the interior and have me choose such items as the buildings flooring, windows,, desk, lab stations, lighting, sinks, and even the size of the blackboard to be used!

Over the course of the next two months, I worked on a daily bases with the Arab Contractor for the finalization of the interior of the school's new science lab. This was a very demanding and trying mission as the main contractor did not speak a word of English, and I did not know Arabic except for the basic greetings.

The entire furniture requirements were to be handmade in the local market, and a few items were simply purchased from the local souk such as the following electrical items: fluorescent lighting, electrical switches, sockets, and air conditioner/heater. The desks, chairs, lab stations, bookshelves, cabinets, and even the sinks were all to be locally sourced and manufactured. This took a great deal of time as a sample of each was submitted for my approval and then if I had accepted the sample, then it was manufactured!

Another daunting task was the assembly of the science equipment such as the microscopes, chemistry glassware from test tubes to the Erlenmeyer flasks, and the graduated cylinders to glass beakers.

The school had some of these basic Science laboratory equipment, but the challenge was to locate them and then to make an up-to-date inventory so if any additional items were needed I could either order them from the local market or have them sent to the school via the US Embassy.

Weeks upon weeks had passed before the interior was completed, finalized and I had a fully stocked and operational Science Lab.

A very positive factor for me was realizing that even though the school was an 'independent' school, yet it was well connected to the US Embassy in Damascus. I soon found that it was a nice 'safety net' for all the teachers. Also, the US teachers had the authorization to use the Embassies Diplomatic Pouch, thus making the mail delivery to and from my family very, very fast and safe. Today, the local Syrian mail service is still unpredictable and irregular. The old joke was that the Syrian Postal Authority was still using the camel for its mail delivery. Most of the time this joke proved to be very true.

Also, we were always invited to various US and foreign diplomatic functions and events. These were usually held at the Ambassador's Residence or for the very large activities at one of the five-star hotels in Damascus.

During my time at the school, the US Embassy had built two great tennis courts located on the school grounds. The funding came from the funds which allocated the embassy to have an emergency helicopter evacuation area. These two tennis courts were surrounded by a very, very high chain-linked fence with one extremely large double chain-linked gate. The reason for these two courts was a serious issue as if the US Embassy was required to evacuate their personnel, they could fly out their diplomatic staff in a time of a crisis and then use the tennis court area to store their diplomatic vehicles. I personally made great use of these tennis courts as I was able to manage some tennis instruction on the weekends plus I helped organize various tennis tournaments throughout the school year.

Immediately, I found the school's local staff to be very congenial and extremely amiable. They were all Syrian, and one could immediately recognize they loved teaching and adored their students. I had a solid teaching relationship with the staff, and this was very important.

Remember this science curriculum was completed twice within the first four months as we didn't receive our new science textbooks until two and a half months into the first school year.

The school had classes from nursery till the ninth grade, and all the class sizes were extremely small. My eighth and ninth grade consisted of only twelve and nine students respectively and compared to my class sizes in California, these were extremely small. In the States, my average class size was twenty-five students. In addition to the small class size in Damascus, the majority of the students were all children from diplomatic families. Many of whom have been to various worldwide postings and hence they attended various international schools, thus making their interest very global.

My weekly teaching schedule was very conducive to a great deal of free time as we taught from Monday till Friday, and Friday was a half-day, and we had both Saturday and Sundays free. Before I purchased a car, each Saturday and Sunday, I would go to the old city of Damascus and simply discover new and interesting areas.

I also discovered that walking in Damascus was always an easy option as from our apartment to the main gate of the school was only a four-minute walk, and to walk to the old city was only a fifteen to twenty-minute walk. I quickly found that everything of interest in Damascus seemed to be a walking distance from our apartment.

Once I purchased a car, we were able to begin touring the entire country unabated as with a two and a half-day weekend, there was no limit to our Syrian destinations and adventures.

The school had also planned many student field trips, and these were normally available for only the upper three grades due to the ages of these particular students. These field trips were real adventures for me and made my appreciation for the school, the country and of course, the Syrian people more pronounced. Even more, it gave me a new and direct insight into the entire area of the Levant as we completed several field trips to the neighboring countries of Jordan and Lebanon. All these trips occurred during the first six months of my first school year.

The schools field trips included: a train ride on the old Hejaz Railroad; then a tour of Petra in Jordan; we followed that trip to the famous Roman city of Baalbek in Lebanon; our next two Syrian field trips were first to: Palmyra, and then we followed that trip with another field trip to encompass the two cities: Hama and Aleppo, both in Central Syria.

The first school field trip was at the end of September. This school trip was a round-trip ride on the old Hejaz Railroad, which included: a one-way three-hour train ride on the old

Hejaz Main Station in Damascus

Hejaz railroads spur line from the main Hejaz Station in Damascus to the small town of Zebdani. The train was driven by an old 1896 steam locomotive. This was the only field trip in which we took the entire school population as it was a fun trip and an adventure that all ages would enjoy. We departed from the original Hejaz Main Railroad Station just outside the Old City in Damascus. This station was built by the Ottomans and was completed in 1913 and was the starting point of this famous Turkish Hejaz Railroad. This narrow-gage railroad line traveled over 1,300 km to the Saudi city of Medina. It was originally planned to end in the holy city of Mecca, but the start of the WW I plus a lack of funding had changed that idea. The Hejaz Railroad line was built for two prime reasons; first, it had strong military ties for the Ottoman Empire and second, it would transport the Muslim pilgrims traveling to Saudi Arabia to attend the annual Hajj.

Before we got on the old train, we had a guide explain to the students all the historical details of both this famous station and the railroad line that we were to travel on. This was the main branch or spur line for travel from Damascus to Beirut and this line was opened in 1894. We boarded the vintage passenger cars and we were off. The railroad tracks were from the rear of the Baramke Station through many areas of the city of Damascus. At each street intersection, there were the flashing lights and a small gate that would be manually closed keeping the cars from crossing the tracks. The students were all hanging out the windows and waving to the people as we passed. We had seven stops at very small stations before getting to our destination Zebdani. The train tracks followed the Barada river valley and our first small station was Dumar. After Dumar, there were many trees along the railroad tracks plus the Barada river and since our trip was in the morning and during the fall season, many wet leaves had fallen on the track. For this reason, the Railways had hired several young boys with cans of sand to run in from of the steam engine and to place sand along the top of the tracks, thus keeping the large steel wheels of the engine from slipping on the wet leaves! To this day, I have never ever seen this action take place anywhere in the world.

We then stopped at the following small stations: Hame; Jedeide; Ain Fije; Deir Kanum; Suk Wadi Barada and Et Tekkie Hatt. It was also amazing that between many of these tiny stations, the tracks would crisscross the main Beirut/Damascus Highway, and again at each crossing, there would be a crossing guard that would manually lower the small gate across the roadway.

From that last station of Et Tekkie Hatt, there was a very long stretch of rail that was very flat and time-consuming until we arrived in the small city of Zabadani. We had an hour or so to walk around this city, and during this transition time, the stream locomotive engine was filled with water and somehow reversed itself. We returned on the train and this time it felt faster as most of the journey was downhill. I know the students and all the teachers had a very informative and nice adventure that day riding an old turn-of-the-century steam locomotive.

In the middle of October, the school had planned a great three-day weekend field trip that consisted of a tour and two-night stay in Petra, the ancient Nabatean city in Jordan. For me, it was my first trip to Jordan, and I soon realized that it would not be my last as I found Jordan quite interesting and adventurous. On this trip, we traveled with the students from the seventh; eighth and ninth grades as it was for two nights and these students were more mature and more keenly interested in this famous city called Petra and also called the 'Rose City'. We also had on this trip many of the students' parents as they too had never seen this amazing Nabatean archeological site.

From Damascus, it took our bus just over five hours to reach the entrance to Petra. There were no challenges at the Syrian/Jordanian border as both the Syrian and Jordanian authorities realized that we were a student group, thus making our exit and entrance procedures in an expeditious manner. Once we got to the main gate of Petra, the school hired one of the many English speaking guides that were available, and then we began our adventurous trek into the most interesting and fascinating ancient cities. The city was believed to have been settled as early as 9,000 BC, and it was possibly established in the fourth century BC as the capital city of the Nabataean Kingdom. The Nabataeans were nomadic Bedouin Arabs who invested in Petra's location to the trade routes by establishing it as a major regional trading hub. We walked into the ancient city through a very narrow winding passageway. Some of the parents rode horses and camels thus making their journey much easier than the students and teachers. Midway along this narrow passageway, we came across the most beautiful structure in all of Petra the Treasury. The amazing structure was carved into the sandstone mountain and still has many of the beautiful features remaining. Also along this narrow passageway, there were carved into the stone water channels that harvested the rainwater to be used for drinking and agriculture by the Nabatean people. It was estimated that at the height of Petra's prosperity, there were 20,000 inhabitants. We continued our hike along this narrow passageway and then we came upon the main city of ancient Petra and the figure of inhabitants was most likely accurate as there

Petra

were a great number of houses and tombs carved into the mountainside for great distances inside this ancient city.

We discovered that the Romans had taken over Petra around 106 AD, and you could see the many additions the Romans added to this ancient city such as the large Triumphal Arch; a Roman Amphitheater; many temples including The Great Temple of Petra and the large Colonnaded Street.

At this time, there was a large rest house available with rooms for rent and a simple restaurant. For the students, we had decided to rent several caves to spend the night. These caves were adjacent to the rest house. This was quite an adventure for them, and I guarantee many of these students still have a fond memory of their primitive two-night stay in a Petra cave. The parents and teachers were far less adventurous and we stayed within the Petra rest house.

There was so much for us to see and so many trails to hike. I guarantee that by the afternoon of our second day, we had explored every single square meter of this colossal site. All-in-all this field trip to Petra was an amazing journey of discovery and adventure. Since this first trip in 1975, I have visited Petra and the surrounding countryside more than ten times and each time I see and discover new sites and locations.

The third field trip was to the Roman Archeological site in Baalbek, Lebanon, and was taken in early November. Baalbek was probably the best Roman site in all of Lebanon. It is also widely known as one of the largest of all Roman temple complexes existing in the world today. This was a very short trip as the Lebanese civil war was exploding in many areas of the country so we were very careful to select a secure and safe weekend to begin this third most adventurous field trip. We took a bus from the school as this fabulous archeology site in Baalbek was only 56 km or 35 miles from Damascus. The border crossing was quite fast as the minute they knew we were a school group, the entry visa process was quite fast. Once we got to the main entrance of Baalbek, we immediately hired a guide as we wanted the fastest and most professional explanation of the full site. We immediately discovered that there were two main temples in the main temple complex the first being: The Temple of Jupiter and the other to the lower left side is the Temple of Bacchus The God of Wine. We started the tour at the Temple of Jupiter by climbing the many high stairs leading to a lovely 'Hexagonal Forecourt'. Then we walked to the massive 'Great Court' which you can still see the many detailed reliefs along the top of the many columns. Then you must ascend a wide set of stairs to the site of the original Temple of Jupiter.

We then descended a few stairs to visit the massive Temple of Bacchus. This temple was much better preserved than the Temple of Jupiter, and I was impressed that it was in a much better state of preservation. As our guide had mentioned that during one of the massive earthquakes, both temples were damaged, but the Temple of Jupiter was later ransacked at a greater amount due to the ease of removing the many stones and arches from that temple. Nevertheless, these two temples were in extremely good condition considering their age. Our tour was then quickly shortened as we were told that there may be some fighting developing along the road back to the Syrian border. On our way out of the main temple complex, we discovered a smaller and less defined temple just outside the main complex. This much smaller temple was dedicated to Roman mythology

God: Venus. She was the Roman God of love. She would have been comparable to the ancient Greek goddess Aphrodite. We concluded this field trip a bit earlier than expected, but notwithstanding this field trip was very informative and quite interesting as to see such a well preserved and large Roman site so close to Damascus was impressive. We did make it back to our school with no challenges along our return trip. Amazingly that was my only trip to Baalbek in the past forty-four years and then in April of 2019, I returned for my second visit. I was just as impressed now as I was some forty-four years prior. Plus now they have added a major and very impressive museum at the end of the self-guided tour. I also discovered that the entire site has been declared a UNESCO Heritage Site in 1984. This was much deserved as this site is still one of the best-preserved Roman temple sites in all the Levant region!

Our forth school field trip, which was taken in mid-November to the ancient city of Palmyra to see the well persevered Roman ruins in the Syrian desert. This trip was an overnight stay as the overall site of Palmyra is simply too

Arch of Triumph in Palmyra

massive and it was about 215 km or 134 miles from Damascus. Being an overnight stay, we had many of the parents accompany our seventh, eighth, and ninth graders. When you enter the city of Tadmur or spelled Tadmor, you are first struck by the enormous Oasis of Palm trees in a Wadi (valley) with a very large freshwater spring that surrounded the city. Because of this large oasis, the city of Tadmor dates back to the second millennium BC. The Greeks had changed the name to the name: Palmyra around the first century AD. Palmyra was famous because it was on the old Silk Road so it became a very important commercial center for trade. The Romans expanded the city and built the famous: Temple of Bel; the Great Colonnade which is over 1.1 km long; the Monumental Arch or also called the Arch of Triumph and the Tetrapylon, which is a rectangular set of four towers each with four columns and in the center was a statue.

We spent two days in Palmyra as the total site area of this fantastic ancient site is colossal. In addition to visiting the enormous old Roman city, we drove to the opposing hill where we visited the many famous Tower Tombs and the thirteenth century Palmyra or Tadmur Castle that overlooks the ancient city below! Finally, while we were visiting Palmyra, we stopped to see the well-known Palmyra Museum that contained a vast amount of the antiques found in the ancient city of Palmyra. So a two-day visit was not nearly long enough to take in the entire area.

We stayed at a very famous hotel called the Zenobia Hotel as it was the only hotel located within the Palmyra ruins. For their reception desk, they used the Ionic Capitals or tops of two columns, and in the small adjoining garden, all the tables were all the capitals of many old Roman Columns! Quite an interesting hotel and the only hotel you could look out your hotel window and see the ancient ruins simply meters away!

Today, a major part of Palmyra has been effectively and deliberately destroyed by ISIL or the Islamic State from 2015 until the Syrian government recaptured the city for the final time in 2017. Initially, after its' capture of the city by the militant group 'Dash,' it had promised the citizens of the city that it would not destroy any of Palmyra's famous monuments. Within days of this promise ISIL destroyed the famous: Lion of Al-lāt and many other statues and began to ransack the famous museum. The Islamic State then began destroying the famous monuments within the ancient city. The Temple of Baalshamin, which was one of the most complete and perfect ancient structures in Palmyra, had been completely destroyed. Then ISIL continued their destructive and devastating rampage as they destroyed the main cella or inner room of the famous Temple of Bel, the main center façade of the Roman Amphitheater; the Tetrapylon had originally sixteen columns only four remain standing today due to their damaging; relentless and unremitting destruction. Originally ISIL was destroying only religious statues and monuments, but in October 2015, news media reported that ISIL was destroying buildings with no religious meaning, including the Monumental Arch. In 2017 and only after the Syrian government had finally eliminated ISIL from the city and in full response to the destruction of this magnificent site, many organizations began the process of restoration of the damaged and ravaged artifacts of Palmyra.

Regarding the restoration, the discoverer of Ebla, Paolo Matthiae, stated that: "The archeological site of Palmyra is a vast field of ruins and only 20 to 30% of it is seriously damaged. Unfortunately, these included the important parts such as the Temple of Bel and the Temple of Baalshamin, while the Arc of Triumph can be rebuilt." He added: "In any case, by using both traditional methods and advanced technologies, it might be possible to restore 98% of the site." I am currently planning to make a visit to Palmyra as soon as possible to see for myself the unnecessary destruction of this magnificent site.

The school's fifth and final field trip during my first year of teaching at the Damascus Community School was a combined two Syrian city field trip that was taken towards the end of February 1976. We departed from school and drove directly to the city of Hama. There we saw the old Roman Water Wheels or "Norias" on the Orontes River. These water wheels would raise the water from the river up to a large aqueduct

Roman Water Wheels in Hama

to be distributed throughout the area. When we were there in 1976, many of these famous Norias were still turning. Unfortunately, I have been told that today only a few are to be seen and none are working.

Again, I am planning to revisit Hama and see for myself if indeed these celebrated water wheels are still standing and turning.

The second city on this two-day school field trip was to the 'Second City of Syria: Aleppo.' Aleppo, like Damascus: 'is one of the oldest continuously inhabited cities in history.' There were many, many interesting sites to visit in the city of Aleppo, such as the Aleppo Citadel,

Aleppo Citadel

which was built between the third millennium BC to the twelfth century AD. It is said that the Aleppo Citadel is: "one of the oldest and largest castles in the world." It was very, very impressive as it sits on a high hill in the center of the city, and you have a commanding view from its ramparts.

Also, we toured the old covered Al-Madina Souq, which is said to be the largest covered souq or bazaar in the world and compared to the Damascus Souqs, the Al-Madina Souq was much larger. One could buy almost anything within this souq. The main Al-Madina Souq contained many smaller souqs each specializing in a certain product such as silk to soaps. Also within the souq were several of the city's famous khans or caravanserais spread around the old souqs. These khans were numerous because Aleppo was the meeting point from as far away as China and Mesopotamia to the east, Europe to the west and the Fertile Crescent and Egypt to the south. This prime location-enabled Aleppo to be the major Middle Eastern commercial link in trade for many, many years. On the second day, we spent a great deal of time in the city's famous: Archeological Museum. We were all amazed at the number of antiquities and relics within this building!

We stayed at one of the most famous hotels in all of Syria. It was called the Baron Hotel and was famous for many reasons: first, it is one of the oldest hotels that was currently operating in all of Syria and second it was the hotel of choice for such famous people as T.E. Lawrence; Theodore Roosevelt; Agatha

Baron Hotel in Aleppo

Christie who wrote part of her book *Murder on the Orient Express* during her stay; Charles Lindbergh; David Rockefeller; etc. all stayed at the Baron Hotel.

I have just discovered that the Baron Hotel had closed its doors in 2014 as the Syrian Civil War was very close, and the building had sustained a bit of war damage. Now all the rooms are empty and have only one last guest and that was the great-granddaughter of the original owner and she was staying in the hotel up until 2014 or 2015. The current fate of this famous hotel property is now completely unknown.

Personally, these five adventurous school field trips were extremely interesting as they taught me a great deal of the history of this fascinating region of the Middle East and broadened my knowledge of the local Syrian population and historic sites. I was also gaining a deep love for the people and places within the Levant region of the Middle East.

Plus it was also an amazing learning experience for my students as they also discovered that education was not only found within their classroom but on these great field trips of adventures. Few students would have the chance to experience such trips during their school year, let alone during their entire lifetime. This was a very special method of learning that my students had experienced while attending the Damascus Community School.

I was also very, very lucky as during my first four months at the school, there were three long religious-based school vacations. The Islamic Holy Month of Ramadan started on September 7th, 1975; this was followed in early October with a long eight-day school vacation to celebrate the end of Ramadan, and this holiday was called: Eid al-Fitr. There was another Islamic holiday in early December called Eid al-Adha which marks the end of the annual Hajj pilgrimage. In late December, there was the Christian holiday of Christmas to celebrate the birth of Jesus Christ, who the Christians believe is the Son of God.

So during those first few months at the Damascus Community School, I was able to plan and travel on three personal trips, and then you add the five school field trips so this short period accounted for many great journeys and expeditions. Each of these eight trips was very special, quite unique and all filled with great fascination and adventure.

On this first long personal school vacation, I decided to fly from Beirut to Larnaca, Cyprus. I had heard so much about this famous island called Cyprus that I really wanted to discover it first-hand. The best flight schedule was to leave from Beirut International Airport as that flight was only a thirty-minute flight on MEA (Middle East Airways). So after school, I left Damascus by taxi to Beirut International Airport. I immediately discovered that there was a major problem that I did not expect. Lebanon was in the initial stages of a civil war and that in the past 24 hours, fighting was flaring up in certain parts of the capital. By the time I entered Lebanon, it was becoming dark, and my taxi ride through the many darkened streets of Beirut was terrifying. There were many street battles in various areas of the Beirut, but especially between the downtown parts of the city to the airport. My driver and I could hear the sound of machine gun fire the minute we arrived at the inner city. We turned around many times simply to avoid the many fire-fights directly in front of us. After many hours of dodging danger, we finally reached the airport. When I was getting out of my Syrian taxi one could hear the shelling and small arms fire from the city center. To this day, I never knew if my driver had made it back safely to Damascus that night.

That evening the airport was quite busy as it appeared that many of the local Beirut residents were fearful of the street fighting in their neighborhoods and simply wanted to exit the city. For the Muslims, it was also the start of their Eid Holiday, so there were many passengers in the airport that evening. I soon discovered that Cyprus was their ideal location as they were still very close to Beirut in case they needed to quickly return yet far enough to avoid any imminent and forthcoming danger.

At the MEA check-in counter, they announced that our flight was to depart thirty minutes early as the airline was informed that the city fighting was increasing at such a swift pace they wanted to get the aircraft in the air as soon as possible. I had never had a flight depart early, so this was a real first for me in my years of air travel.

Once I arrived at the departure area, I could sense the anxiety and the trepidation of the passengers. We did depart early as announced, and most of us were pleased as the fighting remained a short distance away from the airport. Little did I know at the time that this would be my last occasion for using Beirut International Airport as for the next several years, the Beirut Airport was operational a minimal amount of time.

Upon landing at Larnaca International Airport, there was a general feeling of relief and safety throughout the aircraft. What I soon discovered and what I didn't realize before coming to Cyprus was that the island of Cyprus had suffered an invasion from Turkey one year before, and over 36% of the original island was under Turkish control. Cyprus was also suffering from a major refugee problem as around 150,000 Greek Cypriots were expelled from the north to the south of the island and when I arrived in October of 1975, the Turkish Cypriots living in the southern part of the island were being displaced from the south to the north or Turkish controlled part of the island.

What a disruptive and troublesome time for me to visit Cyprus! I found that I was in for a major adventure during my short stay in Cyprus.

I found an airport taxi to take me to my hotel, which was on the main Corniche road along the sea in Larnaca. I had made my hotel booking with a small Damascus Tour Office, and when I entered the hotel, they initially had no reservation in my name. This was not the best way to start one's vacation. I was very lucky as just an hour earlier they had a room cancelation so they gave me this room. My room was facing the main street with a small balcony. Unfortunately, the street noise was quite intense thus making sleep extremely difficult.

I was quite hungry as I had nothing to eat since I left Damascus that morning. The front desk manager suggested a great seafood restaurant near the old seaport which was walking distance from the hotel. I walked to the restaurant and enjoyed a very delicious seafood dinner. To add to the atmosphere of the restaurant, in the front window, they had a large octopus hanging over a pot of boiling water. The chef would simply cut off a large tentacle and serve it directly. It was delectable as I had three servings of octopus that night. As a matter of fact, it was so good that I ate there another five times during my stay. I also discovered that Cyprus had good local white wine, but you had to be very careful as some of their white wines were on the sweet side. Also, they had a nice local beer called: KEO which I usually had with my seafood luncheon meals.

The next morning I hired a car, and the driver took me to the capital Nicosia. This was very interesting as just over a year earlier, the Turkish forces came very close to capturing this city. The partition line or now called the: 'Green Line' is very near to the center of Nicosia. We drove very close to this separation line and we could see UN Peace Keeping forces on both sides of this estrangement line. At this time, there was not a great deal to see and tour in Nicosia as they still had the war on their minds and many of the shops had remained closed since the hostilities broke out some fourteen months earlier. So only after a short tour of Nicosia, I asked the driver to take me back to Larnaca to my hotel. So my first real tour of the island of Cyprus turned out to be a major disappointment.

I arrived back at the hotel, and that is when I decided to take a much-needed nap. That same early evening I decided to walk around the old seaport as it was very interesting, and also I simply needed to relax and look at the various powerboats and sailboats moored in the old seaport.

While walking, I spotted a very nice sailboat attempting to back in an empty slip. On the pier were four of five Cypriots all yelling in Greek to the captain, and it appeared that he was getting frustrated and a bit annoyed with the incoming shouts. I decided to try to help and began yelling at him in English with clear and proper directions. The owner of the sailboat made it into his slip quite well. I helped him with his various lines to tie down on the dock and then he thanked me and asked if I wanted to come on board to have a glass of wine. I said: "Why not?" I discovered that this captain in distress was a Professor of Oceanography at the American University in Beirut called AUB; his name was Dr. George and the name of his Canadian registered sailboat was the: Atoll II. He discovered that I had solid experience in sailing and very quickly we became good friends. After an hour of relaxing on his thirty-seven-foot sailboat, I suggested that we try the seafood restaurant that I had tried the night before. Dr. George had also eaten there several years earlier so he was keenly interested in joining me. We walked to "my seafood restaurant" and once again the seafood was fantastic and we talked until almost midnight. We departed and I went back to my hotel whereas he walked back to his sailboat and his five cats.

The next day I had booked a taxi to have a full-day tour of Cyprus's second city Limassol. Dr. George and I made plans to have dinner once again that evening at this fantastic seafood restaurant.

When I started off, I told my driver that I didn't want to be "A typical tourist" and for him to show me the special places that supposedly made Cyprus and Limassol famous and also that he personally liked. So my driver took me first to the famous and well preserved ancient Greek ruins of Kourion. This large Greek Amphitheater was outside the city of Limassol was very impressive and had a beautiful view of the Mediterranean Sea. I remember seeing the remains of some very old mosaic floors and statues within the Kourion Museum. Then after Kourion, I said, "OK, what should we see next?" From there, we drove into the old city of Limassol and first stopped to see the Limassol Castle. This was located very close to the old harbor and in humble opinion, this citadel was quite small relative to 'Syrian Standards'. It was built on top of an old church or cathedral and yet there were no excavations on site. Then he said, "I will show you the 'old city of Limassol'." I was really expecting to see something along the lines of the old city in Damascus. The old city of Limassol was nice but was nothing compared to the old city in Damascus. Again, I was a bit disappointed. Even the stones used in the construction were different than the Damascus stones; they simply did not look that old. After our short tour, we then went to a 'local Greek Taverna' directly on a beach just outside of the city. I had invited my driver for lunch and it was quite enjoyable as again I had seafood and a great traditional Greek Salad.

After lunch, he wanted to show me his favorite area of Cyprus…the Troodos Mountains. This part of the trip really complimented my tour as the mountains were very green and covered with vast areas of pine trees. We passed by many old villages which contained very old churches and interesting buildings. There were so many hidden valleys to discover, and finally, we drove to the top of Mt. Olympus, not to be confused with the 'real' Mt. Olympus in Greece. We stopped along the way to see many unbelievable views and I took many photos to document the beauty. By late afternoon we finally arrived back at my hotel. I then decided to check with the MEA travel office to reconfirm my return flight to Beirut that next afternoon. At the MEA travel office, they informed me that all the flights in and out of Beirut Airport had been canceled that day and they were 'expecting' the airport to reopen the next morning.

Now my first holiday trip was turning into a real-life adventure! What was I to do if the Beirut Airport remained closed? How was I to travel back to Lebanon and Syria?

That evening, as expected, I met Captain George at the seafood restaurant, and I informed him of my airline challenge. He told me, "Thomas, don't worry as I am planning to sail back to Beirut tomorrow afternoon and if you discover the Beirut International Airport is closed, you can sail with me back to Beirut."

After another great dinner, I walked back to my hotel, and then all of a sudden, I felt excited about the possibility of sailing back to Beirut instead of flying back. Needless to say, I could not sleep well that night as I knew that I was to start school in Damascus in two days and if that option of sailing to Lebanon turned into a reality, I would miss my classes.

Needless to say, as soon as the MEA travel office opened that next morning, I was standing and waiting at the front door. I went up to the same travel agent, and she told me: "Mr. Webber, it does not look good as the fighting in Beirut had intensified and there is a strong probability that all flights in and out of Beirut Airport would be canceled that day."

I then took a bold and decisive move and asked the agent to cancel my return ticket, and I requested a refund. I told her that I would find 'another way' to get back to Beirut. The agent had a very apprehensive look: how was I to return to Beirut if not by air. I informed her of my meeting with a sailboat owner and we were planning to sail together back to Lebanon that same day. She wished me luck that I would succeed in this strange endeavor.

From the travel office, I went directly to the old seaport and found George on his yacht and informed him of my decision to cancel my air booking.

I think he too was hoping that the Beirut Airport would be closed as he wanted to have a crew member with him for his return sail to Beirut that late afternoon. I then returned back to my hotel, packed my bag, checked out of the hotel, and headed back to the sailboat that was hopefully going to take me back to Lebanon. From there, I would find a way back to Damascus. When I climbed aboard the Atoll II,

Professor George was very happy to see me and he then asked me about my previous sailing experience. I told him while I was in college, I had sailed a few times from Newport Beach to Catalina Island and twice sailed on a Transpacific Yacht Race ('Trans Pac') famous participant called *Kialoa I* which was moored in Newport Beach. While at college, I was working in Newport Beach in a 5-star restaurant and the owner of the *Kialoa I*, a 50-foot Ketch sailboat, had routinely invited the waiters and other employees for a day sail as the *Kialoa I* was tied up directly in front of the restaurant. So I did have some sailing experience which was a comfort to Captain George.

We had a lot of time before our departure, so again, I suggested that we have our last lunch at my favorite seafood restaurant near the seaport. After another great and final lunch, we both felt sad as we were going to miss these great meals we shared at this fantastic restaurant.

As we departed the Larnaca seaport, we had to stop by the Cypriote Immigration Control Office to 'officially depart' Cyprus and have them stamp our passports.

My US Passport Stamps

Then in the late afternoon, we sailed towards the small port of Ayla Napa to refuel, as we planned to sail for part of the night from the island to Lebanon, and we felt there would not be a strong enough sea breeze for us to sail entirely to Lebanon. We planned to use the sailboat's inboard motor to power part of the way to Beirut. We found that directly after sunset, the winds had subsided so we lowered the sails and turned on the engine.

The sailing was one of the most beautiful adventures I had ever encountered as the seas were calm and the sunset extremely magnificent. I had taken many photos during our sail, and I had treasured them for many years.

We arrived in Lebanon by early morning, and we decided to moor the sailboat in the small Lebanese port city of Jounieh which was safer than any anchorage or marina close to Beirut. We immediately checked into the immigration office at the seaport, where I received a three-day transit visa. We found a nice little Lebanese restaurant for a light breakfast and then we called the American Community School (ACS) near the large American University in Beirut (AUB) as Professor George had a female friend there and I had a girlfriend that I wanted to see since I was in Lebanon. We told both of them that we would be coming into the area by sea on Professor George's sailboat and for them to be ready for us to collect them around four p.m. that afternoon at ACS. We were planning to disembark from the boat at the small St. Georges Hotel's Marina, where Capitan George had always berthed his yacht. We had a nice lunch in the port of Jounieh and afterward, we sailed south to Beirut and to the St. Georges Hotel. Along the sea route, we heard a great deal of gunfire especially near the Port of Beirut. We were both hoping and praying that once we got closer to the Hamara District and the hotel's marina, the gunfire would subside. We were under sail for most of the trip and once we got closer to the St. Georges Hotel and Yacht Club, we lowered the sails and proceeded under engine power. George asked me to pilot and steer the Atoll II as he was leaning forward in order to throw the mooring lines to the attendant at the marina. Along the way, there was the sound of intermitting small arms fire and mortar shelling onshore, but we decided to ignore them and proceeded to the marina. As I was maneuvering the sailboat to the entrance of the marina towards the main pier, the hotels Maître and two waiters all dressed in tuxedoes and carrying their Kalashnikovs or AK 47's suddenly ran towards us as we were approaching the dock. "Professor George, Professor George" the Maître screamed, "it is not safe here as there is fighting outside our hotels front door!" I quickly pushed the throttle forward and spun the yacht away from the marina as George was rushing back to assist me in this crucial maneuver.

We went a sufficient distance from St Georges and then we both noticed a small fishing boat with two Lebanese fishermen onboard. We pulled up alongside this small craft and asked them to take me to the shore. Reluctantly, they agreed as we guessed the fishing that evening was not very good, plus they were going to make some US dollars simply in my transport. I quickly scrambled aboard and we started to the shore. Within minutes, our small fishing boat came under gunfire. I still recall that every sixth bullet was a tracer bullet and the pinging sound the bullets made in the water was extremely eerie. Sounds that I have long remembered. That was the first time that I was being shot at and unfortunately, not my last! George and I talked about this incident later and we both agreed that if the men shooting at us wanted to kill us, they could have, but they must have thought that we were bringing in guns or ammunition as to them this entire episode was very well choreographed. 'In comes a large sailboat tries to dock at a famous Beirut hotel and then heads out from shore a short distance then they transfer their 'cargo' to a smaller boat and proceeds to come ashore' The other rationale for not killing us was maybe they did not know which 'side' we were on, so they didn't want to kill 'one-of-their-own.'

We did make it to the shore, and on the street, we saw five well-armed 'militants' above us. One had binoculars so I guessed he saw that there were only three people in the boat and we had no cargo.

As we landed at an old fishing village, I paid the driver of the fishing boat: $10. USD and told them that I would be back in ten or fifteen minutes and asked them to wait for me! I then headed towards ACS along the Beirut Corniche or promenade. Again there was light arms fire in the immediate area, but I could not tell from which direction they were coming. Along the Corniche at every intersection, there were checkpoints made of sandbags and manned by well-armed local militia. They watched me running towards them, and once I came nearer, they had the most puzzled and bemused looks on their faces as they must have thought: "Who is this crazy person running in a war zone and with no weapon." I also guessed that they thought that I was not an immediate threat to them as I was unarmed and apparently looked harmless.

ACS was about a kilometer or two from where I was dropped off in the old seaport. Finally, I did make it to ACS unscathed and intact even though it was the most terrifying experience that I had ever encountered in my entire life!

The guard at the school's main entrance was astonished when he saw this American running towards the school and then asking to see two of their teachers. The girls were waiting in the reception area of the school, and when I walked in, they looked baffled. I thought they were going to faint. They honestly thought no one would be crazy enough to come to fetch them during the heavy fighting within the city. I had promised to retrieve them earlier in the day, and I had to live up to that promise, right?

Well, they both had small carry-on bags, and I said: "Are you ready? Let's go." We were now set for a new adventure as now there were three of us running back to the small fishing village a few kilometers away. Thank goodness we were all wearing trainers or sneakers as if they had high heels we would not have made it. I ran in front and we stayed on the main lit streets as I felt it was safer than the dark side streets. We passed in front of the Saint Georges Hotel and I was ready to go inside and inform the hotels Maître that I had made it safely from the Atoll II, but there was no real reason for that gesture. We continued to sprint past the Phoenicia Hotel and onward to our rendezvous point. There was a sense of relief as we approached the old seaport and then there was disbelief and astonishment as our small boat was no were to be seen. They either got tired of waiting or they did not like the idea of being shot at. Nevertheless, we could see Atoll II, but it was way too far for us to get to without a boat. Within the old fishing village, there were a few shacks and one and only one had a small light on inside. So we went to this occupied hut and began knocking on the old wooden door, our only salvation. We knocked and knocked and it seemed like an eternity before this old man appeared. He spoke no English, but one of the girls spoke Arabic and she then explained slowly and clearly that we needed to get to the boat way out there. At first, he had no interest in helping us as it was late and there was the constant sound of gunfire in the immediate area. Somehow she convinced him of our plight and utter despair and he put on an old sweater over his dirty and tattered ghalabiya and we proceeded to his small scruffy fishing boat. We made it on to the Atoll II and I believe we paid him ten Lebanese Lira or the equivalent of about three US dollars. Today, ten Lebanese Lira is useless and worth much less than 0.007 US cents!

We were now safe aboard the sailboat Atoll II was going to be our home for the next two or three days. The only thing remaining for the four of us was to travel back to Jounieh and enjoy a nice weekend in peace and harmony.

Once we arrived back to Jounieh, we discovered a new restaurant on the Jounieh mountainside which was perched on a cliff overlooking Jounieh Bay. It was called La Creperie and we had dinner there the first night and again a lovely lunch the next afternoon as the food, interior design, and views were fantastic. I have eaten there many times since 1975, and each time the food and service appeared to improve.

Our two days together seem to have passed extremely fast as we enjoyed this complete change of pace and newfound security. It appeared that Jounieh was spared from the devastating fighting at this time. On the third day, there was a lull in the fighting, so we decided to travel back to Beirut by taxi. George kept his yacht moored in Jounieh until he could size the current security situation in Beirut and see if it would be safe to keep the Atoll II at the St. Georges Marina. We also wanted to stop by the old fishing village to thank the old fisherman for taking the three of us out to the Atoll II. In addition, and most importantly for me, I went back to Beirut in order to arrange a taxi to drive me back to Damascus. The four of us made it safely back to Beirut, and later that morning, the American Community School had organized a taxi to take me to Syria. That afternoon I returned safely to Damascus and during this extended holiday, I had gained a multitude of adventures to talk about with all my friends and colleagues for many years to come.

Today, that old fishing village no longer exists as it has been replaced with the upscale Zaitunay Bay restaurant and yacht marina development. The St. Georges Hotel has never reopened even after the end of the Lebanese Civil War. There is a large sign on the side of the hotel stating: "*Stop Solidere.*" Solidere was a large redevelopment vision by the late Lebanese Prime Minister Rafik Hariri for the war-torn and severely damaged Central Business District of Beirut. Apparently, the owner of St Georges never believed in the validity or legitimacy of this massive Solidere project and had vowed to leave the hotel closed and in a state of disorder.

We now had almost two full months of classes before the school had scheduled any new school breaks. In the first half of December, we had our second Islamic holiday, and this was again another major school holiday. This vacation started on December 11th and continued to the 18th of December. The name of this second religious holiday was Eid al-Adha, and it followed the end of the Islamic Hajj or pilgrimage to Makkah, Saudi Arabia.

On this vacation, I decided to fly to Madrid as I had really enjoyed my previous four trips to this magnificent city in Central Spain, especially the last journey to Madrid in August on my way to Damascus. On this school holiday, I decided to leave Amman, Jordan, instead of Lebanon as now Beirut was out of the question as the fighting had intensified throughout the country and the Beirut International Airport was closed more than it was opened.

As soon as the school closed that Wednesday afternoon, I was packing my suitcase and getting ready to revisit this exceptional capital of Spain. The next morning, I had arranged for a taxi to drive me to Amman. Unfortunately, my flight to Madrid was not until Saturday morning, as many of the flights during the start of this holiday season were fully booked. All the same, I had planned to spend the next two nights with a friend I had met in Damascus. Mello Mehl was the head of communications at our American Embassy in Amman. It turned out that my two-night stay was exciting and most interesting as we soon discovered that we had many common interests. We loved to try new food, and we enjoyed sampling new and interesting wines. Those two days in Amman passed very quickly. Soon I discovered that it was time to be on my way to Amman's International Airport to catch my flight to Madrid.

The flying time to Madrid from Amman was only four and a half hours, and I had arrived in Madrid in the early afternoon. I collected my suitcase and headed out to the arrivals area of the Madrid Barajas Airport. There waiting for me was my girlfriend, whom I had met while in Madrid on my previous trip in August. She was an English teacher in an international school in Madrid and we had been corresponding ever since our initial encounter that summer. She had been teaching in Madrid for the past two years and knew the city quite well. So instead of taking a taxi from the airport to the city on this trip, she found a local bus that was going to Plaza Mayor de Madrid. We jumped aboard and headed to this most beautiful and exciting city. We walked from the famous plaza to my favorite area of Madrid: Plaza de Santa Ana.

My girlfriend had made my reservations at the same pension that I stayed in 1967, 1971, and then in August of 1975. After I checked into the hotel, we spent some time together catching up on her teaching in Madrid and my teaching experience in Damascus. That early evening I insisted that we have a cold draft beer at the Cerveceria Alemana which was very famous as this was the 'favorite hangout' of Ernest Hemingway. We recalled one of Hemingway's favorite sayings while we were enjoying our cold beers: *"Never go on trips with anyone you do not love."* That is such a true statement concerning anyone's life and anyone's travels, as the majority of my travels have been with people I loved.

After a couple of beers, we then went to the famous Tapa Bars in the area of my two-star 'hotel'. My favorite food without question was the fresh black mussels or in Spanish *'mejillones'*. In the five nights that I spent in Madrid, we had enjoyed many of our meals in these famous Tapa Bars in and around Plaza de Santa Ana. Yet, on this trip, we added several new Tapa Bars for those delicious mejillones in the surrounding streets on the way to and close to Plaza del Sol. This public square was a very short and interesting walk but is quite large especially in comparison to Plaza de Santa Ana, yet the streets between these two plazas have many great tapas bars. I was glad that I was with a person who spoke perfect Spanish as these side streets were not commonplace for the 'typical tourist'.

The next morning, we decided to walk to the famous Plaza de Mayor. During my entire stay in Madrid, I only took bus transport twice, coming from the airport and going back to the airport. Madrid is a city to walk as there are so many small streets connecting to the famous plazas. As a matter

Prado Museum in Madrid

of fact, Plaza Mayor has eight or nine main gates to enter this large enclosed rectangular-shaped square. All the buildings have very similar architecture, and all are a bit ornate but quite beautiful.

From the Plaza de Mayor, we decided to visit the very famous Prado Museum. On my previous trips to Madrid, I had always visited this fantastic and massive museum. Believe it or not, on each visit, I discover something new within the Prado.

On this visit, I discovered that throughout the Peninsular War which was the war between Napoleon's French armed forces and the Portuguese, Spanish and British forces from 1808 until Napoleon's defeat in 1814, the original premises of the Prado had been used as headquarters for the Napoleonic troops based in Madrid. Napoleon's cavalry had used the Prado as a gunpowder-store during the war. The Peninsular War was a long war that eventually led to the defeat and abdication of Napoleon in 1815. The French had dedicated over 200,000 of their troops in the futile and unsuccessful effort to defeat the Spanish and Portuguese, with assistance from the British. In addition, in 1812, Napoleon led a disastrous invasion of Russia in which his army was forced to retreat and suffered massive casualties. At the same time, the Spanish; Portuguese and British forces drove Napoleon's armies from the Iberian Peninsula to end the Peninsular War in 1814. This was one of the main reasons for the ultimate defeat of Napoleon in 1815 at the Battle of Waterloo.

That night we enjoyed our favorite Tapa Bars and retired a bit early for Madrid standards, as we were planning to travel to the amazing city of Toledo some 68 to 70 km or only 42 miles north of Madrid the next morning.

We woke up early and had a light breakfast at my pension. I had discovered over my previous trips to Europe as one travels further south in Europe, the breakfasts get smaller and smaller. In the UK, Holland, and the Scandinavian countries, the hotels usually serve a large and hearty breakfast, but as you travel south to Spain and Portugal, the breakfast served at the majority of the hotels is simpler and less robust than their northern neighbors.

After breakfast, instead of us being 'typical tourist' and taking the usual tourist bus tour of Toledo, we decided to take the train from Madrid to Toledo. It was also an opportunity for both of us to rediscover this remarkable Spanish city on our own terms and to see exactly what we wanted to see and not what a tour guide wanted us to see. From my pension to the train station was a very short distance so, of course, we walked. The trains to Toledo all departed from the famous Atocha Train Station, which was the largest train station in Madrid. As a child, I developed a fond love for train stations as my father worked on the New York Central Railroad and each summer, he had a pass to travel anywhere on their network. The Atocha Train Station is a real architectural gem as it was built in 1851 by several famous Spanish architects and in one instance in collaboration with Gustave Eiffel. The Atocha Train Station is located at the large Plaza del Emperador Carlos V, a plaza at which eight streets converge, in Madrid. I feel like a child when I enter any train station and it was no different when I entered this magnificent station. I still remember the large wrought iron ceiling which covered many of the train platforms. I simply wanted to see all of this famous train station prior to our own train's departure. The journey to Toledo was fast as we elected to take the "Express" train and not a "local" or much slower train. I personally feel one can see more of the countryside from a train than from a bus or a car.

Toledo is known as the "*City of three cultures*" as it has always been a mixture of Christians, Arabs, and Jews. Immediately upon entering the old city, I found there was a striking resemblance to the old city of Damascus. First, because of the three main cultures which were found in both; each city has an old city wall surrounding the old city plus this wall had many beautiful gates and finally a great deal of both the old cities' architecture was, of course, Arabic in form and substance. Specifically, Moorish architecture in Toledo as the Moors had ruled Spain, as some historians believe, for over 800 years. The Moors were originally a mix of Arabs from Arabia, North Africa, Spain, and Berber origins. The Moors created the Arab Andalusia civilization between the eleventh and seventeenth centuries.

What astonished me the most was the similarity between the old city of Damascus and the old city of Toledo. On my first trip to Toledo in 1967, I had never seen Damascus, so this resemblance was unknown to me, but on this trip, it was quite conspicuous as I had lived in Damascus for the past four months. I could make a logical and reasonable analysis of this deep-seated resemblance of the two cites on this trip.

Within the remains of the old Moorish, old city Wall were many gates, and I particularly liked the cities three main gates: the Bisagra Antigua Gate which leads into the old city; the Alfonso VI Gate or also called the Bisagra Nueva Gate as it was built much later in 1559 and the Sol Gate or also known as the: Gate of the Sun. Our favorite was the old Bisagra Antigua gate as it was dated back to the tenth century and it had an unusual horseshoe-shaped archway. When you pass through the Bisagra Antigua Gate,

Bisagra Antigua Gate in Toledo

you enter the famous Plaza de Zocodover and the origin of this plazas name *Zocodover* comes from the Arabic language "*sūq ad-dawābb*", which means "market of burden beasts."

We spent a great deal of time admiring these famous gates, the small alleyways within the old city, and the numerous mosques, synagogues, and churches within the city. I had always loved the works of El Greco and the city of Toledo was the home of this great artist.

During this tour of Toledo and my constant comparisons of Toledo to the old city of Damascus was when and the main reason my girlfriend had decided to visit me in Damascus that coming April during her Easter break. We had spent the full day touring this great city, and we took a late afternoon train back to Madrid.

My remaining days in Madrid passed very quickly, and before I realized it was time to head back to the Middle East.

We decided to return to Plaza Mayor to catch the airport bus that took us to the international airport, and during that bus ride, she had pledged to me that she would come to Damascus during her Easter Holiday. For the next four months, we continued to communicate by mail and she lived up to her commitment. This visit did prove to be a big mistake as my life in Damascus would change over that same period.

I departed Madrid heavy-hearted and found myself thinking of her quite often. I landed in Amman on December 18th and headed back to the US Embassy friend's house, Mello, to spend a few more days enjoying Amman like a real tourist in Jordan. I wanted to visit the many touristic sights offered such as the Dead Sea; Jerash, the ancient Roman city; Aqaba; Kerak Citadel, etc. That next day was a Friday, so Mello and I spent time in Amman enjoying good Jordanian cooking and tasting some great Jordanian Wine.

I had an extra ten days' vacation as the Damascus Community School combined the two holidays into one long December school vacation. It turned out that the school's third and final holiday in 1975 was Christmas, so I had almost a three-week school break that December. So when I returned to Amman, I decided to spend some additional time in Jordan as I was in Jordan only once before, and that was on our school's three-day field trip to Petra. I soon discovered that Jordan was from a very rich and historical country on par with Syria.

Every evening I would consult with Mello as to what activity I should plan for the next day. This system worked very well as he had been to all the major tourist sites in Jordan, and his advice was valuable. He also was working six days a week at the American Embassy as he was the head of the Communications. He first suggested that I travel down to the Dead Sea, as this place was like no other place in the world. "Why?" I asked, and he simply said that the Dead Sea was the lowest point on earth and that I would really enjoy my visit. I hired a local taxi and the journey from Amman to the shores of the Dead Sea was simply amazing. The road was only a two-lane highway and it was in constant descent with very interesting geological formations and scenic views along the entire drive. When I was there in December of 1975, there was only one hotel and that was along the Northern Shore of the Dead Sea. Unfortunately, today, this same hotel is abandoned as the shoreline of the Dead Sea is actually three to five kilometers from this same hotel. The shoreline has been receding at an alarming rate.

When we arrived at the hotel, the outside temperature was very hot yet dry as the sun was very bright. I never thought of bringing my bathing suit on this vacation as it was during the month of December, and I had just arrived from Spain. I was lucky to be able to purchase a bathing suit at the hotel, and I was warned not to get the saltwater in my eyes as the salt content is ten times greater than that of the ocean. I slowly walked into the 'slimy' water and it felt slick as the salt content was very high. I soon discovered that you cannot swim in the Dead Sea, but you can float on the surface. It was and remains today a real and unusual pleasure to float in the Dead Sea.

I also discovered two interesting facts from my taxi driver; first, that the Dead Sea is not really a sea but a lake as it has only a single source of water being the Jordan River, and it is not connected to an ocean.

Second, it has a special type of asphalt or bitumen being released from the seafloor, and this tar in the past has been used by the Egyptians in their mummification and by the Romans in boat repairs. As a matter of fact, the Romans used to call the Dead Sea: *"Asphalt Sea."* I returned back to Amman and had found that this first day of being a Jordanian Tourist was quite an educational experience. Also, it was only the second time I swam in a salt lake as the first time was many years earlier in the Great Salt Lake in Utah.

I returned to Amman very hungry and found that Mello was also starving, so we decided to enjoy an early dinner out on the town. During our dinner, we discussed my next day's adventures. Mello strongly suggested that I use the same taxi driver, and we drive north to the old Roman city of Jerash

Jerash in Jordan

in the morning. The distance was about 48 km and took us about an hour to reach this large and well preserved Roman city. I decided to hire a tour guide as when we were driving to the entrance, I discovered that this city was really enormous. I was very impressed with the current state of preservation of Jerash. The tour lasted over three hours on foot. By the time we had completed the tour, I felt that Jerash was a very well preserved city, but I remembered our school field trip to Palmyra in Syria and I truly felt that Palmyra was more impressive. Despite the fact, I did enjoy my tour of Jerash.

That evening Mello and I enjoyed several bottles of great French Wine, and we talked about many things including how I was enjoying my life in Damascus even with the lack of available single women.

Now I was becoming somewhat homesick so I wanted to return to Damascus. I also wanted to return to enjoy Christmas in Damascus's Christian Quarter and possibly tour other parts of Syria that I had not seen up to now.

So I asked Mello if he could arrange a taxi to drive me back to Damascus the next morning. I thanked him for putting me up for so many days both at the start of my vacation and now at the end. I also discovered that not having the added expense of a hotel stay in Jordan was a true godsend as by mid-December, my funds were running very low. Finally, I discovered that Jordan was a great tourist country, but still, it was simply not Syria.

I made it back to Damascus safely, and the taxi dropped me off at my apartment. Steve, my roommate, was not in Damascus as he was enjoying his long vacation out of Syria. So I had the apartment for myself, so I thought...

The next morning, I received a call from our American Embassy as they had been flooded with calls from our US Embassy in Lebanon, AUB, and ACS in Beirut all requesting if they knew of any temporary vacant apartments in Damascus for their professors and teachers. It appeared that the Beirut International Airport was closed due to the fierce fighting and many of their staff were trying to travel home for the

Christmas vacation. They were making flight bookings out of Damascus and in many cases, there was a long layover in Damascus due to the holiday and the overbooking of many flights. Our American Embassy in Damascus thought of Tom and Steve's apartment as we did have three bedrooms and there were only two of us living in it. I straight away said, "Yes, why not?" Never did I realize that my acceptance would mean that we would have one guest staying for the next 286 days! It appeared that after the Christmas holidays, many professors returned only to find that the fighting had intensified and soon, both AUB and ACS would be cutting the number of students and slashing the number of staff members. AUB even had enrollment agreements with various universities in the United States in order to preserve the continuity of their studies. This led to an even greater number of staff and students fleeing Beirut.

For me, this influx of foreign expatriates began that same evening. Around 7 p.m the doorbell rang, and there was a couple standing in front of our door with their suitcases in hand. I opened the door, and they said: "Steve?" I said my name was Thomas and that Steve was out of the country. They were both teachers at ACS and their flight was not until the next evening. So then began our 'open door policy' of accepting expatriates into our apartment. I must admit looking back at all these guests that stayed over the many months, the majority of them were very interesting, and it was a pleasure for both Steve and me to help them in their time of crisis.

Needless to say, I did not get to see any new areas of Syria over the Christmas holiday, but I did visit the old city and had many meals with our 'refugees' over the following months. The majority of our 'house guests' had never been to Damascus, so they all wanted to see the old city of Damascus, of course, only if they had a day or two prior to their flight. In addition to the old city, many of our visitors wanted to enjoy a good meal while in Damascus. We had a wide variety of restaurants to select from, and that list usually included my favorite restaurant the

Chevalier. I don't remember anyone ever complaining of either the old city of Damascus tour or any of the restaurants I had selected.

It was funny as I had made the decision to allow the guests to stay in our apartment without my roommate's consent. When Steve returned to Damascus, he was shocked that we had five guests staying in our apartment. He later told me that he was in favor of my offer, and his acceptance made the following months pass very quickly. Our guests were not just leaving Damascus, many of them were returning from their holidays and, of course, would stay at our humble abode before heading back to war-torn Lebanon.

As you can see and understand that everything I discovered in Syria really contributed to my total enjoyment of living and working in Damascus, yet, there was one new and major factor that changed my life forever and also continued my deep love for this most beautiful city.

During the first couple of months in Damascus, I soon discovered there was a major shortage of available single girls to date. This was partially due to the fact that the foreign embassies and NGOs based in Damascus recruited foreign staff members not on a family status but on a single male's status only. The lack of foreign women became so serious that each weekend we would go out with our male friends and acquaintances to discover a new bar, pub or club. This was getting very boring as each weekend we would see the same group of male colleagues. Thereafter, on one of our Thursday night's outings, I took the initiative to tell our group that the following Thursday, each one of us was required to bring a female date, and I would reserve a large table at one of Damascus's top clubs. As the week ensued, I received many calls from our group, and each thought that this was going to be a great evening and thanked me for the clever and astute idea. By Tuesday, I had completely forgotten about the thought that I too needed a date! I then remembered that in the American Embassies General Services Office or GSO, there was a very attractive Syrian employee who had helped me with my paperwork for the purchase of my car a few weeks earlier. I had no idea of her name so I called a friend at the embassy and asked him if he knew her or knew her name. He said that her name was Salma and she was a new local hire employee and she was single. I then asked him if he could invite her, in my name, to our Thursday night gathering. The next day he confirmed that she had accepted. All I knew of her was that her first name was Salma, she was very attractive and she accepted to be my blind date.

On Thursday afternoon after school, I went home very sick as I had a very severe case of diarrhea. I was taking the local prescription for diarrhea, but the pills were not working. At seven, Steve was getting ready to go to the club, and I was still in bed. I told him that I wasn't feeling up to it and that he should try to find Salma and apologize for me. Around eight, I forced myself and got out of bed and decided that it was not fair for Salma to be stood up by a total stranger. So I planned that I would go to the club, find her and tell her directly that I wasn't feeling well and then to return home and back to bed.

By the time I got to the party, I was the very last one to arrive. I found Salma and apologized for being late. I explained my desire to head back home. One or two in our group overheard my comments and insisted that I stay for at least one drink. One drink led to a second drink, and one dance led to many dances with this most beautiful young lady.

Throughout the night, I discovered that she had just started working at the US Embassy as before she was studying for her Master's degree in English Literature at AUB. Her dad had insisted she leaves Beirut because of the hostilities and dangerous conditions for a single girl. This entire evening was a combination of fate as she accepted this date without knowing me and came to the party thinking that I would spend a few minutes due to my server case of: 'Montezuma's Revenge'!

I believe for both of us it was love at first sight as we talked as well as danced well past midnight. We were one of the last couples to leave that party, and I had my car, so I volunteered to drive her home. In this manner, I was able to find out where she lived and I was able to set a time to meet her the next afternoon after school for our next date.

The next day was Friday, and I taught until 1:30 p.m. then Steve and I went to our usual Friday restaurant to have lunch. We then went back to our apartment and I changed clothes and walked to Salma's home.

Then I stopped by her family's apartment, which was very close to my own apartment in the Abu Roumaneh district of Damascus. I rang the bell and assumed that it would be answered by Salma, so I said: "Hi Salma, how are you?"...She replied, "Sorry, I am Salma's sister, Rima! You must be Thomas." I said I was sorry and then I simply waited for Salma to appear. To this day, both sisters continue to look very similar and both remained beautiful ladies. When I think back about that day, I still feel it was a very simple mistake to have made.

We decided to go out for a walk that afternoon and try to get to know each other better. Salma, I discovered, was originally Palestinian, and her father was a successful Palestinian/Syrian businessman. Her father was a true 'success story' as he was one of the first Palestinians to graduate in Agronomy from France in 1937. He then set up his original agricultural company in Palestine and was able to secure many international distributorships that the company still holds today. As in Palestine in 1937, many of the large western agricultural companies wanted to have both an Arab and a Jewish company representing them, as Palestine was in the middle of an Arab revolt that had lasted from 1936 until 1939. Even with this lengthy uprising of the late thirties and the renewed fighting between Palestinians and Zionists from 1947 till 1948, his agricultural business was very successful and was doing quite well up until early 1948.

In a very interesting yet upsetting entry into his diary, the Soviet Ambassador to Court of St James in London between 1932 and 1943 was Ivan Maisky. He had maintained a very detailed, unique, and assiduous daily diary. In his book: *The Maisky Diaries* which was edited by Gabriel Gorodetsky, he entered in his diary a meeting that the ambassador held with the Zionist leader Dr. Weizmann on February 3rd, 1941 in which Weizmann was explaining his 'plan' to save the Central European Jewry and he stated: to move a million Arabs now living in Palestine to Iraq and to settle four or five million Jews from Poland and other counties on the land which the Arabs had been occupying…I expressed some surprise about how Weizmann hoped to settle 5 million Jews occupied by 1 million Arabs. 'Oh, don't worry,' Weizmann burst out laughing. "The Arab is often called the son of the desert. It would be truer to call him the father of the desert. His laziness and primitivism turned a flourishing garden into a desert. Give me the land occupied by a million Arabs, and I will easily settle five times that number of Jews on it."

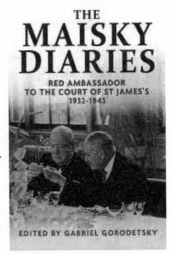

The Maisky Diaries

Weizmann shook his head sadly and concluded: "The only thing is how we could obtain this land?"

Up until now, I had never thought that any Jewish leader had such strong negative opinions of the Palestinian people. I remember my father-in-law telling me that the agricultural company that he had established in 1937 was flourishing and very successful.

The Palestinians knew and understood that the British Mandate for Palestine was going to be terminated on May 14th, and the Jews were going to proclaim their Israeli Declaration of Independence on that same day. So many Palestinians prepared to leave their homes and country prior to that infamous and loathsome day.

So was Salma's father's safety concerns too as he knew the fighting between the Arabs and Jews would intensify and possibly lead to a major war. His family's safety was paramount. Also, at the same time, my future mother-in-law was nine months into her pregnancy. So in mid-Apri, they had left their home in Jaffa and were planning to drive directly to Amman, Jordan. They thought that they would be gone for only a few weeks, so they packed very little of their personal belongings. As my father-in-law would tell me "Just enough clothing for a short sojourn to neighboring Jordan." We all know and realize that today it has been over seventy years since they left their home in Jaffa.

Shortly after they left Jaffa, my mother-in-law developed strong labor contractions. The baby was coming. My father-in-law immediately stopped in a hospital in Nablus, and a short time later, she gave birth to a beautiful girl. So my wife was actually born in Nablus, Palestine, on April 20th, 1948. A day or so later, they left Nablus and headed to Amman, Jordan, with one additional family member.

They stayed in the Amman area for a few months, simply waiting for the military coalition of the Arab states to defeat the Jews. Well, the main armies of Egypt, Iraq, Transjordan, Syria, and a handful of troops from Saudi Arabia, Yemen, and Lebanon were defeated in just over ten months. It was a major defeat for the Egyptians and of course, the Palestinian Arabs plus a major victory for the new state of Israel. Salma's family was a part of the 700,000 Palestinians that either fled or were later expelled from their homes in the area that became Israel and they became Palestinian Refugees. In the three years following the Arab-Israel War about 700,000 Jews emigrated to Israel, many of whom had been expelled from their previous homelands in the Middle East.

Salma's father felt from the onset that the Arab Armies would be defeated, and he saw no future for his family and his agricultural business in Transjordan. So a few months later, he relocated his entire family to Beirut. Then in Lebanon, he re-established his company, and once again he gradually became a very prominent businessman. Lebanon was experiencing an economic boom and he took full advantage of this prosperity and expanded his company to several offices within Lebanon. In 1958, he foresaw that Lebanon was going to disintegrate into a major sectarian war. So for the third time, he gathered his family and they immigrated to Damascus. His prediction about Lebanon did not immediately come true as he only missed the start of the Lebanese Civil War by only a few years.

So again, for the third time, he re-established his agricultural company anew, and Damascus was his final location until his death in 1980. So once more, he was very successful as he expanded his agricultural business into twelve countries and had opened three European offices in London; Versailles and Verona. Today, his two sons have taken over the family business and have expanded their father's company to over sixty countries worldwide.

Salma and I continued to date on a regular basis over the coming months, and we developed a very strong relationship. We were married some eight months later.

So as one could see, my love for Damascus had many contributing factors, Initially for me, it was simply the developing love of the Syrian people, the beautiful old city of Damascus, and then my love of the school that I taught in for the next three years. Then everything else helped contribute to my overall love of Damascus that still exists today. Paramount was the meeting with my beautiful wife that continues today to be the main and overriding contribution of this strong love of Damascus.

Chapter Six

Comparative Religious Studies

Islam was completely unknown to me until I came to the Middle East in 1975. As a matter of fact, many other non-Christian religions were new to me before this first trip to Damascus. I guess I lived in a religiously sheltered life as we never had neighbors or classmates with other religious faiths in Western New York. My dad was raised Lutheran by his German parents, and my mom being of Polish descent was, of course, raised Catholic. My dad had switched when he married my mom, in his second marriage, and would remain a Catholic until his death.

I was the only Webber sibling that did not attend Catholic school while growing up in Orchard Park. Why? Well, my brother had failed kindergarten at Nativity School. My parents were so upset that they took my brother Don out of the Catholic school and enrolled him in a public school. So when I was ready for kindergarten, I was automatically placed in a public school.

I would actually describe my parents as: "Sunday Catholics", oh yes, I was Baptized at birth, received my First Holy Communion at the age of twelve, and went to church with my parents every Sunday. But as a family, we never gave up anything for Lent except candy and chocolates and only for a few days. The only other times we would go to church were for weddings, deaths, and special religious celebrations.

I enjoyed Christmas Midnight Mass as after the traditional mass, we would rush home to open our presents. Oh yes, there was always a day set aside for me to make my monthly confession. I still remember that I always had a hard time trying to think of any "sins" that I had committed since the last time I was kneeling in the confessional panel. My mom always had us memorize her favorite prayer. It was called *"Father Baker's Prayer"* and mom had insisted that we would learn it verbatim as it was

the prayer that she claimed she had written. I had believed this story for many years because that was what she led us all to believe.

I had always loved to go to Our Lady of Victory Basilica, in Lackawanna, New York, especially for Christmas mass.

Our Lady of Victory Basilica, in Lackawanna, New York

This special basilica was so big that for many years I had never seen a larger church in my entire life. All that changed when I first visited Rome and went into St. Peter's Basilica in the Vatican.

Our Lady of Victory Basilica was built by Father Baker and was opened in 1926. It was the main church that my parents and grandparents had worshiped every Sunday and every special holy day. A couple of years ago, during a stateside trip, I stopped by Our Lady of Victory and went downstairs to the basilicas gift shop. There I found a copy of *"Father Baker's Prayer"*, and I had asked, "Who was the author of this famous prayer?" The sales attendant was shocked as she answered me saying: "Of course Father Baker!" Well, my mom had my entire family believing that she was the author and I was probably the last in the family to discover the truth. Anyway, it did help us with our memorization skills. I could probably recite the entire prayer today if I tried and put my mind to it.

During my college years, I was drawn away from the church even more for various reasons. My exodus from the Catholic church was expanded and hit a pinnacle just before my first marriage. I was to become the only offspring not to have married in a Catholic church. Diane and I both wanted a civil marriage as it was faster and less expensive. My parents were not too upset with our choice, so I guess they were moving from the strict doctrines of the church as well.

I always loved to visit churches, from my first trip to Rome to the small church in Ulm, Germany, that has the tallest wooden steeple in the world. Even today, I enjoy going into a famous church.

During junior college, I had met a strange fellow student who was a concert pipe organ player. He and I drove to over twenty churches in California and Utah during our vacation. He knew where the most famous organs were located, and we simply asked permission from the priest or pastor, in order that my friend could play that church organ. He even played the most famous pipe organ in Salt Lake City in the Mormon Tabernacle. That pipe organ is one of the largest in the world.

Recently, I have come back to enjoying organ recitals when played in one of the various churches in Damascus. Maybe it was a residual or enduring influence from my college days.

I have not prayed in a church for many, many years, but I am still a keen admirer of different churches around the world.

During my first year of teaching at the Damascus Community School, I discovered my roommate Steve was a Southern Baptist Minister. During the year that we roomed together, he had performed several weddings in Damascus. We rarely discussed religion or politics as a rule of the house. We both felt that the people that discuss these two sensitive subjects usually end up with their same views and not talking to each other. This house rule would be challenged dramatically over the next ten months.

In early 1975 Lebanon, our Syrian neighbor was in their early stages of its own civil war, which would last over fifteen years. This was a multifaceted civil war in which you had Christian, Shia Muslims, and Druze, all forming their own militias and each trying to control a different area of both Beirut as well as Lebanon. Actually, it appeared that the start of the Lebanese Civil War started around February 1975 with the Sidon Fisherman Strike, and continued with minor clashes throughout the country. Soon the Lebanese central government was divided and disintegrated. Once this happened, the Lebanese army was split, and the militias ruled the city. I feel it never really got bad in Beirut until October 1975 with what they coined: *"The Battle of the Hotels."* Many times during the initial fighting, the Beirut International Airport would be closed for a day or two, but now the airport would be closed for longer periods of time.

As the fighting intensified within Beirut, the majority of the expatriates were now faced with the challenges of how to evacuate Lebanon. The only way out was by land via Syria because the Beirut seaport witnessed severe battles as it was one of the main areas of receiving smuggled materials such as arms, modern weaponry, and food. The apartment of Thomas and Steve in Damascus was considered to be a stopover and a "safe refuge" for all foreign expatriates fleeing Beirut and catching a flight from Damascus International Airport. The majority of these 'refugees' were professors from AUB (American University Beirut) and teachers from the ACS (American Community School). I recall that we had at least one expatriate staying in our apartment continuously for 286 days. The highest number for one night was an amazing seventeen overnight guests. You could not move from room to room that night.

And what do professors and teachers like to talk about when they are together? Religion and Politics! We would have the most stimulating and interesting conversations, especially when it pertained to religion. I still remember how well-versed many of these educated professionals were and their ability to clearly define various religious doctrines and beliefs. During our conversations, we discussed major religions such as Hinduism, Buddhism, Church of the Latter-Day Saints, Judaism, the various sects of Christianity, and of course, Islam. I participated in many of these thought-provoking discussions, and I slowly evolved and found that Islam could be a new and enlightening religion for me to discover.

The results of these extremely interesting conversations and more importantly, when Salma and I decided to get married is when I chose to 'revert' to Islam. Now many are probably wondering why I used the term: 'revert'. The word 'revert' means to go to a previous state. Islam considers everyone to be born Muslims since it is supposedly the only true religion from the one true God. So 'revert' implies that one is returning back to the original state of being within the Islamic faith.

I still remember that during my appearance at the Courthouse in order for me to make this change in religion and become a Muslim, I needed to announce my faith by reciting the Shahadah or confession of faith. The Shahadah is the first Pillar of Islam, of which there are Five Pillars. It must be recited in Arabic and states the following: "There is no God but God (and) Muhammad is the messenger of God." It is essential to say this phrase to become a Muslim and to revert to Islam.

I still remember that I had to memorize that Shahadah and with my Phonic Dyslexia; I had a very difficult time pronouncing that saying in a coherent manner. I was able to recite it, but to this day can't remember how I did it to the approval of the presiding magistrate.

I discovered while signing a large book that I was the seventh foreigner to revert to Islam that year, 1976, in Damascus. I discovered that Salma's sister-in-law was number six that same year. That would have been two out of seven Muslim conversions from the same Syrian family.

I ran into Steve by accident many years later on a flight from Cairo to Washington Dulles Airport, and we talked, and I discovered that he too had reverted to Islam. We had a chance to talk further, and I asked him if that reversion had anything to do with our nightly conversations in Damascus. He too felt that they influenced him to make the change from being a Southern Baptist Minister to a Muslim.

I often think back to those many nights in the Fall and Winter of 1975 and the Spring of 1976 and wonder how many others had changed their religious beliefs due to our many conversations.

Chapter Seven

The Drive of My Life

Still, to this day, I cannot believe that I had lived through this harrowing and nerve-racking experience that still ranks in a 'once-in-a-lifetime' experience for me and my family.

The year was 1977, which was the year Syria was being tormented by the Muslim Brotherhood, and their common method of terror or modus operandi was drive-by car shootings. It seemed that each city had at least one attack per week on a government official. In the government's attempt to curb these techniques, they began forbidding vehicles having tinted glass plus increased vehicle inspections. All attempts to curb this method of terror were in vain, as they continued throughout the spring and summer.

This was the backdrop of my traumatic experience.

The American Embassy had planned a large pool party in a private club along the Barada river near the resort city Zabadani to celebrate the Fourth of July. My wife had given birth to our first son Omar in early June of 1977, so she did not want to go to the club too early to attend the party. Two female employees of the embassy asked if I could take them to the club so they could help to set up this Fourth of July party. Since my wife didn't want to go until the early afternoon, I accepted and we left the embassy around ten in the morning. The club was about forty kilometers away on the old Damascus/Beirut highway. The drive to the function was non-eventful and I dropped the girls off and went inside to see how the arrangements were getting along and then drove back to Damascus to collect my wife and newborn son, Omar.

I had owned a secondhand 1974 Plymouth four-door sedan for the past year and a half. It was colored gold, so the students at the American School nicknamed it: *"Mr. Webber's Golden Goose."* It had a powerful V8 engine, and I

1974 Plymouth

had toured a great part of Syria in my Plymouth for the past eighteen months.

When I'd left the venue and was driving back home, I was dressed in shorts, had the windows wide open, and was listening to the radio at a high and deafening volume.

Once I left Zabadani, you needed to climb a steep hill to reach a long and level plateau on top. Without paying much attention, I passed three cars and continued in my cheerful way. I had reached the apex of the hill and was simply driving happily along minding my own business. Then without warning, one of the cars I had just passed came alongside me, it was a dark blue Peugeot, and I glanced over, and to my bewilderment, there were four men and the one in the front seat was holding a large knife and shaking it at me. I rolled up my window and then sped to get away as I did not want anything to do with this car or its occupants. Once again, without hesitation, the blue Peugeot 505 came alongside me and this time, he rammed his car into the side of my car, trying to push me off the road. I sped and for the next thirty-five kilometers, it was a race to Damascus. All I knew was that I had to stay in front of this car or else he would be able to control the situation and my car. He kept pulling alongside hitting my car and I started defending myself and started pushing his car away. On the plateau straight away, it was not too difficult to continue in front of this madman as I had a much stronger engine. In hindsight, I should have pushed his car off the road as my Plymouth was much heavier and was much larger. But, still, I had no idea of who or why this car was acting in this strange and bizarre manner.

At one time, I remember it was like a movie and I was starring in the 'chase scene.' My heart was beating a million times a second. My mind suddenly remembered the defensive driving class I had in Zandvoort, Netherlands at the Formula One racecourse. I should use what I was taught. I remembered that no matter what happens, I should stay in front of the other vehicle and use my more powerful engine and better driving skills to maintain supremacy.'

We then entered a small village, and there were a lot of cars and pedestrians. He was then able to just overtake me and pulled his car in front of my car. I remembered the only way out was to make a hard right turn onto the sidewalk, and then I was able to get away from this monster. Within seconds, he was right behind me and again trying to pass me. After that small village, the road then ran along the sides of both the Barada and Tora Rivers and was very sharp; twisting; winding and much narrower. Many oncoming cars were forced to hit the side of the road to avoid collision with both our cars. We were coming into the outskirts of Damascus and all I could think about was to get to the American Embassy where there would be safety.

We drove very fast through the area called Al Rabwe, and I knew I was getting ever-so-close to my sanctuary within the walls of the US Embassy. One last red light to overcome, and I would be almost to the gates of the embassy. Then when we approached that traffic light, it had just turned red. There were cars approaching and backed up at the red light. I was forced to stop. The dark blue Peugeot came upon me and quickly rammed into the front of my car, stopping any possibility of escape. All three passengers got out of their car and one man stood in front of my car with his pistol drawn and was shaking yet aiming his gun directly at me. He then lowered his gun and shot my front tire flat. The man with the large knife then used the butt of the knife and shattered my window. He then punched me breaking my sunglasses and giving me a bloody nose. The next thing I remembered was the middle car, a large black Mercedes sedan pulled up and the rear window was rolled down and the person asked: "Where are you from?" My hurried and only response was: 'Alsifarat Al'amrikia' in Arabic for the American Embassy. Immediately, the man in the back of the Mercedes rolled up his widow and drove away. The three in the chase car got back in their damaged car and all simply raced away.

I had urinated in my pants, was bleeding from the side of my face and my nose. I had a blown-out front tire, and the entire side of the car was smashed and dented. I had glass shards all over me, and I had to fend-for-myself. No one was willing to come to my aid or assistance. So I pulled my car to the side of the roadway and proceeded to change the damaged front tire. Then I drove ever so slowly to the main gate of the American Embassy and to the safe refuge within.

Most of the US Embassy personnel were currently out of the embassy as it was a holiday. The US Marine Guard seeing my car and my face immediately called the Duty Officer and asked him to come quickly. Mr. Bob Pelatro was the Charge-de-affair at the Embassy as well as the Duty Officer that day. Our Ambassador Richard Murphy was in the States on holiday.

I remembered sitting in my car, waiting for Mr. Pelatro to arrive and simply kept asking myself over and over, "What just happened? What just happened?" When he arrived, he was astonished that I was alive as the damage to the car was extensive. He listened to my story with great interest and then wrote his initial report on the incident. He suggested I immediately go home with one of the Embassy drivers, clean up and not talk to anyone except my wife about what had transpired.

When I arrived at our apartment, and my wife opened the door, she was shocked to see such a sight! After a much-needed shower and a change of clothes, I explained the entire incident to her. She immediately guessed that it must have been a major governmental official and their reaction was simply self-defense. Self-defense against what? I simply passed those three cars and had continued on my merry way.

The embassy sent an official complaint to the Syrian Ministry of Foreign Affairs to which there was never a reply or an apology or even recognition that an incident had taken place. No compensation for the extensive damage neither to my car nor for my mental and physical abuse or damages was ever received. We soon learned from "certain channels" that the "official" in the back seat of the Mercedes was indeed a top, key governmental executive and was a direct and close family member of the current Syrian President. I remember being told that I was indeed one lucky person and that I should be thankful that I was alive and not shot.

Needless to say, we did not attend the American Embassies Fourth of July party that year.

My car stayed in the embassy's compound for the entire summer. I traveled to the States for my annual vacation, and during my stateside holiday, I had purchased a replacement side window. On my return to Damascus, I had shipped this large side window along with the replacement molding, side mirror, etc. as simply extra pieces of luggage.

This "incident" was the 'talk-of-the-town' for many years to come.

Chapter Eight

Iran – An Amazing Place

Iran, Iran, Iran, what a great yet short experience in my life.

I taught at the Damascus Community for one additional year after my car incident, as I still recall today as "The Drive of My Life," which occurred on that eventful Fourth of July in 1977. I was in no clear psychological state to continue teaching at the American School beyond this fourth year. I had realized, throughout the school year, that that this harrowing experience had taken its toll on my clear mental state, my family's safety, and my love for Syria. I now felt that I needed to travel and teach as far away from Syria as I could possibly find.

I had applied and was interviewed with four different international schools for the coming new school year of 1978–1979. The four international schools were in Lahore, Pakistan; Kabul, Afghanistan; Kathmandu, Nepal and Sar Cheshmeh, Iran. Each had advantages and disadvantages, so what I have always done in the past, whenever there was an important decision to make, I completed my 'Benjamin Franklin Table' for each school. This table would provide a fast and efficient method to resolve my decision as to the selection of my next teaching position. To make my decision, I completed my Benjamin Franklin Table and how I completed it was simple. I merely found four clean pieces of paper; on each, I drew a line down the center and then placed the advantages of that particular school on one side and the disadvantages on the other side. I would simply add up the total advantages and minus the disadvantages and whichever school had the greatest number, that would be my selection. Today, I still use this 'Benjamin Franklin Table' for each major decision I currently need to make and I have found my two sons also employ this same technique in their decision making the process.

My final selection was: Sar Cheshmeh, Iran, but if I had been keeping up with the current events at the time, it most likely would not have been Iran. Remember this was the spring and summer of 1978, and there was some small sporadic protest beginning in a few cities of Iran. I had always known that the Shah was a 'key ally' of America, and they would never let him down, right? Wrong…

My wife's family was also against this move as they did not want to see their daughter and newest grandson move so far away and at this potentially trying time in Iran. They would say: "Why not stay and enjoy the comforts of Damascus?" They knew that the Shah was very pro-American, so they felt our family's safety should not be a major concern. I kept telling them, "The experience we all will gain should overcome the distance we were to travel."

At this time, I was also in contact with my first wife and my son Thomas II. They were still living in San Diego, and she too felt that this new overseas travel would be beneficial and advantageous for Thomas. So she accepted my request for Thomas to join us and to complete his following school year in Iran. Thomas would be attending the 6th grade, and I felt positive that he would be exposed to a different and very British method of schooling.

Nevertheless, I had completed my final contact with the American Community School in June of 1978, and then we prepared to leave to the States for our annual holiday. We would be back in Damascus to pack for Iran later that summer.

It was a great summer holiday as we saw my mom for the first time after my dad had passed away in March of 1978. She was doing well, but was quite lonely, which one would expect after the man you had been married to for fifty-plus years had passed away a short time earlier. I had informed my family about the news about moving and teaching in Iran. There were no comments about the current small civil disturbances in some cities of Iran, as there was really no current news coverage of such small disturbances in this faraway country. And for my family, Iran was just as distant and unknown as Syria once was some four years earlier, so what was the difference? I tried to explain that this new school was located some 800 km south of Tehran near the city of Kerman and not near the capital city Tehran. Also, it was located on a mountain top some 9,500 feet above sea level and was an Australian-run operation to open a Copper Mine. When it would open, it would be the second-largest Open Pit Copper Mine in the world.

My family had heard of the Shah of Iran as he was 'Americans most trusted ally and friend' in the Middle East, apart from Israel. Plus America had a lot of two-way trade with Iran, so this must be good, right? Many of my older family members still called Iran Persia, and for my mom, Persia sounded so exotic and mysterious, so would it be a good place for her son Tommy to teach. Only time would tell.

The Shah or officially called: Riza Shah Pahlavi was always traveling to American and was always seen on American television. That summer, for most Americans, no 'red flags' were set off about a few protestors in faraway Iran.

Our summer vacation continued to be wonderful as we saw all of my family as well as my wife's family during that holiday. We would normally visit my family first in Western New York, and then we would travel to see my wife's family in Ohio. Then it would be a cross-country trip to visit my favorite sister Anita and my first son Thomas II and his mother in Southern California. So each summer holiday in America would be a journey from the East Coast to the West Coast. Today, in all my current stateside vacations, I still follow this same unwritten statute.

When we finally made it to Southern California, Anita's husband Bill was the first to alert me to the potential danger of traveling to Iran at this time. He was always an avid reader of various newspapers and watched a great deal of international news broadcast, so he was more up-to-date on the current news than we were. Once again, I assured

Bill that the Shah had formidable armed forces, and he was American's closest comrade in the region. All the same, he warned me to be careful, remain safe, and stay in contact with them.

We then drove down to San Diego to see Thomas and his mom and some close friends like Jerry Johnson and his family. It was another great stay in San Diego, my adopted "home" as Omar was old enough to appreciate the San Diego Zoo and other amazing sights of San Diego.

While we were packing Thomas's two suitcases, I was thinking about Diane, as she was such a brave and accepting mother. For her to be alone for the next year must have been problematic.

When we drove from her driveway in La Mesa, none of us had any idea that this Iran expedition would end in total disaster.

We headed back to the East Coast, and during our drive back, I was very happy to see the bonding between Thomas and Omar, his half-brother. There was about ten year's difference in age and yet Thomas got along with his younger sibling and Omar with his older brother.

Once we got back to Western New York, it was nice to introduce Thomas to his grandmother, all his aunts, uncles, nephews, and cousins. Dr. Tom and his new wife were visiting his parents in Buffalo, so we had a chance to meet them while in the area. It was Tom's first chance to meet Omar and also the first time he had seen Thomas after his birth in Buffalo during our dental school days.

All-in-all it was an excellent and exceptional summer holiday. That summer, time simply flew by as not only had we traveled from coast-to-coast, we also visited many of our family and close friends.

At the onset of our summer vacation, we had flown in from Damascus via Geneva and on to Boston.

On our return to Damascus was exactly the same. We stayed in Boston for a day or two in order to show Thomas the sights of that great city. Then our flight was first from Logan Airport in Boston to Geneva. Again, I had planned to spend two days to relax and enjoy this great Swiss City. We finally arrived back in Damascus at the end of July 1978.

During the next two weeks, we were busy packing for our Iran trip, plus we were showing Thomas the sights of Damascus. I felt he was really impressed with the Damascus, especially the old ramparts and ancient city walls of the old city.

Well, the day came that we were to fly from Damascus to Tehran, and we all had great hopes yet certain anxieties.

The new school had sent us tickets on Swiss Air directly from Damascus to Tehran and then connecting to an Iran Air flight to Kerman, which was again 800 kilometers south of the capital Tehran.

The first leg from Damascus to Tehran was fine. The next flight from Tehran to Kerman was simply amazing, as the first half of the flight we were passing mostly dry and arid landscape. As we got closer and closer to Kerman, I noticed the landscape changed to more green and agricultural land use. Surprisingly all along the land surface, you could see hundreds of these round open pits that resembled 'bomb craters'. They were all in long straight lines and all separated by what appeared to be about 30 to 35 meters. What were these? I told Thomas to look out his window to see these astonishing and bewildering objects. When we arrived at Kerman Airport, we were taken immediately by bus to our final destination, our mountain top village called Sar Cheshmeh.

I asked our bus driver what those round pits were. He told me that they were Old Persian Water Wells or freshwater aquifers, and each was called a "Qanat." I never forgot this word and then I soon started researching these bewildering wells. "Qanat" which is the Arabicized version of the original Persian Word, and they date back to the First Millennium BC.

After we had settled into our new housing in Sar Cheshmeh and in late September, I had rented a car and drove some three hours from Kerman to view these qanats first hand. They were amazing as they were man-made, and the tunnels looked to be over 30 to 40 meters deep. Unfortunately, all of our photos were lost during our departure from Iran.

After our flight landed in Kerman Airport, we collected our luggage, and we were met by our Iranian driver from this Copper Mine. When we left the airport, I was surprised to find that the temperature was not that bad as it was sunny and only around thirty degrees Celsius. We were also very lucky that day as we were the only passengers ascending up the mountain to our new home. The driver loaded our suitcases into the companies mini-van and we were off to discover our new home supposedly for the next year.

On that first trip, we never entered the city of Kerman as the airport was outside the city limits, but it appeared to be a very large city. On many follow-up trips, we were to do a great deal of shopping in the Old Market Area and the Old City Souq of Kerman. A very interesting city as it was a mix of the old and modern Iran.

On the initial trip, we then drove from the Kerman Airport about 65 kilometer's or just over a two-hour drive to our final stop at the Camp Headquarters building located at the base of the main mountain in the Zagros Mountain Range. It was nice as they were expecting us, so we completed all the registration forms and documents before proceeding up the mountain to our new home in a mountain top village called: Sar Cheshmeh.

My teaching contract was with an Australian company called Anaconda Group, which had been the management company for this new Copper Mine under construction in Sar Cheshmeh. We verified the fact at the company's headquarters that indeed the new mine in Sar Cheshmeh would be when completed, the world's second-largest Open Pit Copper Mine.

I then discovered an interesting fact that I did not know before. The small mining town of Sar Cheshmeh was located on top of the mountain at an elevation of 2,600 to 3,000 meters above sea level. This would be over 8,500 to 9,800 feet in elevation. We had been living and working in Damascus, which had an elevation of only 700 meters or only approximately 2,300 feet. How were we going to manage? How were our bodies going to adjust to this 'thinner air' and much dryer air? Will it take much longer to cook our food, and would they dry out much faster than in Damascus? And what about sports such as tennis, how fast would that tennis ball travel in this thin air? All these questions were in part due to the fact that at this very high elevation, there was much less oxygen and a much lower atmospheric pressure.

Were we ready to face these new challenges of living on this extremely high mountain top?

We did discover, along with all of our preliminary worries, that we were able to adapt and enjoy our time 'closer to heaven' as we later called this experience in Sar Cheshmeh.

It took quite a while climbing this mountain as we were in a mini-bus, yet, we enjoyed the changing landscape as we ascended higher and higher. Once we arrived at Sar Cheshmeh, our first surprise was the newness of all the buildings, houses, and the infrastructure in general. I found that this was really nice as my initial expectations were that this was going to be an Old Iranian village located on the very top of a tall mountain. Our driver took us around town so we could get a 'feel' of the town before we went to our new home. The town had a supermarket, center, a few restaurants, and the school. It appeared to be very newly constructed. He then took us to our home. All the houses were four alongside each other and were therefore considered semi-attached. We were in the third house of the four, and as we entered, we were quite surprised at the size of our home plus the nice furnishings. The driver explained where all the switches were for the lights, hot water heaters, air conditioners, etc. He was very helpful and he finally asked if we needed anything else and then he was off.

As we were unpacking, the doorbell rang, and to our immense surprise, our three neighbors were at the front door welcoming us to Sar Cheshmeh and giving us food so we could have our first dinner without a fuss. The three couples were teaching at the school for last year and they remembered when they had first arrived, there was no food or provisions stocked in the house so they made sure that we had enough food for a nice dinner. What a great way to meet and get to know your neighbors and fellow teachers. They also mentioned that there was a compound bus that would come to our neighborhood in the morning and if we wanted to join them, we could take the bus to the supermarket and the 'downtown area'. We enjoyed our dinner and then completed our unpacking. All of us retired quite early, as it was a very long day for the four of us.

The next morning, we prepared ourselves for our compound bus trip, and we went outside waiting for its arrival. All of our neighbors joined us for our first bus ride and again, they proved to be very helpful and knowledgeable. The bus came on time and we then proceeded to ride to the 'city center'. It was no more than a 'village center' or at the most a 'town center.' We were able to exchange our American dollars for Iranian rials. Iranians commonly express amounts of money and prices of goods in "tomans." For this purpose, one "toman" equals 10 rials. At that time, the rial had a floating rate and was pegged to the US dollar. In 1978 the exchange rate was about 71.50 rials to one US dollar. On January 1st, 2019, the exchange rate was a staggering 11,200 tomans or 112,000 rials to one US dollar! By mid-November 2019, the Iranian riyal has leveled out to a respectable exchange rate of 42,000 rials to one US dollar. There are many factors for this poor exchange rate. Most importantly, it has been the stifling American sanctions against all the Iranian governments that had caused this week's exchange rate. The first US sanctions were originally imposed against Iran in November 1979 after a group of radical students seized the American Embassy in Tehran and took the people inside hostage. More recently, the current American President Donald Trump in August 2018 reimposed even stiffer sanctions than the previous administration and warned that anyone doing business with Iran will not be able to do business with the United States.

The supermarket was really a supermarket and had most everything that we required to set up our kitchen. At the time, what really impressed me was their wide selection of seafood. Remember we were living on a mountain top a thousand kilometer's for the Persian Gulf. During our short stay, I ate more jumbo shrimp than at any other time of my life.

After our shopping excursion, we had lunch together at a typical Iranian restaurant. We quickly learned that the Persian language was very different than Arabic, and they seem to place an "es" in front of all words beginning with an "s." So a simple 'Steak' was pronounced 'essteak'...and so on...

That evening we had a very nice home-cooked meal, and we went to bed fairly early as I was scheduled to see the new school the next morning and examine the school's science curriculum for my: general science classes.

So far, everything seemed to be very organized and well-disciplined as the school bus collected us exactly at the appointed time. I was scheduled to teach third to ninth grade General Science using the British/Australian teaching program. The textbooks and the lab books were good, and I soon became very familiar with the British approach of teaching science. It was different from our American system, but for me acceptable and I adapted well to the new syllabus. I had two more days to acquaint myself with my new classroom; laboratory and books.

Then it happened, my first day of classes! I had a full schedule as I was the only science teacher in the school. I can still remember the first day of classes. I was totally impressed with the caliber of the students' knowledge and interest in science in general. I soon discovered that many of their fathers were key engineers or top managers working at the new mine. I enjoyed teaching in Sar Cheshmeh and looked forward to the start of each new school day.

It was also interesting to have my son in my science class, and this would be the only time that I would be teaching any of my sons.

Our family quickly developed a solid routine, breakfast each morning together, then lunch at school, and finally the entire evening together as a family unit. Our weekends were spent playing tennis and exploring the beautiful country called Persia or as we know as Iran.

One of our neighbors and coworkers at the school also had a keen interest in the Iranian culture and rich history. We were able to rent a vehicle in Sar Cheshmeh, and we would travel down the mountain to discover new and interesting sights. On one of the first trips, I insisted that we try and find an area that had numerous qanats. This was not a difficult task as Sar Cheshmeh was only 50 or 60 kilometers South of Rafsanjani and only a bit further from the large city and provincial capital of Kerman. Plus we were in the Zagros Mountain Range which we knew was the source of water for many of these old Qanat Water Irrigation Systems. I can still remember my excitement as we approached our first qanat.

They are actually a series of man-made underground irrigation canals or channels, and each qanat is the opening of a vertical shaft that goes down many meters to reach the underground aquifer. All the qanats are connected by

Qanats

man-made tunnels connecting each other. These appear to be originated in Persia, and each delivers clean, cool, and fresh drinking water. All are underground for many kilometers. This obviously keeps the water from evaporating and will flow year-round to many villages a long distance away from the water source. It appears that each village developed a great deal of fertile agricultural land around each and every qanat!

I researched the present-day usage of the Qanat system, and there appears to be just 37,000 qanats still in operation in Iran today!

Later, I discovered and read a book titled: *Blind White Fish in Persia* in which a group of four undergraduate students from Oxford University came to Persia in 1950 on a small school grant to f study these famous and unusual Blind White Fish.

Unfortunately, they never found any blind fish, and most of the book turned into a travel book in which they described the rural way of life found in Persia at that time. To my surprise and astonishment, no one has discovered these Blind White Fish living in the qanats of Iran.

Blind White Fish in Persia

Our first visit to a qanat appeared to be very deep, and the air rising from the lower level was very cool almost cold. We were also lucky in this first visit as this qanat had a water bucket and pulley system to extract the fresh, clean and very cool water. I also remember wishing that our first bucket of water had contained a Blind White Fish. No such luck as we met the same fate as Anthony Smith some twenty-five years previously.

Over the next three and a half months, we discovered and explored Iran on regular weekend bases. The artifacts that we purchased were exceptional, and we had planned to take them with us after our contract ended. My only regret was that we never had the time to explore the various Zoroastrian sites located a bit too far from Sar Cheshmeh.

The Iranian Revolution was a series of events involving the overthrow of the 2,500 years of continuous Persian monarchy under Mohammad Reza Shah Pahlavi, who was supported by the United States.

Unfortunately, each night we would hear and see both on the television and on the radio broadcasting the troubling news of massive demonstrations taking place in Tehran, and then as the weeks quickly passed, expanded to other major Iranian cities. All the same, we felt confident that the Shah, with his formidable military, plus the strong American backing, would soon have everything under control throughout his country. We were also confident that we would never encounter any demonstrations or troubles in our village because we were located on top of this high mountain in Southern Iran. We felt we were far away from the major hostilities.

As the weeks rolled on, the demonstrations were increasing, especially in the capital city Tehran. Again there was no indication that our small local Iranian community had an interest in creating any problems here in Sar Cheshmeh. We thought the local Iranians were all well paid, had acceptable accommodations, and were very happy as they had secure jobs. Unfortunately, between August and December 1978, the strikes and demonstrations paralyzed most of the country.

The Shah maintained a close relationship with the United States as both regimes shared a fear of the expansion of the Soviet/Russian state, Iran's powerful northern neighbor.

Leftist and Islamist groups attacked the Shah's government often from outside Iran, as they were suppressed within for violating the Iranian constitution, political corruption, and the political oppression by the SAVAK or the Iranian secret police.

The Shah was thought to be heavily protected by a lavishly financed army and the top security services. At the time, one international reporter analyzed the situation as: "Few expected the regime of the Shah, which had international support and modern army of 400,000 to crumble in the face of unarmed demonstrators within a matter of months."

At first, the Iranian Revolution was in part a conservative backlash against the westernization, modernization, and secularization efforts of the Western-backed Shah and a more popular reaction to social injustice and other shortcomings of the ancient régime. The Shah was perceived by common Iranian people as a puppet of the United States under the Shah's rule, western powers exploited Iran's natural resources blatantly. To the people, the Shah's regime was oppressive, brutal and corrupt and it also suffered from basic functional failures, like overly ambitious economic programs that brought economic bottlenecks, shortages, and inflation.

The Shi'a cleric Ayatollah Ruhollah Khomeini, the leader of the Iranian Revolution, first came to political prominence in 1963 when he led the opposition against the Shah and his program of reforms known as the "White Revolution", which aimed at breaking up landholdings owned by some Shi'a clergy, allow women to vote and religious restrictions, etc.

In December, my main concerns were of my planning for the upcoming Christmas/Winter Holiday and had nothing to do with the current situation facing the Shah. Salma and I felt that it would be great to vacation back in Damascus as this would give Thomas the opportunity to revisit this famous city and for Salma to see her family. A big challenge was developing in making the airline reservations and flying out of Tehran back to Damascus. Many of the local travel offices were closed due to the strikes, and there was no internet back in 1978. The various travel offices were having difficulties in contacting their main offices in Tehran as well as the various airlines. For us, this was very upsetting as we had heard it was bad in Tehran, but could it really be 'that bad' in a way that we could not make a simple airline booking?

At that time, Ayatollah Khomeini was exiled from Iran in 1964 by the Shah, and he left Iran first to Najaf, Iraq, and later to Paris. I believe on December 11th, 1978, Ayatollah Khomeini called for a massive countrywide strike and immense demonstrations throughout the country. This call was heeded to by the majority of Iranians and the entire country was paralyzed.

On that same day, the Iranian Revolution reached our small hamlet of Sar Cheshmeh. That morning a large group of locals had marched to the British Club and set it ablaze. Once the news reached our school, the school's administration closed the school and sent the students and instructors home. Each bus had an armed security guard in the front, ensuring that we would arrive safely home. My wife was shocked to hear of the demonstrators and of the burning of the British Club.

The school's administration felt that this was simply a one-off conflict, so the next morning the school busses collected the students and teachers and again, each bus had an armed security guard stationed at the front of each bus. That morning we tried to teach in a normal manner, but that was virtually impossible as rumors were running wild from every student and faculty member. Then that morning the news came that there was another large group of demonstrators marching in the streets of downtown Sar Cheshmeh. The administration again reclosed the school and everyone was sent home. That morning was the last time we were ever to enter the school, as over the next twenty-four hours, the demonstrators took to the streets and created havoc within our rural community.

The camp administration then feared for the safety of its employees and families; thus, it unswervingly announced that we would begin a mass evacuation the next morning. We had less than 12 hours to prepare ourselves so we began frantically packing our personal belongings. We were told that we were allowed only one suitcase and one small carry-on bag. It was very difficult for us to decide what we wanted to take and what we wanted to leave behind. We were also told that this would be a 'temporary departure' as the administration was expecting to resume full work 'after the disturbances' subsided most likely at the start of the New Year, 1979. This was comforting news that we would be returning so many of our collectibles; personal effects and toys were simply left behind. I still remember that I had insisted that Thomas leave his full collection of Lego blocks and that they would be here waiting for his return. He never returned and today, I feel there is still a small personal resentment of my son towards me over my mandate and decision concerning his precious collection. Each family was simply told to merely lock their doors and windows of their homes.

The next morning a multitude of buses arrived at the camp compound, and we were all collected and our suitcases placed below, and we were hurriedly bused down the mountain. Our first stop was the company's base camp where all information was gathered from us and we were asked our required destination from Tehran. This process took hours as the buses contained 'non-essential' company employees with their families as well as all the school teachers, administrators, and their families, plus a security contingent who was to escort us to Tehran and finally to the Tehran Mehrabad International Airport. All evacuees were given a light lunch in the base camps small cafeteria and by three p.m., we were all instructed to rebus and our entire group then traveled to Kerman. Kerman was the largest city and had the only opened and operating Iranian Railroad station in the region. The demonstrations had really started to affect the domestic travel as many of the airports' employees were out on strike and we were very lucky that the main rail lines were still operational. The camp administration had rented three train carriages to take us the 800 kilometers to Tehran. I still remember that train ride as if it had just occurred yesterday. That night, as the train passed through many small villages along the route, I noticed that each small town and village had some sort of electrical power and many had nice new school buildings. It did indicate that the Shah had promised his people that he would modernize his country even though he was accused of major corruption and bribery at the time.

Once we arrived in Tehran, we had our one-way air tickets waiting for each family all arranged and paid for by the company. Those families who had immediate departures were directly taken to Tehran's Mehrabad International Airport. Those that had late departures were placed in a local hotel and later taken to the airport. We were lucky as our flight was within five hours, so we were taken directly to the airport. The airport was in a state of turmoil and disorder, yet we were able to obtain our family's boarding passes and then to finally board our airplane and fly safely back to Damascus.

Our directives were simple, we were told by the Anaconda Group to simply wait for their announcement of the schools' reopening, and the camp's company would forward to us our return air tickets to Tehran, and then we would restart teaching in Sar Cheshmeh.

Once we returned to Damascus, we were staying at my father and mother-in-law's house. Each day we were glued to the television in order to gather news and information about this "Iranian Revolt" taking place in Iran. On January 16th, 1979, it was disheartening to hear that the Shah of Iran, Mohammad Reza Pahlavi, had fled his country that morning. He had left a caretaker government in place, but the strikes and demonstrations continued in his absence.

Shortly thereafter, the camp company sent me a telex message indicating that the school would be closed "until further notice" and that they would try to arrange for the collection of our personal effects as best as they could. I realized that all our 'personal effects' were neither packed nor ready for collection.

I went immediately to the Swiss Air office in Damascus and purchased a round-trip ticket Damascus-Tehran-Damascus. All international television stations were reporting that on the twenty-sixth of January, Ayatollah Khomeini had declared he was to return to Iran from his exile in Paris, but there

Air France Commercial Flight with Khomeini at Tehran Airport

were too many protests and strikes and strong concerns for his safety. He finally returned to Tehran on February first, along with over 120 journalists on an Air France Commercial Flight!

Khomeini knew that the Iranian military would not shoot down a commercial aircraft with so many civilians on board, and he was right.

I had made my Tehran flight for February second and a return date of February seventh. I planned to complete my mission in six days. I would return to Sar Cheshmeh, pack our personal effects, and give away the food we had in our refrigerator and cupboards. Then return somehow back to Tehran and finally Damascus.

Swiss Air was still flying from Damascus in and out of Tehran's Mehrabad International Airport. I knew that there were no domestic airline flights or trains operating at this time in Iran due to the ongoing strikes. The arrivals area at the Mehrabad Airport was empty, and I was lucky to have found an airport taxi outside the arrivals area. I was also very fortunate because the majority of passengers were leaving the country and not arriving to Iran. The arrivals area was empty, but there was a major shortage of taxis in this area of the airport. I did find one taxi and he took me to the large Bus Terminal and I bought a one-way ticket to Kerman. I remember that trip down to Kerman was very slow and very long. Once I arrived in Kerman, I was able to get in touch with the companies base office and they happened to have a car leaving to Sar Cheshmeh in a couple of hours. The driver dropped me off at our house and the first thing I did was to turn on the heating system as it was biting cold and quite wintry inside the house. The second thing I did was to have a very nice deep sleep.

In the morning and for the next eight hours, all I did was to get everything organized and ready to pack.

Months earlier, we had gotten to know several local Iranian Engineers and their families. So that morning I called them to see if they were still in Sar Cheshmeh and if they could bring some much-needed empty boxes for my packing. In return, I gave them all frozen and dry food in our kitchen. It was great talking with these two engineers as they were both American educated and they had sent their families back to their home cities so they too were bachelors. They were both indispensable as they had cars in Sar Cheshmeh plus they had solid contacts within the company of the camp.

I had by now packed everything, including my son's beloved collection of Lego blocks. His blocks were carefully packed and placed

in a secure box. All-in-all I believe I had over ten boxes and one very
prized old leather Iranian chest. We had found this old chest on one of
our excursions to the countryside months earlier. I still remember when
we found this Iranian chest in a small town market place we thought it
was a solid wood chest as it was hard to distinguish the covering material.
Once we got it home, I carefully cleaned the exterior and discovered that
the covering was old leather with amazing calligraphy and designs on
the top surface. We then lined the inside of the chest with some rich-
looking velvet material. When our friends saw the finished product,
there were amazed at the beauty of this old Persian Chest. I carefully
packed my two large telescopes inside our chest. All-in-all I was very
happy about my packing and I placed everything next to the front door.
They were simply waiting for the shipping company to collect them and
forward them on to our Damascus home. We were later informed that
the shipping truck did come by our houses and by the time they reached
our front door, the truck was full and they said they would return…That
never materialized. So all our precious items were lost and now only
remain in our memory.

Upon completion of this mammoth job of packing our personal
effects, I had arranged with the companies logistics department
transportation back down the mountain and on to Rafsanjan to catch
a domestic bus to the capital Tehran. That bus ride was very scary
and threatening as in each small town or village, our bus was forced
to stop, and the local religious demonstrators climbed aboard to place
photos of Ayatollah Khomeini on the bus and to hand out various Shia
religious leaflets to the passengers. It was terrifying as I was in the front
seat of the bus and I did not look quite like an Iranian, as a matter of
fact, I really looked quite American. Since the Shah's departure, many
Americans were targets of these religious fanatic demonstrators. The
young man next to me spoke perfect English and suggested that at
each unscheduled stop that I place a newspaper in front of my face and
when the demonstrators entered the bus not to talk or say anything to

anyone. My identity was especially tested when we entered the holy city of Qom as this is one of the main cities for Shia Islam's pilgrimages and the location of the Shrine of Fatimah bint Musa. Our bus was stopped multiple times in this city alone. My concealment seemed to work as I was never accosted or approached by any local demonstrators. Also, at each food and rest stop, this young Iranian student was always with me doing all the talking and speaking to me in English in a very quiet manner. This Iranian student was a real godsend as I feel that without his help and assistance, I may not have been so lucky on this frightening journey. What was scheduled to be a nine-hour bus ride took well over eleven hours because of all the unscheduled stops.

We did arrive at the capital, and I left the bus and took a taxi to a three-star hotel that this young Iranian student had recommended. Ironically my hotel room and balcony faced the rear gate of the US Embassy.

I vividly remember watching television in Damascus that early morning in November 1979, a group of Iranian students seizing the US Embassy and taking fifty-two hostages. Till now, I can still remember that interesting view from my Tehran hotel room.

On February seventh, I left my hotel mid-morning and traveled to the Mehrabad International Airport to catch my return Swiss Air flight back to Damascus. I was warned by the manager of my hotel that the situation was very bad at the airport, and I should try to arrive four hours before my scheduled departure time.

Words can never describe the disturbing situation that I found in the airport departure area. It was overcrowded, and people were hysterically looking for any airline that had available seats to leave the capital. I never expected to see such despair and angst among so many people desperately trying to leave their country. After a lengthy search, I did find the Swiss Air check-in line and that line was so long that I thought I would miss my flight.! Finally, I reached the check-in counter and my ticket was in order and I was given my economy boarding pass.

On my way to the passport control, a man approached me and offered me money and even his wife's mink coat simply for my boarding pass. No way was I going to face this catastrophic and disastrous situation again, so I smiled and said: "No, thank you."

I had finally made it to the main departure area near my gate, and that journey from the entrance of the airport to the departure area took over three hours.

I noticed on the departure board that our flight was going to be delayed by thirty minutes. I had my boarding pass, so I was not worried and was simply ready to wait that extra time. There was an announcement over the public address system saying: "Mr. Thomas Webber, please report back to the Swiss Air Ticket Counter." My heart sank, what was this? What was the problem? I reluctantly walked back to the Swiss Air Counter and the young lady asked: "Mr. Webber, can I have your boarding pass?" I immediately and directly said: "No!" She then explained that she has a First-Class boarding pass for me as an Iranian family was traveling and the husband was booked in First-Class and his family was in Economy and he wanted to sit with his family. I candidly said: "Let me see the First-Class boarding pass" as I have always been a 'Doubting Thomas'. She presented me with my First-Class boarding pass and as I was leaving the counter, the husband and his family warmly thanked me. I felt that I should be thanking them.

Well, it was a very comfortable and relaxed flight back to Damascus that I will long remember.

That was the last time I had been in Iran, but to date, despite our losses, I still feel that Iran is an amazing place.

Chapter Nine

Back to Damascus

When I first stepped off my final return flight from Tehran back to Damascus in February of 1979, I had no idea of how or where my future would develop. Were we going to stay in Damascus and start a new life? Would I look for a new teaching position? Would I consider teaching at the Damascus Community School once again? Or should I look for work in a different field?

The good news was that my answer would not be rushed as we had time on our side. Of course, my wife's parents wanted us to stay in Damascus. We decided to stay with them for the time being and to look at opportunities that would avail and benefit both of us.

My son Thomas was living with us in Sar Cheshmeh, and of course, he was evacuated along with us back to Damascus in mid-December, 1978. Once my family and I arrived back to Damascus, my top priority was, of course, his continuing education. I did not want him to miss any additional schooling since our hasty departure from Iran he had only completed half the school year. I was in touch with his mom by mail ever since the difficulties started in Iran and she was aware of our return to Damascus that December. We both felt that it was best for Thomas to return back to San Diego as soon as possible so he would be able to continue his studies and complete his sixth grade in California. The schools were currently on holiday due to Christmas. We knew the Swiss Air Station manager in Damascus very well and since Thomas was only twelve years old, he made special arrangements for my son to travel to California alone. A few days later, I took Thomas to the airport and he traveled solo as an 'unaccompanied minor' from Damascus through

Switzerland and finally on to the States. He later told me in private that he hadn't been too sure that he would be able to travel alone, but when he arrived safely in San Diego, he was quite proud of himself as he had gained a great deal of self-confidence and assurance during that long solo journey. He also gained experience by living in a foreign country that would help him in later his life and work.

My next priority was to finalize my current employment in Iran as we were simply evacuated out of Iran, and I was still employed as a science teacher. We had given the management company in Sar Cheshmeh our contacts in Damascus and shortly after I arrived back in Damascus in mid-February I received a telex from Anaconda informing me that 'the school would be permanently closed and they had no plans to reopen due to the current political situation in Iran.'

My contract would be respected, and they would cover my outstanding wages for the next several months. They also informed me that our personal effects that were left in our house in Sar Cheshmeh would be collected and sent to our address in Damascus in a 'timely manner'.

I informed them by return telex that we also had a shipment of over forty boxes that were sent from Damascus, and these were never received in Sar Cheshmeh. They promised to look into this second shipment.

At this time in the late 1970s and early 1980s, many international communications were completed via the telex network and telex machines.

The telex provided the first common method for international communications using standard and proven signaling techniques. Telex was

A Telex Machine

the major system of sending written messages electronically between businesses in the post-World War II period. Unfortunately, its usage went into decline as the fax machine grew in popularity in the mid-1980s.

I still vividly remember that I would need to type and hole punch my message upon a paper tape and then place this tape into a 'reader' and only then would I be able to send my message. Whenever we sent or received a message, the message was printed on copy paper, thus giving one 'original message' and the second page was the sender's copy. I also recollected that the office telex operator kept the original message in a binder and the copy was given to me. Also, after a short period, that copy would fade and be barely legible after a few months.

I believe that the original telex operators started exchanging informal messages thus, they became the first 'texters' long before the introduction of mobile phones. They would use such abbreviations as WRU "Who aRe yoU" code or CU L8R for: "see you later." Oh well, those were the days…

Concerning our two shipments, the first which was left in our house in Sar Cheshmeh in February. The company had informed me, some two months later that the moving truck which was collecting the personal effects from each of the teacher's homes had finished with our two neighbors shipments, and unfortunately, the truck was full and they were planning on returning the next day to continue their job. Regrettably, due to some major local disturbances, the driver and his truck never returned. Sadly we discovered that everything we were expecting from Sar Cheshmeh was lost and we would never see them again.

The second shipment had better news. It seemed that the US Embassy in Tehran had realized that there were a great number of American citizens whose shipments were delayed in the Iranian Customs. So they hired a fleet of giant cargo planes and started dispatching all freight that was listed as owned by an American family living in Iran. All freight was loaded onto these aircraft and transported out of Iran to a massive warehouse at JFK Airport. Sometime later, I was contacted by the freight forwarder at Kennedy Airport that indeed my consignment of forty boxes was being stored in this warehouse. A few weeks later, I flew to the states to retrieve our shipment. I made an appointed to collect our belongings and was successful in locating this giant storehouse near JFK Airport. When I arrived, I was overwhelmed at the enormous size of this building and as I entered, the forwarder pointed to a distant corner and said: "that's your shipment!" Yours is one of the last to be collected, as months earlier, this building was totally packed with shipments only from Iran. We walked to this distant corner and I was immediately struck that there were only a few boxes present. To my dismay, I counted only eight boxes. "What happened to the other part of our shipment?" I asked. He then proceeded to tell me how chaotic the entire situation was as each giant 747 cargo aircraft were simply unloaded and then the workers chucked and threw each box, carton or suitcase into this warehouse. It was simply in a state of chaos and pandemonium as many of the suitcases and boxes were accidentally opened and a great deal of the contents was spewed on the floor. He said it was a total mess as the entire warehouse was in a complete state of disarray for weeks on end. So your other boxes may have been taken by accident or simply were removed or gotten rid of to save space.

I then looked inside each of the remaining eight boxes, and there were only a few kitchen utensils; junk and unwanted items remaining. The old carpets, antiques, keepsakes, clothes and all our collectibles were missing. I did not find one item that I wanted to take out of the warehouse and salvage. This entire trip to the States was a true waste of time and money. I immediately changed my ticket and that same evening, I flew back to Europe and then on to Damascus extremely disappointed and dismayed.

On my flight home, I was trying to convince myself that this situation with our personal effects was not that bad, and yet, I knew that it was a true tragedy, and we would never see those precious and beloved items again.

Only one positive outcome came from my return flight, and that was that I had met the new General Manager of Marathon Oil for Syria. We sat next to each other on our flight from Geneva to Damascus. He was very impressed that I knew a great number of people in Damascus, and some may be able to help him in this new endeavor.

A couple of days later he contacted me, and we arranged to meet. I decided to bring my best friend, Nabil, along with me. This proved to be a very positive and tangible business opportunity for Nabil as over the following thirty years, he had personally worked, not only with Marathon Oil but with many of the new oil companies entering the newly established Syrian Oil Market.

A short time later, Nabil introduced the General Manager of Marathon to my wife, and he hired her immediately as Office Manager for his newly opened workplace.

So my flight to and from the States did have somewhat of a 'silver lining'.

After I returned to Damascus, my father-in-law asked me if I were interested in working in his agricultural company to establish a new landscaping division. I thought about it for a short time and agreed to begin work to create this new Landscaping Department. For me, this would be my first entry point into a part of the business that I would truly enjoy for the remainder of my life, and that is new business development.

We had many meetings over the coming weeks to select the full scope of this new department. We decided that we would concentrate on the landscaping, horticultural, and gardening fields. Specifically in the following areas: landscaping projects, project maintenance, introduction and importation of new garden and horticultural products plus indoor plant propagation and production.

My father-in-law also wanted the new garden products to be available for sale in all his AMC stores inside and outside of Syria.

He then arranged for me to study horticulture, plant propagation, and simply develop a full understanding of all indoor plants from their names to each plant's needs. My educational and business stay was arranged by my father-in-law to take place in Belgium in a small and very quaint town called: Lochristi, which was just outside of Ghent in East Flanders.

This region is noted as the *"Begonia Capital of the World"* and the village of Lochristi is the main area's hub for all the nurseries specializing in Begonia's, Azaleas, and many kinds of ornamental plants. He felt that it would be ideal for me to gain first-hand knowledge of all aspects of indoor plants and horticulture with a stay at one of the largest nurseries in Lochristi.

The name of the large nursery was Philip Sonneville n.v. and was owned and operated by a great young Belgian, Philip. He and I got along very well, and we developed a strong friendship over the three months of my 'internship'. During the week, it was all work at the nursery and on the weekends, we would explore the many fine restaurants in both Belgium and Netherlands. These two countries are both very small so driving to the Netherlands from Lochristi for one evening's entertainment was not out of the question.

I stayed at a very small three-star local hotel in Lochristi called Hotel Begonia. This was a great choice as the hotel was located only a few kilometers from his nursery and was clean and inexpensive.

Each morning I would have my breakfast at the hotel, and then Philip would collect me, and we would go to his nursery. I would begin to work within the large glasshouses and he would concentrate on his Begonia and Azalea production

Hotel Begonia,
Lochristi, Belgium

and sales. I always had lunch with Philip and his elderly mother and then after work, either Philip or his secretary would drive me back to the hotel.

I usually had my dinner in the hotel, and then afterward, I would enjoy a nice Stella Artois Belgium draft beer and review my daily written notes or study the various books on ornamental plants.

Soon we started visiting various agricultural and horticultural suppliers so I could have a better understanding of horticultural in general. Not to waste any time, whenever I found a product that was currently not found in the Middle East, and I felt would have a promising sales future, I would discuss distribution with that specific company on behalf of my father-in-law's large agricultural company. One day Philip suggested that we travel to the Netherlands to visit several peat moss companies and for him to introduce me to several very prominent Dutch Peat Moss suppliers. Peat moss was found throughout the Netherlands and especially in the North-Eastern provinces of the country where there were vast bog fields. A *bog* or bog field is a wetland that accumulates peat, a deposit of dead plant materials often mosses, and in a majority of cases, sphagnum moss.

I discovered that in the 1870s and 1880s, peat was used primarily for heating homes and industries. Just before the start of the twentieth century, coal had started to supersede peat as a fuel. The extraction of peat in the Netherlands virtually ceased after 1992, ending many centuries of exploitation of Dutch peat lands by man for energy and industrial purposes. So when we visited the peat factories in 1979, the majority of the peat suppliers in the Netherlands were using their peat products primarily for garden peat and potting compost.

I was lucky to find many of these peat companies were extremely eager to sell their peat products to the Middle East and especially to my father-in-law's company. So during these very educational and informative trips to both Belgium and the Netherlands, I found many other new and interesting garden products. For example, the Jiffy peat products company from Norway, their: Jiffypot® and the very popular Jiffy-7® peat pots. I started the distributorship and to date, these products have a high sales volume in many of the Agricultural Machinery stores around the world.

With Philip's help, I made contact with a UK company called Lune Aluminum Plant Containers. They were the manufacturers of the very modern-looking brushed or polished aluminum planters of various sizes.

Lune Aluminum Plant Containers

So a great deal of my time wasn't simply learning about the various indoor plants, but it entailed discovering new and prominent horticultural companies that wanted to start a business within the Middle East and especially in the Levant region.

I soon discovered that Philip enjoyed three passions: fine food, great wine, and fast cars. So each weekend, we would always find a prominent and well-known restaurant for dinner; visit their wine cellar so Philip could purchase some distinguished and notable wines for his own wine cellar and then speed on to our next bar or club.

These months passed by very quickly as towards the end of my internship, I was becoming very homesick. My wife and I were in constant contact as we would write many letters on a weekly basis so we knew what the other was doing and experiencing.

At the end of my training, I bid a tearful goodbye to Philip and his mother. I then left Lochristi to fly back to Damascus. I did see Philip as he visited Damascus a short time later, but unfortunately, I never saw Philip's mother again as she passed away a few years later. I also had heard that Philip had married his secretary, and they had a son, whom I understand was named Thomas.

Once I landed in Damascus, there was so much to talk about with both my wife and her dad. Her father and I decided to open a small landscaping office at their farm just outside of Damascus and we started to immediately look for suitable employees. The first employee we hired was a young Agricultural Engineer named Hadi who spoke excellent

English. He was quite talented in garden design and he worked with me for the following two years. We did many projects including the expansion of the Miqdadi Farm and many villas in the immediate area surrounding Damascus. The reputation of our small landscaping company was quickly spreading and the number of jobs kept increasing. Two years on, when I decided to leave Syria and move to the United States we kept Hadi as the new General Manager, a title which he held for many years.

Our second son was born in June 1980 in the same hospital as his brother some three years earlier. So our family was expanding.

Life in Damascus was very interesting during those years as the Syrian Oil industry was increasing with the arrival of many major American and European Oil Companies. Syria was booming, and this created a fantastic social life. During the summers, membership in the Sheraton Hotels swimming pool was a must as it was where anyone who was anybody was to be seen.

The American Embassy had countless functions along with the other major embassies in Damascus. Our social calendar seemed to always be overflowing with events. In addition, we would often travel to the new beach resorts opening along the Syrian Mediterranean Sea Coast. During the winter months, we had many trips to Lebanon to enjoy a long weekend of skiing.

What really made life pleasant while living in Damascus were our weekly visits to the Miqdadi Farm. My wife's family had purchased this simple farmland a few years earlier and had developed it into a true: *"Garden of Eden."*

Imagine visiting a place where everything's almost perfect. As we know that the Garden of Eden is used as a symbol in literature and art to represent paradise and of the all-elusive nature of happiness and peace. This was indeed the Miqdadi Farm!

It contained a great number of various fruit trees, so throughout the spring, you would see many of these trees in full blossom and by early

summer, you would be able to simply
pick the fresh fruit directly from each
tree.

Our Foal and Her Mother

The farm had a large horse stable
with a very large riding paddock
adjacent. Usually, once or twice a year,
there would be several young foals
born from the group of three or four
fillies and stallions.

The horses' were very friendly and could be fed by hand. All the
visitors to the farm truly enjoyed watching, feeding, and simply enjoying
the horses in this area.

In addition to the horses, there was a special smaller area for rabbits.
This was the favorite viewing area for my two sons in the entire farm as
they could always feed the rabbits grass or carrots and simply observe
their funny behavior on each visit to the farm. The number of rabbits
was increasing at a very fast rate, so at all times of the year as the farm
had a large number of both bucks and doe. So on each visit to the farm,
we always saw new and beautiful 'kittens' or bunnies to enjoy.

Near the rabbit enclosure, the
farm had a large enclosed area of
perches and nests for many pigeons.
It was always fun to count the
number of small eggs and then guess
to see which egg would hatch first to
produce such an ugly newborn squab!

**A Newborn Squab and a
Pigeon Egg**

Both my sons seemed to always
have questions when we were looking
at the farm animals. For example:
"Dad, why do the pigeons keep bobbing their heads, it looks so funny?"
Then I explained that pigeons have their eyes mounted on the sides of
their heads, not like we humans or even like owls that have forward-

facing eyes. Plus the pigeons have monocular vision rather than binocular vision like humans. I told them that monocular vision is when both eyes are used separately. By using their eyes in this way, as opposed to binocular vision, the field of view is increased, while depth perception is limited. So the pigeons simply bob their heads to create a better depth of perception. Monocular vision does have its advantages, as it enables the animal to see its surroundings better and to detect predators that might be ambushing from their sides. Also, pigeons are considered to be one of the most intelligent birds on the planet and able to undertake tasks previously thought to be the sole preserve of humans and primates.

I then said to the boys that we should go back and see the rabbits. We will look at their eyes, as they too have a monocular vision as they can see almost 360-degree eyesight and with this fantastic eyesight, and these rabbits can see almost all the way around themselves as well as above their heads. "You see, they were able to spot us coming from very far away, so when we arrived close to their yard, they were already waiting for us to feed them."

So now it's my turn to ask you both a question. "Why do you think these rabbits twitch their noses?" Both boys answered correctly: "Because they want to smell us better." That's right, rabbits have an excellent sense of smell, and this twitching simply brings more air into their noses.

Most importantly, at the farm, my wife's family had developed a large grass picnic area, so each Friday, there would be a large BBQ with many of the family and friends being invited.

This grass area also included over 200 rose bushes, an original,

One of the Farm's Grass Areas

and old Bedouin Tent, a full-service kitchen and a large man-made stone waterfall with a stream running from it. Along the course of this small stream, they had placed decorative water fountains and water bubblers.

The Miqdadi Farm was truly a "Paradise on Earth" or as many people would describe it as: *"Heaven on Earth."* It was so relaxing and peaceful that normally each Friday, the majority of the guest simply did not want to leave.

Finally, after my second son's birth in Damascus, I began getting strange and bizarre feelings...that we should live in America! Omar was only a little over a year old when we left Damascus to live in Iran. Ramsey now

Round Black Volcanic Stone with Bubbler

was just over a year old, and he had only visited America once just after he was born the year before. So both boys really did not know America and did not their family living there.

My wife had lost her father in late 1980, and this was devastating for her. So I felt maybe a change of scenery may be the best for her and in addition, her sister had moved to the States also in early 1980. In 1981 my wife's eldest and youngest brothers had moved to Amman to re-establish their father's agricultural business headquarters in Jordan. What was left in Damascus for my wife? It was only her mom and her middle brother that was left in Damascus.

And for me, I left the United States back in 1975, which now felt like an eternity. Since that year, I had only gone to the States during the summer on holiday. My dad had died in early 1978 while I was working at the American School in Damascus, so my mom was now living in a retirement home. I definitely wanted my two sons' to know their other grandmother much better as she was now getting to be close to her eightieth birthday. I must honestly admit that I was getting homesick.

So I felt for my family and me to live in America was a viable and worthwhile option.

Chapter Ten

Let's Try Living in America

Why America?

Well, a lot of safety issues went through my mind, especially after we were evacuated out of Iran in 1978. Then the somewhat volatile situation we faced in Syria upon our return enhanced those fears. We had our second child, Ramsey, born in 1980, so my family's safety and security issues were keenly becoming very apparent. Plus, to be honest, I really missed the States and simply going back on holiday wasn't the same as living in 'the good old USA.'

I hadn't really lived in American for any long duration of time, beginning with my departure to Europe to live for one year in the summer of 1971 and my return back to the States in 1972. I then departed to Damascus in late August 1975. So during this period, I had only lived in the States for just over three short years.

I had accomplished many diverse actions within the States during that short three year period. First, my first wife and I divorced in late 1972. I returned back to San Diego State University and received my California Lifetime Teaching Credential in the spring of 1973. I got my first US full-time teaching job in September 1973 till June of 1974 in Irvine, in Orange County, and finally, I completed my first two books by the end of the summer of 1975. In August 1975, I was headed to Syria. So many major changes had transpired during those three short years.

To be honest, I really missed America and had a strong desire to educate my two sons and my wife on the 'True American Dream' and where else to learn these values than in the States.

It was a decision that I had made on my own as there were many other factors that had also entered into this major decision. My wife and I, since coming back to Damascus from Iran in late 1978 and her finding a solid job with an American Oil company in Damascus, started to have major challenges with our marriage. So my self-centered brain thought: "a new life in American will heal all those problems" that we both faced in Damascus. Well, our living in American did the exact opposite. Our lives in the states from 1981 until 1983 were one of the most turbulent and disappointing times for both of us.

It took us three months to get everything organized and packed for our imminent departure. You don't realize how many items one family could accumulate in just three short years. OK, our last son was born in 1980 in Damascus, but the sheer quantity of 'things' was mind-boggling. What to take and what to give away? So the simple packing process took over three months as we were both having full-time jobs, which still entailed many social commitments. I remember we had a carpenter make a large wooden shipping box for all our valuable items. This large box looked like a large casket and soon became the joke with all of our friends and neighbors. "Why are you taking your casket?" they would ask. It was so large and heavy that indeed we had to hire a large crane to take it down from our rooftop apartment to the waiting truck below.

We did finally complete this massive packing project, and then we simply placed everything in temporary storage in Damascus until we knew our final location in the States.

I was able to turn over the landscaping company that I had set up in Damascus to my Syrian General Manager, and he had promised to look after it and not to have it fail. In fact, Hadi had grown that small local company into a flourishing business.

The selection of our final state to live in America was not too difficult to ascertain. I wanted a state with mild winters, unlike Western New York, which had very cold and snowy weather. I wanted a state where Salma could find a job that would use her translation skills and abilities.

I wanted a state that I could have a work opportunity to create a possible export company as I thought and envisioned that I could find American goods and services to export back to the Middle East, therefore it should be along the East Coast. For the boys, I wanted a state with the top-notch and solid elementary schooling system. Also, we wanted a state that we would have a short drive to simply visit both our families.

So finally, my decision was to find a state near Washington DC, not Washington DC itself as I was told there were way too much crime and lack of safety within those city limits.

Prior to our departure from Damascus in May, we all traveled to Amman to say goodbye to Salma's two brothers. And then, on our way to the States, we stopped in both the UK and Belgium to see friends and family.

So now, it was time... We departed with great hope and some anxieties for a new life in America. We landed at JFK on the 25th of June, 1981.

We hired a car and drove directly to Western New York to see my mom, sister, and brother. And then it was onto the Cleveland Ohio to visit Salma's sister and half-brother in the area. Salma's sister and her family had departed Damascus for the Cleveland area in 1980, and her husband had set up his medical practice. They, of course, wanted us to stay in the area around them, but I was confident that Ohio was not for us and felt that further south would be our better choice for our new life in America.

We then drove to our final location: Washington DC/Northern Virginia Area. We found a nice clean motel and began to look for our new "home." Someone in Damascus who was with the US Embassy had recommended Reston, Virginia, as it was a new development, it was a planned community and had very good transport links to downtown Washington, DC.

I later discovered that their definition of a "planned community" was one that "has man-made lakes, big shopping areas, very good schools, great transport links, and a solid mix of both blacks and whites."

We immediately fell in love with Reston, so green, so clean and well planned. We looked for an apartment to rent to find a house to buy would require a lot of time and effort. Initially, the only negative for Reston was its' high humidity, yet we found it wasn't simply a challenge for Reston but for the entire state. July and August in the greater Washington DC area are brutal. High temperatures and equally high humidity.

We bought a new car, a Volkswagen Rabbit, 4 door Hatchback, so we would not have a continual high monthly car rental fee. It was also a smart purchase as it proved very useful in transporting many large construction materials that were later required to build

Volkswagen Rabbit, 4 Doors
Hatchback – 1982

our basement. It also saved us a lot of gas during our many trips to Ohio and Western New York.

This Rabbit also gave us the ability to explore the many new areas within the state. We were also a bit "green" in our decision to purchase a new car as the car licensing in Virginia had a campaign for: 'special designed' license plates, and the extra fee would go towards a new state ecological approach to recycling. So our license plate was selected to be: OMAR. Our son was very proud of 'his car' so it was always called: *"Omar's Rabbit"*!! I do believe that Omar still has the original license plate.

We focused our attention on finding a nice house to buy so that we could enroll Omar into an elementary school a walking distance from home and possibly a daycare center for Ramsey also close to our new home. We were lucky as the housing market was fairly soft in the Northern Virginia area, and our search and final selection took only about one month to complete.

Our realtor was very professional, and she did not try to show us a property that was above our budget. The minute we entered this house on Turkey Wing Court, I fell in love with our new home. It was a split level detached house that had three bedrooms and a large living room and a nice enclosed back yard. The full basement was not finished and I immediately began to dream about how I could finish off the basement by possibly adding: a large family room, additional bathroom, a fourth bedroom, a storage room and of course, a wine cellar. We moved into our new home just prior to the start of the new school year.

Our home was a very wooded area of Reston as it appeared they built the homes around the trees, so as not to disturb nature. Unknown to us at this time, this extensive wooded area in our Dogwood subdivision of Reston would cause our neighborhood to have a fairly high crime rate. Six homes were burglarized during our short two-year stay at this location. The concept of our "planned community" had not planned for this crime factor as no one had told us the simple fact that the potential of the: 'have not's' wanting to take from the haves was accelerated in our subdivision. After we moved and settled in, we heard of the first burglary. I'd become fixated in making sure our new house was not going to be the next target. Luckily for me, during a shopping trip to a local Kmart, I noticed when we were entering the store, the manager was carrying a slightly damaged female mannequin out of the store. I thought quickly and asked him if he was throwing it away. He said yes, and so I asked if I could have it. He mentioned to me that he must take it out of the store in order to give it to me, and so I followed him back out of the store and then placed our "new house guest" in the back of our car. My wife and kids thought I had gone mad and made fun of my latest folly.

That evening I repaired the mannequin's arm and set her up in our basement. I made sure that she would be seen and is highly visible from the three basement windows. The mannequin was also exactly the same dress size as my wife, so I asked Salma for some old, used clothes to dress up our new house guest. For two years, she stood guard in a short black mini skirt, a white blouse, and high heels. I even went as far as to add a small, empty wine glass in her left hand. Therefore if a prowler was to look through the basement windows, they would see a woman in the house. I am not sure how many burglars had been frightened away by our house guest in those two plus years, but all I know was that our house was safe and we had no break-ins.

One very interesting scene took place when we had a water meter man ask to read our water meter, which was in the basement. He asked if anyone was downstairs and I told him no. A few seconds later, I heard this loud scream. He was frightened to see this sexy girl standing there as he was not expecting to see anyone downstairs. Thank goodness he did not have a heart attack. We sold our mannequin at our garage sale two years later for five US dollars.

The elementary school system in Reston was one of the top three in the entire state. We were really pleased with Omar's progress and development at Dogwood Elementary School. Ramsey was too young so he was placed in a Day School Nursery for the first year, and then he was a nursery student the second year at Dogwood.

Almost immediately, Salma had found a great translation job in Rosslyn, Virginia, with a company called CACI. She was perfect for this position as she was highly trained and had advanced degrees in both English and Arabic. Plus the company had many large contracts with several Gulf States so she stayed for the full two years in which we lived in the States. The Reston area had a great transportation system so she could take a commuter bus from Reston to Rosslyn. So she was now a true 'American commuter'.

When I first departed Syria in June of 1981 to live in America, my initial business goals in the States were to establish an import company to bring to America the many Syrian made products I had discovered during my years in Damascus.

When we arrived in the States, I had continued to plan to set up this new import/export company in the state. Soon I discovered that importing Syrian products such as can goods, handicrafts, soap products, etc. were already soundly established in the States. It became apparent that the states of New York and New Jersey were the centers for the Syrian importation. I actually drove up to New Jersey to meet first-hand with these current importers. After multiple meetings, I quickly realized that there would be no possible penetration into this mafia-like operation. The importation was connected with two or three Syrian/American families and apparently wanted nothing to do with this newcomer.

I then reversed my business concept from importation to exportation. It was a lengthy and time-consuming process that took me close to a year to establish. I had to find those niche products that the US manufacturers were producing and were willing to export overseas. In addition, I had to develop those foreign markets that required these same key products.

It did surprise me that so many US manufacturers were content to sell strictly within their large and bountiful domestic market. Many simply did not want to add the encumbrance of doing international business with all the burdens connected with international export such as using the metric system, completing Letter of Credits or complying with and sometimes in great detail new shipping regulations such as Bills of Lading; international insurance plus stamps and seals from each countries' embassies that they were being shipped. Even so, I was able to find several lucrative products and was successful, to a small degree, to earn a living over the next year and a half. Things were doing fine as my new export company was exporting virtually everything.

Unfortunately, with my last order, I had arranged for three 20' containers to be shipped from an East Coast Port to Beirut, Lebanon in May 1982. These three shipping containers held a wide variety of products from car parts, traffic signs to beehives. The various products were all consolidated into these three containers and shipped together to Lebanon. Little did I know or realize that prior to shipping my containers what was about to happen in Lebanon.

My containers were shipped from the States and arrived in Lebanon around the first of June, 1982. On the sixth of June was the start of the 1982 Lebanese War and the Israeli Invasion of Lebanon.

This latest war and invasion in Lebanon lasted until the Israeli withdrawal in 1985, and during this time, the PLO had withdrawn from Lebanon in August 1982. Thousands of Lebanese civilians were killed especially during the time that the Israeli army laid siege to Beirut. The Lebanese civil infrastructure was destroyed and it was pure chaos and pandemonium during those years.

Needless to say, my three containers were lost while in the Port of Beirut, and I soon discovered that the insurance that was purchased for their travel did not cover my containers in a 'War Zone'. Also, there was a term known as 'Force Majeure' and this is literally translated to mean 'unavoidable accident' or 'chance occurrence'. Under international law, it refers to an irresistible force or unforeseen event beyond the control of a state making it materially impossible to fulfill an international obligation. This happens to free the insurance company of all or any liability or obligation, hence the shipper loses everything.

Unknown to me at the time in my insurance policy, there was also a 'war exclusion clause' specifically excluding coverage for acts of war such as invasion, insurrection, revolution, military coup and terrorism.

Insurance companies commonly exclude coverage perils on which they cannot afford to pay claims.

I was forced to close my small export company and absorb all the financial losses. It was good while it lasted, and then I began working in a few odd jobs in Virginia.

It seemed like my life was facing another: 'timing challenge.' The first timing challenge was when I passed those three cars in 1976 and had my 'drive of my life'. Maybe if I had left a bit earlier or a little later, I would not have been placed in that dire and life-threatening situation. The second was the timing of my new teaching position in Iran. Remember it was August of 1978 and obviously, I was not paying attention to the news about potential Iranian Crises and the inability of the Shah to handle this major uprising. And now, this third timing challenge may have been a blessing from above as it gave me the opportunity of finding a new job in a new city...Jeddah.

Chapter Eleven

How to Survive in Saudi Arabia Without Even Trying

Our decision to leave America was a unanimous choice, and it was now only two very simple questions: Where and When. We found after our two years of living and working in America, it was a total case of ups-and-downs and unfortunately, the downtimes outweighed the good times.

With the loss of my three shipping containers in June of 1982, I lost everything, and I was forced to close my new company. For the time being, I was handling odd jobs in the Virginia area. I must admit that there must have been a silver lining to this Israeli Invasion of Lebanon that appeared less than a year earlier. The following April, a university girlfriend of my wife had informed her that she and her Saudi husband were coming to the Washington DC area and they would like to see Salma again and to meet me. The next night they called from the Four Seasons Hotel in Georgetown and invited us to dinner. During dinner, her husband asked me: "How are you doing Thomas?" I gave him a direct and honest answer: "not very well Saad!" I then explained what had transpired in the last months and all he said: "I will see what I can do."

Over the next few nights, they had invited us out and on our last visit, the husband told me about a company that he co-owned in Jeddah which was in urgent need of a General Manager to run the company. He asked if I was interested and of course I said yes. He then told me that he would send a Saudi Visit Visa to the Royal Saudi Embassy in DC. I remember that on our way back to our house, I asked my wife if she trusted his promise. She said that she did not know him too well and that she knew that he was a very busy Jeddah businessman and that he may forget about this business offer and his promise to send a visa.

One week later, I received news from the Royal Saudi Embassy in Washington DC that there was a visit visa in my name and that I should come to collect it. So this job offer was for real.

My wife and I talked about this potential job, and we decided that we should look into this work opportunity as the odd jobs I was doing were simply not working out for us financially. I made an appointment at the Saudi Embassy and I had the Saudi Visa stamped on my US passport on April 12th. Then came the difficult decision of when I should travel to Jeddah. The timing for me to leave my family alone was not right as there was a reported rapist in our neighborhood. He was molesting and assaulting many women of various ages and the police simply could not apprehend or capture him. How could I leave my family with this mad man on the loose in our vicinity?

We both felt that this job opportunity may not remain vacant as the Saudi economy was booming in the early nineteen eighties. The price of oil peaked from approximately $36 per barrel in 1980 with a production of almost 10 million barrels. But from that high, we would soon discover it would continue to decline, and by late 1986 their production dropped to about 2 million barrels per day and the price dropped on the world markets to approximately $14! This fall from the early eighties was initially because the demand began to fall as a result of recessions in many industrialized nations and the more efficient use of oil that also produced a surplus. So in the mid-eighties, the Kingdom of Saudi Arabia helped to create a worldwide oil glut. As a result of the oil glut and the pressures of decline in production, after 1985, Saudi Arabia began enforcing production quotas more harshly for OPEC members.

In early 1983 my timing to travel to Jeddah proved to be critical and a godsend as over our first three years in the Kingdom, its economy was in an incessant and austere decline.

I selected a date around the fifteenth of April for my departure from Washington National Airport to JFK Airport. I then took BA on to London with a short stopover at Heathrow Airport and then directly on to Jeddah. What I recall of my flight was that it was a most uneventful journey until we approached the Saudi Air Space and then all alcoholic service was stopped onboard prior to landing in Jeddah. As it was then and continues to be today, there is no legal alcohol being served in the Kingdom outside of the various embassies and consulates.

Jeddah International Airport or also called King Abdulaziz Al Saud Airport has four terminals. Since I arrived on a British Airways flight, we landed and were bussed to the 'North Terminal' which is near the very large Hajj terminal. This Hajj terminal has won numerous awards with its architectural beauty and as the name implies, is used only during the active Hajj season. It is dedicated to handling the thousands of yearly pilgrims that perform the Hajj. This Hajj terminal was for quite a while, among the 'world's largest airport terminals' (460,000 m^2). But today it is superseded by many new airports with huge terminals such as Dubai International Airport Terminal #3, which is still considered the world's largest by size (1.713.000 m^2), with the new airport terminal in Istanbul and of course the new terminal at the old Beijing Capital Airport taking second and third place internationally.

King Abdulaziz Al Saud Airport has a third terminal called The Royal Terminal and of course, was only used by the Royal family and by all state visits. The fourth terminal is called 'South Terminal' which handles all the Saudia flights. The sad part of this original Jeddah International Airport was that they were still using busses to transport you from the aircraft to the terminal and vice-versa. The good news is that the New King Abdulaziz Al Saud Airport has had a soft opening in early 2019 and will do away with both the North and South terminals and those horrible busses that have been used since 1981.

When I landed in the evening at the Jeddah International Airport, the ambient temperature was in the low forties Celsius, and the humidity was quite high as Jeddah is located directly on the Red Sea! When my bus arrived at the North Terminal, it was extremely busy as the majority of international flights were arriving at Jeddah between 8:00 to 11:00 p.m. So the passport control lines were quite long and at that time, they had no distinction in the passport lines between the incoming passengers, the unskilled new labor contract employees, and others like myself who were first-time-visitors with visit visas and other who were foreigners with Saudi Residency Visas/Cards. So it took over an hour to reach the front of the queue. Thank goodness my visit visa was in order as I then passed the passport control with relative ease. I could see my suitcase just arriving as I left the passport control officer. There has always been a 'challenge' with the luggage delivery in Jeddah at both terminals as the aircraft are parked quite a distance from the terminal and the off-loading process is quite slow. Today, you still wait for your baggage long after you complete the passport control.

I finally left the departure area and saw my name on a small signboard and a driver waiting for me. The company did make my hotel reservations, and their driver drove me to my hotel, which was conveniently close to the company's office. I slept quite well as when one travels East, you are losing time and the time in Jeddah was seven hours ahead of Virginia time. Then you must add the fight time and the layover in London. I was ready for a solid night's sleep. I had arranged with the driver to collect me the next morning so I set the alarm clock in order not to sleep in and miss my morning pick-up.

That next morning while at breakfast, I thought that I really didn't have a great deal of information about this BMS Company. I only knew it was an electro/mechanical company partially owned by my new Saudi friend Mr. Saad and they were looking for a General Manager.

The company's driver collected me on time as promised, and it was a very short drive to the head office of the company for my initial interview. When I entered the office compound, we walked through a busy workshop and initially, I was surprised at the number of maintenance personal all working on various projects. The second surprise was the majority of these workers were all from the Philippines. I later discovered that there were a great number of skilled Philippine craftsmen employed in Saudi Arabia as they did not demand a high salary and were quite good in their respective professions. I then entered the main office area and I felt that I had my zipper down or something as every office employee stared at me while I was entering. I figured that they had never worked for an American manager and they must have been very interested in gazing at this tall American.

I then met Saad's Palestinian partner, Zachariah, and we had a very productive two-hour meeting. We discussed all aspects of the company, and he gave me a description of the areas of business that BMS was involved in throughout the Kingdom. We spoke about my managerial background, my other qualifications and finally, my educational diplomas. Towards the end of our comprehensive meeting, he made me an offer to join BMS as their General Manager. He promised me that my contract would be ready and given to me the next morning. We shook hands and he then gave me a comprehensive tour of the maintenance facility and maintenance functions that his team performed. I was impressed with this BMS Company as he had established a multimillion-dollar business over a few years.

I then asked if their driver could take me to Mr. Saad's office as he had called my hotel that morning to welcome me to Jeddah and had asked to meet him after my morning interview.

The company's driver was very informative as he mentioned a great number of details about the city of Jeddah, its different districts as well as the names of the major streets. It was unique to discover that most of the Jeddah's new main north/south streets were numbered, for example, Aerbi'in Street or forty street, next was *sitten* or sixty street and finally *saeb'in* street or seventy street. I asked what these names meant. He explained that each was the width in meters of that respective street. Interesting…and as I observed and discovered that indeed *aerbi'in* street did appear to be only two lanes in each direction and only about forty meters wide. Saad's office was on *saeb'in* street and indeed, this was a very large street with three or four lanes in each direction. So this street was seventy meters wide. It also appeared to be the newest of the three as there was major construction on this street for almost three kilometers before we arrived at his office.

Saad was waiting for me and greeted me warmly. Also, working in an adjacent office was Mayada, Saad's wife. I believe that both Saad and his partner spoke just after my interview as he knew all the details of this positive dialog. They both congratulated me and welcomed me to Jeddah. I proceeded to ask them about my predecessor, as I was curious to know what had happened to him. They were both very candid with their replies. I learned that he was British and he did not meet their sales quotas and he did not have a sound relationship with his employees especially his maintenance team. That was useful information to have as I could then avoid those major pitfalls once I took up my position. For me, it was nice to see them again and to thank them for arranging my visit visa and interview.

That afternoon their driver took me back to my hotel, and I spent a lot of time contemplating my morning meeting back at BMS, I had an early dinner and went to bed a short time later.

I discovered the food in Jeddah was good, but not on par with Damascene cuisine. As a matter of fact, I was to live in Jeddah for the next twenty-two years, and I never found an Arabic restaurant in Jeddah equivalent to an Arabic restaurant in Damascus. Yet, on the other hand, in Jeddah, I did discover the opportunity of enjoying other cuisines that simply did not exist in Damascus: Thai, Chinese, Indian, American, and most importantly, very delicious and fresh seafood.

The next morning the driver collected me, and we drove to the office to discuss and sign my contract. At that time, everything seemed to be in order with the contract, but as I later discovered, I was very naïve to the conditions omitted in my first Saudi management contract. Such items as housing and a company car were included. But blatantly omitted were my two son's schooling expenses, medical insurance, home leave for my entire family, specific details as to my sales quota, moving expenses to Jeddah for my family and me, extra income for managing Saad's apartment house, etc. In all subsequent and succeeding work contracts, I would make sure that the above omissions were included.

I was then told that my housing would be a two-bedroom furnished apartment in a large apartment building fairly close to the office. After I signed the contract, they suggested that I visit the apartment and indeed, it was very close to the office. We would be in a nice apartment on the second floor of this new building. The furnishings were modest yet very clean and I felt that my wife and family would enjoy living in this residence.

After my tour of the apartment house, the driver was instructed to give me a full tour of Jeddah. I soon discovered that Jeddah was an attractive and very modern city totally different than Damascus. Then the driver drove me down to Jeddah's old city, and this was indeed comparable to the old city of Damascus in many ways. It also had a different and interesting architectural style unlike that of the Old City in Damascus. Many of the old buildings in the old city called the Balad were constructed of the following materials: coral stones as they were lightweight and readily available from the surrounding Red Sea reefs; a special petrified clay from surrounding lakes which acted as a special water-proofing and Teak wood which was imported mainly from India for the doors: Mashrabiyas and Rowshons. The Rowshons are large screened windows projecting out from each home with carved wood latticework located on the second story of a building or higher and they were often lined with stained glass. The Rowshons are long projected wooden skeleton covered with decorative wooden panels and screens that usually cover the entire elevation of the upper floors. This element of architecture helped the air move and spread around the house as well as cast shade on the walls of the house to alleviate the sun's heat. The final material used in construction would have been Gypsum and it was used to cover the coral stones. Many of the Teak front doors were simply massive well decorated and either painted in special colors to distinguish the well to do families or simply varnished. Many of these old Balad Homes are still standing today, some are over 30 meters in height and a few of them well is over 500 years old.

There are at least two explanations for the etymology of the name 'Jeddah'. The first study of the origin of the name Jeddah is that it was taken from Jeddah Ibn Al-Qudaa'iy, the chief of the Quda'a clan. The more common and accepted account has the name derived from the Arabic word: Jaddah for: "grandmother." According to legend and eastern folk's belief, has it that when Adam and Eve descended to Earth, Eve chose to descend to Jeddah while Adam picked the Indian subcontinent as his destination. The tomb of Eve, the grandmother of humanity, is considered by some Muslims to be the burial place of Eve, but the validity of this claim has yet to be confirmed. Yet, Prince Faisal,

The Tomb of Eve

Viceroy of Hejaz, destroyed this location in 1928. In 1975, the site was also sealed with concrete by religious authorities, who disapproved of pilgrims praying at tombs.

I only discovered the great and fascinating history of Jeddah while doing my research on this chapter. I had never realized, during my twenty-two years of living and working in Jeddah, that this city had such a vast and intriguing past. I felt that this earlier historical period of Jeddah must be well explained within this chapter as firstly, it is very interesting and secondly, I have lived longer in Jeddah than any other city in my entire life.

Jeddah's history is quite unique, as it can be traced back to the Stone Age. Excavations in the old city suggest that Jeddah was founded as a fishing hamlet in 522 BC. According to some accounts, the history of Jeddah dates back to early times even before Alexander the Great visited the city between 323 and 356 BC.

Jeddah first achieved prominence around AD 647 when the third Muslim Caliph, Uthman Ibn Affan, turned it into a port, making it the port of Makkah instead of Al Shoaiba port southwest of Mecca. In AD 703, Jeddah was briefly occupied by pirates from the Kingdom of Axum. Mainly, Jeddah has been established as the main city of the historic Hijaz province and a historic port for pilgrims arriving by sea to perform their Hajj pilgrimage in nearby Mecca. Today, Jeddah remains the principal gateway to Mecca and Medina, two of the holiest cities in Islam.

One of my own most interesting and beloved Berber travelers Ibn Battuta visited Jeddah during his world trip around 1330. He wrote the name of the city in his diary as "Jiddah.""

In Gavin Menzies' very popular and most interesting book: *1421 The Year China Discovered America,* he mentions that the Chinese emperor at the time: Zhu Zhanji allowed one of the most famous Chinese Admirals: Zheng He to visit Mecca.

So this famous Chinese navigator had visited Jeddah as Jeddah was then the main seaport to the holy city of Mecca.

The Portuguese explorer Vasco da Gama, having found his way around the Cape of Good Hope and obtained pilots from the coast of Zanzibar in 1497, was the first Portuguese explorer that pushed his way across the Indian Ocean to the shores of Malabar and Calicut, attacked fleets that carried freight and Muslim pilgrims from India to the Red Sea, and he struck terror into the surrounding rulers and potentates. It was very interesting as, by the late 1490s, King Manuel of Portugal, who commissioned Vasco da Gama, wasn't just thinking about commercial opportunities as he set his sights on the East. In fact, his impetus and motivation for finding a route to India were driven less by a desire to secure more lucrative trading grounds for his country but more by a quest to conquer Islam and establish himself as the king of Jerusalem.

The Princes of Gujarat and Yemen turned for help to Egypt. Sultan Al-Ashraf Qansuh al-Ghawri accordingly fitted a fleet of fifty vessels under his Admiral, Hussein the Kurd. Jeddah was soon fortified with a stone wall, using forced labor, as a harbor of refuge from the Portuguese, allowing Arabia and the Red Sea to be protected. Parts of the city wall still survive today in the old city. Even though the Portuguese were successfully repelled from Jeddah, the Portuguese fleets in the Indian Ocean were at their mercy. This was evidenced by the Battle of Diu between the Portuguese and the Arab Mamluks. The Battle of Diu is considered as one of the most important battles in history. The author William Weir in his book *Fifty Battles That Changed the World* ranks this battle as the 6th most important in history. He says: "When the fifteenth century began, Islam seemed about ready to dominate the world. That prospect sank in the Indian Ocean off Diu."

The Portuguese soldiers' cemetery can still be found within the old city of Jeddah today and is referred to as the site of the 'Christian Graves'.

As territories of the Mamluk Sultanate, the Hijaz, including Jeddah and the holy city of Mecca, passed into Ottoman possession. The Ottomans rebuilt the weak walls of Jeddah in 1525. The new Turkish wall included six watchtowers and six city gates. They were constructed to defend against the Portuguese attack. Of the six gates, the Gate of Mecca was the eastern gate, and the Gate of Al-Magharibah, facing the port, was the western gate. The Gate of Sharif faced south. The other gates were the Gate of Al-Bunt, Gate of Al-Sham (also called Gate of Al-Sharaf) and Gate of Medina, facing north. The Turks also built The Qishla of Jeddah, a small castle for the city soldiers. In the nineteenth century, these seven gates were minimized into four giant gates with four towers. These giant gates were the Gate of Sham to the north, the

Gate of Mecca to the east, the Gate of Sharif to the south, and the Gate of Al-Magharibah on the seaside.

In 1802, Nejdi forces conquered both Mecca and Jeddah from the Ottomans. When Sharif Ghalib Efendi informed Sultan Mahmud II of this, the Sultan ordered his Egyptian viceroy, Muhammad Ali Pasha, to retake the city. Muhammad Ali successfully regained the city in the Battle of Jeddah in 1813.

During World War I, Sharif Hussein bin Ali declared a revolt against the Ottoman Empire, seeking independence from the Ottoman Turks and the creation of a single unified Arab state spanning from Aleppo in Syria to Aden in Yemen. King Hussein declared the Kingdom of Hejaz. Later, Hussein was involved in a war with Ibn Saud, who was the Sultan of Nejd. Hussein abdicated following the fall of Mecca, in December 1924, and his son Ali bin Hussein became the new king.

A few months later, Ibn Saud, whose clan originated in the Central Nejd province, conquered Medina and Jeddah via an agreement with Jeddans following the Second Battle of Jeddah. He deposed Ali bin Hussein, who fled to Baghdad, eventually settling in Amman, Jordan, where his descendants became part of its Hashemite royalty.

As a result, Jeddah came under the sway of the Al-Saud dynasty in December 1925. In 1926, Ibn Saud added the title King of Hejaz to his position of Sultan of Nejd.

Jeddah in 1938

Today, Jeddah has lost its historical role in peninsular politics after Jeddah fell within the new province of Makkah, whose provincial capital is the city of Mecca.

The remaining walls and gates of the old city were demolished in 1947. A fire in 1982 destroyed some ancient buildings in the old town center, called Al-Balad, but much is still preserved despite the commercial interest to tear down old houses such as The Naseef House and Gabil House.

So the history of Jeddah is both interesting and unique as it involved many visits for hundreds of years from the four corners of the world.

After my initial and very interesting tour of Jeddah, I returned to my hotel and requested a late departure as my flight to London was to depart after midnight the next morning. I relaxed in my room, packed, and then had my final dinner at the hotel before heading back to the airport's North Terminal.

Once I arrived at the airport, I received my boarding pass and then spent time simply waiting for my departure on my BA flight. Once airborne, I was again amazed by the fact that once we left Saudi Airspace, the service of alcohol began and was a continuous and unceasing process until we landed at Heathrow Airport. The majority of the flights departing the Middle East usually left between midnight and 2 a.m. in order to connect with an ongoing flight from their European airports. I had only two hours in Heathrow to connect to a direct flight back to JFK and then down to Washington DC to National Airport.

I hadn't talked to my wife since I had left the states five days earlier. Remember there was no internet back in 1983 so phoning was an expensive option. I took a taxi from the airport back to my house in Reston, and I arrived around four or five in the afternoon. Salma and the boys were at home and were a bit surprised as they did not know exactly on which day I would return. As I drove up in the taxi, both the boys ran out of the house to welcome me home. I missed them as much as they missed me. Everyone wanted to know what had happened and I guess they concluded by the happy look on my face that my short trip was successful and positive. We talked for over an hour and then I realized that I was really hungry. Salma had already prepared dinner and all she needed to do was to reheat the food. We all sat around the table talking about our new future in Saudi Arabia.

I told my family there was good news and bad news. The good news, of course, was that I had signed a lucrative contract that would take us to Jeddah, a very interesting city. The bad news was that BMS expected my return to take up my position as soon as possible. In addition, their trip to Jeddah may be delayed due to lengthy and protracted family visa-issuing processes in Saudi Arabia. During my interview in Jeddah, I was warned that the visa process was going to take time. First, it would take months for my own work visit and then additional months for my family's visit visas to enter Saudi Arabia. This entire visa procedure would definitely take a great deal of time.

That evening after the boys went to sleep, Salma and I started making plans and wrote an "Action List" of things that we must accomplish prior to my departure.

We felt that it would be in our best interest to try to rent our furnished home and not sell it. But we had amassed so many antiques over the past two years and had brought from Syria many special Syrian' pieces of furniture that it would not be right to rent our house with so many of these special furnishings. We knew that any tenant would not realize the value of these old pieces and possibly misuse them. When we purchased the house, the basement was completely unfinished. I had spent a great deal of time building-out the empty basement. I had added a twenty-one foot family room, a large bedroom, a toilet, a very large storage room, and a large wine cellar in the deepest portion of the basement.

This unique and matchless experience of building the entire basement surprised me as I never thought that I had the ability to do such a massive job on my own. My eldest brother was always the 'handyman' as I remember growing up that it was always Fred that was building something new or repairing something broken at our house in Western New York. In our basement, in Reston, the only area for which I hired a contractor was when I added the bathroom in the basement. I have never enjoyed plumbing, and to date, I still do not enjoy doing any sort of plumbing job, no matter how simple the task.

Now, all I needed to add in our basement was an additional room between the bathroom and bedroom that would serve as our own private and locked storage room. I knew that this area was the driest in the entire basement and would make an ideal room for all our unique and valuable personal effects. Also, in this manner, all of our 'special furniture' would be locked and stored in safety during our absence.

I decided that I would rent a special space from a professional storage company for my many bottles of wine. We had left the wine within this company's storage for almost two years, and it was really getting financially prohibitive to maintain the wine in such an arrangement. So during one of my visits to my sister-in-law who lived in the Cleveland area, I suggested that I would construct in her basement a nice wooden wine cellar similar to the one I had constructed in our Reston house. And then, after I finished her wine cellar, I would transport all of my wine up to her new wine cellar for proper storage. She liked the idea as her new wine cellar would add value to her property and she would save us the expense of storing the wine in this Virginia's company stowing facility.

This new storage room in the basement would be for all our antique items and other personal effects that we would not take to Jeddah and, of course, not leave upstairs during the rental period.

We then decided on the rental advertisement for our house, and we formulated a nice-sounding advertisement and placed it in several newspapers to run that next week. To our amazement, we had many parties interested in renting our home. We finalized with one nice young couple, and we agreed that they would move in on the first of June.

Then we discussed the boys schooling as at first Ramsey was in a Day Care Center and then they were both enrolled in an elementary school a walking distance from our home. Since this was April, we decided to keep them at the elementary school. Our rental of the house and the boy's schooling had been well coordinated with the end of the school year in mind.

Now I had to plan and arrange for accommodations for my family. I knew that by June first, I would have received my second Saudi Visit Visas. Salma's aunt knew of a great apartment in Annandale, Virginia, that we could rent on a short term basis. So we prearranged to rent that property. Salma and I also felt that if their Saudi Visit Visa process took longer, she would leave the states and take the boys to Damascus to stay for the duration of time with her mom. Since the boys and I only carried US Passports, I then arranged for us to get three Syrian Visit Visas from the Syrian Embassy in Washington, DC, so we could all travel legally to Syria. Salma had maintained her Syrian passport so she didn't require a Syrian Visa even though she carried an American passport.

We then thought of our VW Rabbit and felt it would be best to sell it prior to my departing Virginia. Like with the renting of our home, we had no problem in selling the car and having the new owner taking ownership just prior to my departure date.

I had received my first Saudi Visit Visa from Saad in mid-April of 1984 that I used for my first trip. I now required a second Saudi Visit Visa from the company, which arrived in late May.

Since we first arrived in America, Salma had been working in Rosslyn, Virginia as a translator. She had really enjoyed her time working with this company, and now she had to inform them that she would be leaving the company and America.

Things for us were working out very well with Salma and me as we were completing our "Action List" and all that remained was my starting that new storage room in our basement. The completion of this special room took less than a week as I did not need to add any false ceiling or paneling as I had with the other parts of the basement.

As the middle of May approached, we had completed each item on our Action Item List, so it was time to plan my return trip to Jeddah. I decided to return at the end of May so I could help with moving the special articles to the new storage room in the basement and to conclude the sale of the car, etc.

The rental apartment for Salma and the boys in Annandale was very nice, and they stayed there for a month or so. She then decided that instead of paying unnecessary rent, she preferred to fly to Damascus and wait for their Saudi Visit Visa's at her mother's home. This was a very wise decision as their Saudi Visit Visas were delayed and never received until mid-August!

My trip back to Jeddah was again uneventful, and this time, I traveled to Jeddah via Damascus. I landed back in Jeddah some forty-five days after my first visit. Again on this trip, the company driver picked me up from the Jeddah airport and this time, he took me directly to my new apartment.

The apartment was clean yet stifling hot as the windows had been closed for quite a while, and no air conditioners were used. The driver showed me where all the electrical switches were and most importantly, where each air conditioner switch was located. It was funny as I remember when I first looked in the refrigerator, there was only a liter of milk and one fresh chicken placed as a homecoming gift.

I began emptying my suitcases, but I never completed the full tasks as I was very tired and decided to go to bed. The next morning, I was picked up from my apartment and driven to the office for my first 1 day 'on-the-job'.

I had a meeting with the co-owner in which he explained that he would personally introduce me to the managers of the largest companies that BMS had existing maintenance contracts with that week. I was then introduced to the entire office staff and went to inspect my new office. I felt my first day went extremely well, and the entire staff seemed to like the idea of having an American manager.

That first week went by extremely fast, and by the weekend, I began to feel that I fit the position and worked well with all employees.

I then discovered that the company had a policy of conducting a thirty-day 'trial period' so I had to complete that time portion before they could begin to start my Saudi Residency paperwork. In early July, we began the lengthy and detailed task of preparing all the necessary paperwork for this all-important Work Visa and Saudi Residency Card. Without these, I was not allowed to legally bring my family to the Kingdom.

The company's Government Liaison Officer was not a very active person, and I soon felt he was not too interested in getting my paperwork completed in an expeditious manner. He claimed that he needed the original copy of my Birth Certificate, my University degree, and my Marriage Certificate. These were furnished by mail or post, which was the most time-consuming process, as we must remember that the year was 1983 and it predated the internet era. Once these were obtained, each needed to be translated into Arabic and certified by a Notary. The Notary was at the America Embassy, so this point was not too difficult to complete. After almost two months, I finally obtained my Saudi Residency Card and Work Permit in early August.

I immediately began the process of obtaining a visit visa for my wife and two sons. The Saudi authorities then questioned me on the reason why we wanted to have these three American Visit Visas delivered to Damascus Syria and not to an address in America. We finally obtained their visit visas in mid-to-late-August. In Damascus, the Royal Saudi Embassy was one block from where they were living, and it only took a few days to have their visas stamped on their passports.

There was a great deal of excitement in Damascus as well as in Jeddah once they had their Saudi Visit Visas on their passports. As it had been over three months since we had last seen each other and the wait was excruciating and agonizing for all of us.

The day finally came, and the family arrived at Jeddah on a short two-hour flight directly from Damascus. They all landed in Jeddah in late August of 1983 and I believe their flight landed in the early evening. Unfortunately, they were greeted with a temperature in the low 40 °C and stifling high humidity. You see the average high temperature in August in Jeddah is around 39 °C and the low at night being 27 °C or 28

°C. Both boys' first comments to me were: "Dad, Jeddah is very HOT." I told them never to use the word "hot" as it will defeat you mentally. Simply say, "It is warmer today than yesterday" or "I didn't expect it to be this warm." I didn't want to inform them, at this time, that the highest temperature in Jeddah can reach more than 50 °C which is 122 °F. I would let them discover that in the coming years.

We collected their suitcases and walked out of the terminal into this blistering heat. I then promised them that they would enjoy staying in Jeddah even with this severe temperature, and this promise did hold true for over twenty years. As a matter of fact, my eldest son Omar is still working and residing in Saudi Arabia.

There first impression of Saudi Arabia was quite negative due to the high temperature, so I wanted their second impression of this beautiful city to be positive as mine had been. So I decided to drive them home the long way and to see a few of the many monuments along the way and alongside the Jeddah Corniche or coastal road.

Jeddah is still known today as an "Open Air Art Gallery" as during the oil boom in the late 1970s and early 1980s, there was a focused civic effort, led by the then Jeddah's city mayor Mohamed Said Farsi, to bring art to Jeddah. He had the vision to make Jeddah a beautiful city and began to purchase art to be displayed along the many streets, including the seaside Corniche and many public areas around the city. As a result, Jeddah contained a large number of modern open-air sculptures and works of art by many famous artists such as Henry Moore, Alexander Calder, Jean Miró and the prolific and Jeddah's master architect: Julio Lafuente who has created many sculptures around the city. These monuments are typically situated in and around and on major streets thus making Jeddah one of the largest open-air art galleries in the world. Most of the sculptures depict traditional Saudi items such as coffee pots, incense burners, Arabic calligraphy, Palm trees and a giant Al Qiblah, which points towards the city of Mecca. The fact that Islamic tradition prohibits the depiction of living creatures this has made for some very creative, as well as unusual modern art. These include a giant bicycle, which was made from the old pipes of the first water desalination plant in Jeddah, a huge block of concrete with several cars protruding from it all at odd angles and is called: "Crazy Speed" or the "Accident" and my favorite in Jeddah of over 400 sculptures and monuments is: "The Globe."

So the very first monument I showed my family was the famous Globe, which is in the center of a large roundabout. They were all very, very impressed as we saw it at sunset and I continued around the circle several times so they could really become absorbed with the beauty and uniqueness of this renowned monument. It is basically an Islamic monument as it has a bright beam of green light radiating from Mecca.

Globe Roundabout
in Jeddah

From this spectacular monument, we drove a short distance to the celebrated Jeddah Corniche. This is the world's longest coastal roads, as it exceeds 110 kilometers in total length. It is divided into three sections and we were just entering the Central segment and there is a Northern and Southern portion. By far, the Central section is the most beautiful and has the most number of sculptures and monuments to view.

The city has been poetically and gracefully called: "The Bride of the Red Sea." I personally feel that the Jeddah Corniche must have been a contributing factor for this elegant phrase. While writing this chapter, I was doing my fact-finding and discovered that the Egyptian Red Sea resort called Hurghada also uses the same idiom: 'The Bride of the Red Sea'. I do believe that Jeddah's name was first inscribed over that of Hurghada.

For a first time visitor to Jeddah, I personally feel that the central section of the Corniche is a must-see panorama and seascape. There are so many splendid views of the Red Sea and the continuous fringing or shore reef which runs the entire length of the coastline. We stopped about halfway along the Corniche and walked to a small fishing pier that had lights illuminating the reef face or called reef crest. This area of the reef seems to be the most diverse and contains a great deal of sea life. My two sons were thrilled and very excited as there were so many brightly colored fish that they could not believe their own eyes. Since this first trip to view a reef, we all love to take the opportunity to relax and view whichever reef anywhere in the world.

Then we continued along the Corniche until we came upon undoubtedly the most beautiful sight in all of Jeddah: The Jeddah Fountain. This is the world's highest fountain as it has now attained a height of 312 meters, which is over 1,000 feet.

The Jeddah Fountain

To be honest, the entire family was very excited and thrilled to view this new fountain. We were all lucky as the fountain was inaugurated a few months earlier. When we first viewed it, it was only 120 meters in height, and two years later, they changed and enlarged the pump to extend its height. All the same, even today, I get moved and impassioned when I see the Jeddah Fountain.

It was now time to head home. I was very pleased that my initial tour of Jeddah went so well with my family.

Before I left the house to the airport, I made sure the apartment was spotless as I did not want any negative views to address concerning our new home when they arrived. I was also very smart as I left all of the air conditioners on, so when we entered the apartment, it was very cool and refreshing.

When we arrived, they immediately looked around and they all liked their new residence.

The next day was a Friday, so there was no work and I decided to extend my tour of Jeddah to include the Old City of Jeddah called Balad and to drive along the Southern Corniche. The Balad was nice but again nothing like the old city of Damascus. It was also looking new for us.

The Southern Corniche was a great discovery as it was a brand new four-lane road for the entire length and had absolutely no development along its length. It was unspoiled and pristine, and the Red Sea curved in and out of small bays and inlets. We parked the car often and simply walked along the coastline finding numerous seashells, hermit crabs, and clams. I think we collected over fifty seashells that day.

The day quickly wore on, and it was soon time to head back to Jeddah and have something to eat. When I'd first arrived in Jeddah in late May, I'd discovered that selecting a restaurant was a very easy task as there were many international cuisines including Indian; Chinese; Thai; Italian; French and American. Earlier, I had discovered a very nice Thai restaurant so I suggested that we have a late lunch in this great tasty Thai restaurant. Salma and my sons quickly discovered a very annoying Saudi regulation…all restaurants close 10 to 15 minutes before prayer time and open 5 or 10 minutes after completion of the prayer. This was to allow their Muslim employees time to prepare and walk to the mosque for prayer. It appears to this day that many expatriates living in Saudi Arabia keep an accurate record of each daily prayer time.

Earlier in Jeddah, I was introduced to a very special spicy Thai shrimp soup called: Tom Yum Goong in this same special Thai restaurant. So I made sure that I ordered a large bowl of this fantastic soup for my family. Even after 35 years, my family adores and craves this famous Tom Yum Goong soup. So our first meal out in a Jeddah restaurant proved to be a notable success.

Over the next 22 years, we would enjoy many extraordinary meals, especially in select and well-known Asian restaurants. It was our family tradition to celebrate our family member's birthdays at the Gulf Royal

Chinese restaurant. It remains today a very special restaurant for all of us to enjoy.

In addition to these specialized Asian cuisines, my sons developed a love for two different Saudi fast food chicken restaurants. Their favorite chicken dish is called: Al Baik, which is a special broasted chicken and the other is called: Al Tazaj in which they grill their chicken. Today the local customers simply say "Let's have broast" and the lines in these two top fast food chicken restaurants are long, especially on Thursday nights.

We also discovered many special seafood restaurants that specialized in either fresh local fried or barbequed fish and another fish dish called: Saiyadyia. On this plate, the fish was placed on top of special long rice with a very flavorsome sauce served on the side.

Since 1972 I did not consume red meat or chicken, and thus, I was never a lover of the most popular Saudi cuisine as it contained mainly lamb and chicken. The Saudis' main national dishes were called: Saleeg, Kapsa, and Mandi, plus they commonly served a very heavy Moroccan meat soup called: Hareira. You would also find Kebab's; Shawarma and Mansaf, which is actually the national dish of Jordan and Palestine yet it is commonly served in Saudi Arabia as many of the workforces have emigrated from the Levant region.

Finally, on each return trip to Saudi Arabia, I always order a local takeaway food called Mutabbaq, which is a Middle Eastern flatbread filled with an egg mixture, folded then pan-fried. The name Mutabbaq in Arabic means "folded."

Saudi Arabia's food would not be complete unless I mention Saudi Dates and their Saudi coffee. Saudi Arabia is in the top three leading date producing counties in the world. They have many different varieties of dates.

Their Saudi coffee is very unusual as it is brewed using slightly roasted green coffee beans and a large amount of Cardamom. Most people mix Arabic Coffee with Saudi coffee. They are very different. First of all, this Saudi coffee is not black in color, it is simply a light tan, and secondly, it tastes great as they use an abundant amount of Cardamom to season their coffee. This is the only coffee that I drink as I gave up drinking the traditional black coffee many, many years ago.

Since my family came in late August, we had to think about the school that we were going to enroll our two sons in. We were again very lucky as our apartment was a walking distance to an English international elementary school. My wife had brought their school records from the States, and the following Sunday morning, she walked to the Manarat Jeddah Elementary school. This school was using a British teaching curriculum and we were lucky as they did have room for both boys. My wife registered and enrolled them in their respective classes and we discovered the school would not start for another two weeks so we had sufficient time to purchase their: school uniforms, backpacks, books, etc. They would attend only one semester as we soon found that they were learning their English with a strong Scottish accent as the majority of the instructors were from Scotland. Over the semester, we got to know the instructors and even I had a difficult time understanding their English with their strong Scottish accent.

After their first semester in this English school, we then decided that both boys should be totally immersed in a purely Arabic school setting. We were living in Arabic culture, and till then, their Arabic was quite weak and my wife and I knew the importance of speaking and writing Arabic. So we decided to take them out of this English school system and to find a 100% Arabic curriculum. There were many schools available to the foreign Arab speaking families, plus we had time to search for a suitable school. We came upon a purely Egyptian Arabic school not too far from our apartment. We enrolled them and they started just after the New Year.

This school selection was one of the best choices we ever made, not because of this particular school, but because they were learning in a totally Arabic environment. Their English instructors were both from Egypt, and they had a very strong Egyptian English accent. So much so, my sons were asked to help teach English in their respective classrooms. I also believe that they were the only 'true Americans' in the entire Al Nasr School acting as a part – time English teacher!

Of course, we found it necessary to hire an Arabic tutor for the duration of their first semester. He came to our house five days a week, and the boys assimilated into their Arabic school environment quite well. This was due to many factors: my wife had always insisted on speaking only in Arabic to them, and this tutor was another contributing factor. When we were together, I was always the one speaking only in English to the boys. So they had a great separation of the two languages. This also contributed to their quick success in learning Arabic and them maintaining their strong English language skills.

Over the remaining elementary and middle school years, they both attended purely Arabic schools, and from their first two years at Al Nasr School, they attended a very prestigious Arabic school called Dar Al Fikr. Unfortunately, while they were attending this school, Saudi Arabia was faced with the start of the groundwork of the first Gulf War in early August of 1990. From that date onward, it appeared that everyone in Saudi Arabia was beginning to be on a 'war footing' in preparation for a war within the Middle East. As Iraq had just invaded Kuwait and the Iraqi leader Saddam Hussain annexed Kuwait and vowed not to leave.

For the next five months, 100% of the international attention within the Kingdom was in both Iraq and Kuwait.

My sons attended Dar Al Fikr School for four years, and that last year was very traumatic as there was always the threat of Iraqi retaliation on all parts of Saudi Arabia with their Scud surface-to-surface missiles. Scuds are notoriously inaccurate thus making all parts of the Kingdom at risk of an attack.

Combat against Iraq started on January 17th, 1991, and in less than five weeks, Saddam was defeated by the coalition of over 34 countries. Slowly, life began getting back to normal in all of Saudi Arabia.

In September of 1991, they were ready to attend both middle school and high school, and we decided to enroll them into a pure English school system as our eventual goals were to have them both attend college in either an American or a British university system.

My eldest son Omar attended the British High School in Jeddah called Continental School from the eighth grade up to his graduation with his Cambridge IGCSE qualification certificate. He then attended a variety of US and British Universities and finally decided on completing his study at Ohio State University.

Ramsey, on the other hand, attended his fifth to ninth grades at the SAIS or the Saudi Arabian International School, which is an American School. Originally, this school was called PCS or the Parent Cooperative School and was in operation in Jeddah from 1952. Unfortunately for Ramsey, SAIS had only offered classes till the ninth grade so, for his three remaining grades, he attended Blue Ridge School which is a private, all-boys boarding school located in the foothills of the Blue Ridge Mountains in Saint George, Virginia, near Charlottesville. Ramsey had always been able to cope with the hot weather in Jeddah, but really never enjoyed the high humidity here. So when it came to the time for him to select a university in the States, he chose to attend and graduate from Arizona State University, as it had an arid yet dry climate and still quite hot in the summers.

Soon after Salma and the boys arrived in Jeddah, she answered an advertisement for a word processing position at the US Embassy in Jeddah. She was accepted immediately and had worked at this location for twenty plus years. She also held the job of consulates language instructor and translator both she enjoyed immensely. When we arrived in Jeddah in 1983, it was officially the US Embassy, but in 1984, the Jeddah Embassy became a US Consulate General when the embassy was relocated to Riyadh. We immediately began enjoying the extra benefits that her position offered to her and her family such as the use of the embassies driver to bring her to and from work each day, the use of the consulate's large swimming pool, access to the Dunes Club which was an adjacent swimming club, the consulate's Brass Eagle which was the US Marine's watering hole and sports bar plus many invitations to the numerous consulates' diplomatic functions.

My family really enjoyed taking trips to either the open sea or using a swimming pool virtually every weekend during our total stay in Jeddah. The Dunes Club plus the consulate's pool were our favorite locations for the first few months, and then we would travel more and more to the Southern Corniche to enjoy the open sea. There were very few people using these beautiful beaches and the travel time of 45 minutes was short to reach these pristine and unspoiled beaches. Each trip had always been worth the drive. It was here along these untouched shores that our desire to learn snorkeling first began. We went out and purchased four sets of snorkeling equipment which consisted of a proper mask and a special breathing tube. We never used fins as they seemed to disrupt the sand especially in the shallow waters of the reef lagoon. So that next Thursday after school and our work we all went to the US Embassy's large pool and I helped my wife and sons get acquainted with the snorkeling equipment. At first, it could be a fearful experience as you are free-floating and not holding to any surface. I did not want the boys to develop any fear of snorkeling so I had the boys first start by snorkeling along the edge of the pool back and forth with me next to them. Then I had them snorkel out to me a few meters away in the middle of the pool and then finally to swim across the width of the pool multiple times with their mask and tubes. I made sure that I did not instill fear into them as I knew snorkeling in a swimming pool was very different than swimming in the open sea. When you first swim in the open sea along the reef crest and then you swim out and look down the reef face to the seabed some twenty meters below, you may have the tendency to panic. To date, I get slightly chilled when I cross the reef face and look down into the depths far below me.

We decided to go to the Southern Corniche the next day, which was a Friday. So after our first practice sessions in the pool on our way home, we went to the SCUBA (Self Contained Under Water Breathing Apparatus) Shop and purchased a couple of books on the Red Sea. The first and most important was titled *Red Sea Safety*. It was a guide to the dangerous Marine Animals one encounters while snorkeling or diving in the Red Sea. The other was a nice waterproof book titled: *The Divers Guide to Red Sea Reef Fishes*. That evening we looked at the boys and I felt that they were getting very excited.

The next morning, Salma made sandwiches for lunch, and we had plenty of juice and water. We found an old blanket so we took that to be used as our cover on the sand. We always took beach towels but only used them at the end of our picnic as I found that by the time we would leave the sea and make it to the blanket, our body had already dried. We made better use of these beach towels at the end of our trip as we always brought a large twenty-liter plastic 'jerry can' filled with freshwater and then we would use the water as a shower and the towels to dry off. I had always been interested in this name: 'jerry can'. I discovered that it came from the name: 'Jerry' as that was the name the allied soldiers called their German counterparts and the Germans were using this specially designed container for transporting both gasoline and water. The shape was much more practical than our forces' round gas containers. Hence the name, Jerry cans was because of their German origin. The military jerry cans used by the armed forces were still made of metal as they needed to be sturdy and withstand extreme conditions.

Our first-day snorkeling was a tremendous success as we were in the Red Sea for at least four hours. The water was very clear, and the water temperature was just over 30 °C and we described it as 'bathtub temperature'. The sea life we saw was magnificent plus it was abundant. The boys did not want to come out of the water.

Throughout the twenty-two years in Jeddah, we enjoyed the Red Sea to its maximum. We also progressed in our selection of beaches to visit each weekend. We had started along the Southern Cornish and the various open beaches, and this was utilized for many years. Our Syrian friends were members of various beach clubs along the Northern Cornish so there were often invitations to enjoy the comforts of a nice beach club and to foster many new friendships.

We started weekly visits to the Red Sea initially alongside the open sea along the Southern Corniche. We then found great beach resorts on the Obhur Creek and then finally on the open sea further along the Northern Corniche. So there seemed to be a timely progression during our 22 years of living and working in Jeddah.

In a short time, I developed a keen interest in sailing, and one of the most popular sailboats was the Hobie 16 fiberglass catamaran. It was very easy to sail as it had a trampoline style deck, was very fast and extremely easy to set up. It weighed only 145 kg which was only 320 lbs., so it was quite easy to store and place on

Hobie 16

any platform out of the water. It had a set of two sails, the mainsail, and a smaller jib and these were very easy to raise and to drop by one person.

It also could be sailed solo or with a crew of up to four. Many times we would 'turn turtle' or simply capsize our Hobie, and each time it was fairly easy to right our Hobie with a partner. Being tossed into the water was not too bad as the water temperature was very warm and of course, we always wore a life vest.

I purchased several Hobie 16's during our long stay in Jeddah with a close friend. We soon started enjoying racing our sailboat on Friday afternoon races in the large Inland Sea called 'Obhur Creek' along the Northern Corniche. We enjoyed sailing and swimming on the Obhur Creek in several different beach compounds for many years.

I then went one step further and joined the Jeddah Sailing Club on the open sea, which had beach huts so the entire family would enjoy a full day sailing, barbequing, and simply enjoying ourselves. Sailing and racing the Hobie Cat on the open sea was much more challenging than on Jeddah's Obhur Creek. The winds were always gustier and the waves much higher, consequently making sailing much more exhilarating and exciting. We enjoyed the sailing club for four or five years and during this time, I helped organize sailing competitions between the American Businessmen's Group (ABJ) and the British Businessmen Group (BBG). These sailing contests were so popular that they became an annual event.

Many of the British and American expatriates had purchased a substantial number of Hobie 16's, and a few were sailing the famous Laser sailboat. The Hobie 16 is a bit faster than the Laser as the top speed of the Hobie is around 24 knots whereas the Laser has a top speed of only 16 or 17 knots. This model, Hobie 16 catamaran sailboat, has been the most popular and most competitive cat class sailboat in the world!

When we left the sailing club, we then purchased a membership at the Sheraton Beach Club also along the open sea. This was definitely an upgrade over the sailing club and their beach huts as the Sheraton had a full-service restaurant; very nice deluxe beach chalets, a dive shop, etc. A couple of years later, we learned of a new and unique beach club opening also on the open sea. It was called: Salhia Beach Resort and was owned by the Bin Laden Family. We were one of the first to purchase a membership at Salhia and we were members up to the day that we left Jeddah. This beach resort had a large sandy beach, several restaurants, and the choice of a studio, one or two-bedroom apartments. One other advantage of the Salhia Beach Resort was that they allowed me to keep my new Hobie 16 and sail from their beach.

So surviving in Jeddah for over twenty-two years was not that difficult, mainly due to the Red Sea and its endless types of activities.

But more importantly and what we found to be even more enjoyable while living and working in Jeddah was the ability for us to travel to Mecca and Medina. Mecca is only 86 km or approximately 53 miles from Jeddah, and Medina is just over 416 km or approximately: 258 miles.

Mecca is the holiest city of Islam, as it is the birthplace of Islam. This is where I made both: Hajj which is the Fifth Pillar of Islam as it is compulsory in the Islamic faith and many lesser pilgrimages or called Umrah Mufralah which is not obligatory. Also, we made many trips to Medina to simply visit Islam's second most holy site. Medina is the final resting place of Prophet Muhammad.

During my twenty-two plus years and after my single year of work with the BMS Company, I worked in nine other employment fields from teaching English to developing new business opportunities for private Saudi Families. Each job that I held and retained gave me a great deal of satisfaction and pleasure thus making the twenty-two years run by. I felt like I had just arrived in the Kingdom. Also, I had never felt that it was time to move on or to move back to America during these great years in Jeddah.

Amazingly, during this long stay in the Kingdom, we lived in only three different residences. During our first three years, we were in two apartments, and for the remaining nineteen years, we were in one large villa.

Like most people living and working overseas, we met very interesting and unique friends, but unlike many expatriates, we have maintained a friendship for many years. With one special group, we explored the Kingdom by going on many

Hejaz Railway Station

camping trips. The majority of these camping trips involved spending many days discovering and exploring the Hejaz Railway. I had always had a keen interest in the Ottomans Hejaz Railway since my first few years in Damascus, as that was where I first discovered the Hejaz Railway. So to explore this railroad in Saudi Arabia was a true delight. We discovered that there were forty railroad stations and garrisons each distanced twenty kilometers apart from the Jordanian border to the holy city of Medina.

We had seen and toured every station except number 14. In my humble opinion, this station must be haunted or bizarre as we had attempted to visit this station on three different occasions, and on each attempt, we were foiled by various mishaps. Either our four-wheel vehicles suffered tire punctures, or the GPS navigational system mysteriously stopped working or we got lost or simply could not find the station. It will always give us a new goal and incentive to return to Saudi Arabia and try to locate this elusive station.

The Hejaz Railway was built by the Ottoman Empire, and the main purpose of the Railway was to establish a connection between Constantinople, the capital of the Ottoman Empire and the seat of the Islamic Caliphate to the Hejaz region in Arabia. The Hejaz region had the two holiest sites of Islam; Medina to the north and Mecca to the south. These are the two holiest places of Islam. The holy city of Mecca has been the destination of the Hajj annual pilgrimage. The railway line was never completed to Mecca as construction was interrupted due to the outbreak of World War I. It reached no further than Medina some 400 kilometers or 250 miles short of Mecca. The completed section from Damascus to Medina was just over 1,300 kilometers or 810 miles. Another important reason to build this important railway was to improve the economic and political integration of the distant Arabian provinces into the Ottoman state. It would be a necessity if security in the Arabian region were to be maintained and it would also be a symbol of Muslim power and solidarity as Hajis, pilgrims on their way to the holy city of Mecca, often didn't reach their destination when traveling along the Hejaz route. The hajjis were unable to contend with the tough, mountainous conditions and up to twenty percent of hajjis died on the way and most importantly, it was to expedite the transportation of military forces. This proved very important during the beginning of WW I.

During the war period, there were many attacks upon the Hejaz Railway, and the most famous were the attacks by the British military man T.E. Lawrence who carried out multiple attacks with the help of the local Arab tribesmen. Trains being destroyed during the Arab Revolt of 1916–1918 can still be seen where they fell. I had compiled three large photo albums of these memorable and illustrious camping trips.

There was a small revival effort of the original Hejaz Railway around the year 2000 as they reopened the line from Damascus to Amman, and this was partially successful. The train service departed from the Qadam Station just outside of Damascus to Amman Jordan and they had passenger service and limited freight service for a few years. With the outbreak of the Syrian Civil War, this service was soon discontinued.

In Jordan, they rebuilt the original branch of the Hejaz Railway from Ma'an to the main Seaport in Aqaba for the transport of the phosphate from the mines near Ma'an to the Gulf of Aqaba. Today, you can see these freight trains traveling alongside the main Amman Aqaba motorway to and from the port and city of Aqaba.

Our eldest son Omar was the first to leave Jeddah as he went to both the UK and the States to attend college. It was funny as when he'd completed his schooling and returned to Jeddah, he was the only one to have continued to live and work in Saudi.

Our youngest son Ramsey left Jeddah about two years after Omar as he was attending boarding school in the States and then continued with the university. After he graduated from Arizona State University, his first job was in the UAE. He is still living and working in the Emirates.

My wife had left Jeddah in early 2005, and she retired to Damascus to set up her new home in Damascus.

In 1994, I actually began my business development and franchise career with the Jamjoom family in Jeddah. The family members were the owners of Jeddah's first mega mall called the Jamjoom Center. The mall was not truly designed to be a proper mall as many of the aisles and walkways were either too narrow or simply ended in dead ends. Also, the mall did not have an anchor store, a food court, or a supermarket. It was simply a very poorly designed mall. I was hired as a New Business Consultant in an attempt to revitalize the entire mall. I worked on and developed three new business concepts for the mall. First I had designed a new twenty-one outlet food court. Then I negotiated with four major US and UK Department Stores, such as: Macy's, Saks Fifth Avenue, and Nordstrom's to become an anchor outlet within the mall. Finally, I planned and designed to introduce a "Franchise Corner" and these franchises included: dry cleaning, custom framing, photo finishing, and even shoe repairing. Unfortunately, the mall was losing so much money that the owners did not have the required funds to invest in these new rejuvenating concepts.

A prominent Saudi businessman had seen my name in several newspaper articles concerning my redevelopment plans for the Jamjoom Mall. He contacted me, and we met to discuss my ability to diversify his family's business. They had always been in auto sales and were the General Motors distributor for Saudi Arabia. Soon after our meeting, he made me an offer to work at GMA as Director of Business Development and to begin to expand and broaden his family's business portfolio. I worked for the Abu Jawad Family for three exciting years. During that time, I helped them purchase a US Franchise called: Mail Boxes, Etc or MBE. We were the Master Franchisor for eleven countries of the Middle East and over the next two years, we had expanded MBE in all eleven countries. It was a real income generator as there was no postal service within the Middle East at the time so we had absolutely no competition.

I also established the groundwork for a new joint venture with the American company called: 'NetJets'. This was intended to introduce the executive jet fractional ownership concept within the Middle East.

I also developed a new Solar Energy Division for his parent company GMA. We were the major bidding company for many Yemeni government Solar Energy repeater TV and communication stations.

Finally, I was the lead negotiator in the franchise acquisition with Warner Brothers to open their Warner Brother Stores throughout the Middle East. After months of negotiation at the Warner Brothers London offices, I suggested to Sheikh Mohamed that we should not purchase that franchise because all the Profit & Loss Statements and other important Financial Statements were not realistic and were not representative for our Saudi Market.

In 1997, I made a major switch in my own career as I personally felt that the Saudi government was placing a greater amount of attention to training and what was generally labeled: 'Saudization'. At this time, the Saudi economy had a very high unemployment rate so the Saudi government made a Royal Decree insisting that each public and private company operating within Saudi Arabia was required to hire a certain percentage of their workforce to be Saudi Nationals.

Soon after, I was approached by one of the general managers within the Saudi Binladin Group to develop a training system within the group for training Saudis for the position of security guards. I was told that this was going to be a very daunting and most formidable task as no one in Saudi Arabia felt, at this time, a Saudi would ever accept a job as a security guard.

In my business career, I have always enjoyed facing and solving challenges. So, I started my new position as a Training Manager with the Saudi Binladin Group. I then establish and developed the "Binladin Academy" which emphasized Saudization and Technical Enhancement training and development programs.

My first Saudization Training program handled the challenge of training security guards. We ran an advertisement in the local newspaper, and we received over 200 applications. I had our Human Resource Department handle the final selection of our first class of fifty candidates. I had developed a full one-month curriculum composed of the following subjects: Work Ethics, simple English language, general security related subjects and very basic phone and computer training. On our first day of class, I remembered that a few of our students actually came to the training wearing sandals and some without shoes. Oh boy, I thought this was not going to be easy…I don't know how we did it but thirty days later we graduated fifty students. At their graduation, I made sure they all received a nice framed Graduation Certificate and what I designed was a "Passport to Success" that had their photo and their grades during the training and spaces for them to take additional training if required. After graduation, they were assigned to various Binladin offices and factories around Saudi Arabia.

I still recall that exactly one year after this first graduation class, I asked our Human Resource Manager to check to find out how many of these fifty original graduates were still employed by Binladin. He immediately warned me not to be too optimistic. I asked him and our General Manager how many employees they expected to still be in the company. Both answered: "If we have twenty-five employees, we would be lucky and thankful." A week later, I was called to the G.M.'s office and the HR manager was there and he informed us that of the original class of 50 students, we had still remained at Binladin 49 security guards! That's fantastic…I then asked 'please let me know what happened with number fifty.' A couple of days later, I was informed that this security guard was working at one of the Medina's locations and that his father had passed away, so as the eldest son, he was obliged to take care of his father's business and his immediate family.

I was then asked to put together a business plan to organize what the CEO Sheikh Bakr Binladin had requested, to open a new "Binladin

Corporate University." I laid the groundwork for the foundation for Binladin University. This included a thirty-day long US business trip with three of the top managers at the Saudi Binladin Group. I had arranged personal visits to the US Corporate Universities as: Eastman Kodak in Rochester, Syracuse University, Lockheed Martin in Bethesda, Disney U. in Orlando, Fluor Daniel in Irvine, Texas, NASA Space Center in Houston, Motorola in the Chicago area, etc. With these very worthwhile visits, I was able to set up the groundwork for our future Binladin Corporate University based in Jeddah.

I then decided to get back into both franchising and training, and I found a US company that was great in both. In 1999, I partnered with two Saudi Businessmen, and we bought the franchise rights for an American Franchise called: Berlitz Language Centers for the entire Kingdom. I was working as the Berlitz Managing Director as well as a partner. By 2002, I had expanded Berlitz and opened and sold fourteen new Berlitz Language Centers within Saudi Arabia. In the first year, I had expanded the language business by 46% and during the second year by 52%.

My final position in Jeddah was with another American Franchise called RE/MAX. By chance in 2002, I met the Saudi Franchisor of RE/MAX Real Estate and decided to work for the Saudi businessman who had just purchased the franchise rights from RE/MAX US for the entire MENA region. He became the Master Franchisor of RE/MAX. Mr. Lou' Bougary did not have a strong franchise background, so after we met, he asked if I could help him develop the franchise concept throughout the region. The very first item on my agenda was to have me design, prepare, and publish the new RE/MAX sub-franchise agreements that we could legally use domestically within the Kingdom and another set to be used throughout the Middle East. We sold franchises within the Kingdom as well as within the UAE and then Qatar.

The new franchisees in Doha were five brothers that had just formed their new family business called: Al Jaidah Brothers, W.L.L. While I was arranging for the sale of this RE/MAX franchise in Qatar, there was a major terrorist attack at the US Consulate on the 6th of December 2004. A group of five men associated with the terrorist group Al-Qaeda (Al-Qaeda Organization in the Arabian Peninsula) conducted a mid-day attack on the US Consulate, which killed five Consulate workers. The group was led by Fayez ibn Awwad Al-Jeheni, a former member of Saudi religious police. The attack underscored the ongoing vulnerabilities of Westerners to threats and terrorist actions in Jeddah and environs. At this time, my wife and both boys were no longer living in Jeddah. I remember I was at work at our RE/MAX office, which was located a short distance from the American consulate. Everyone in the office had heard the commotion and gunfire and we all ran to the office roof where we could clearly see the smoke rising from the consulate grounds. Immediate the RE/MAX Saudi owner strongly suggested that his driver directly takes me home and that I should not leave my villa until this attack and bloodshed had ended.

This was the first and only time that I had feared for my life and my own safety while living in Saudi Arabia. I was very thankful that my family was all out of Jeddah. I felt that it was time for me to leave Jeddah after some twenty-two years.

Chapter Twelve

My Five Great Years in Qatar

Actually, there were two real reasons why I decided to leave the Kingdom of Saudi Arabia. The first was a very clear idea that living in Jeddah was no longer as safe as it had been, especially with the increased number of well-known terrorist 'sleeper cells' growing and emerging within the country plus the attack on the US Consulate in Jeddah in late 2004. The second reason and most obvious and important for me was the fact I was offered a job in Qatar by the five Qatari brothers who purchased the RE/MAX Properties Qatar real estate franchise.

While I was in Doha arranging the RE/MAX franchise signing ceremony the night before, all five brothers took me out to dinner and during our meal, they asked if I knew of any other franchises or new business opportunities they could look at investing in and bringing to Qatar. I told them to give me a bit of time so I could concentrate my thoughts and efforts on specifically the Qatar market.

On the way back to my hotel, one of the brothers explained to me that their company, Al Jaidah Brothers W.L.L, was very new and was recently formed to separate their business ventures from their older half-brother. They also mentioned that they were looking at any new business field that I could suggest or recommend to them.

I discovered that each of the five brothers was very successful in their own particular field. The eldest, Abdullatif, is in the upscale retail furniture business and has several showrooms and was now concentrating in the property management field. The second eldest is Ibrahim and is an extremely successful architect and has a very thriving engineering and an architectural company called: AEB or Arab Engineering Bureau.

The middle brother is Salah and he is in the banking industry. He is quite famous and exceedingly successful in all areas of banking and finance. The next to last brother is Tariq and has been at the forefront of the Qatar international advertising and media industry. His current media company is called: Gulf Space International and is recognized to be the media leader within the entire GCC. Finally, Zeyad is the youngest brother of the five and has a flourishing intergraded systems solutions company called Techno-Q and is a leader in the region as well as globally.

So when we arrived at the entrance of the Marriott hotel, I left his car with a solid view of his family, plus I had a multitude of ideas and perceptions of potential new business concepts for the brothers. A vast number of thoughts were racing through my mind at an alarming rate, so much so I knew I would not be able to sleep, so I decided to go to a small disco connected to the Marriott to compose my thoughts. I sat at the bar and asked the bartender for several of those small cocktail napkins. It may seem odd that I would select a bar with loud music, but I was so focused that I knew I would never hear the music or any of the crowd noise that evening. I began writing and writing and by the time I had finished, I had well over fifty clear business ideas on paper. I can't ever recall being so focused on one particular subject in all my life. So much so that when I finished writing at the bar and on my way back to my hotel room, I stopped several times to jot down additional potential business concepts to introduce to the marketplace of Qatar. I was literally 'on-fire' with new and innovative propositions. Today, I still recall that I did not sleep very well that night.

Zeyad picked me up the next morning to take me to the newly opened Four Seasons Hotel for our RE/MAX Signing Ceremony. I had arranged to have our American Ambassador, and his entire Commercial Team present plus the brothers had arranged to invite many of Qatar's top business families and the local press. It was a very successful ceremony and an enjoyable lunch followed. That evening, two local TV stations carried our event and the next morning several of the newspapers covered the signing in great detail.

That night, I was invited to the last dinner with four of the five brothers, and during dinner, I mentioned my experience at the Marriott disco the night before. I had over fifty solid business concepts that may work in Qatar. They then asked me to send them the new ideas the next day and for me to prioritize my list into the top ten which I personally felt would be the most successful. They then asked me one final question: "Would I be willing to leave my current employment with RE/MAX Arabia if they liked my list of business investments?" I thought about my answer for a few seconds and then emphatically said, "Yes." I then proceeded to give them my thoughts on why I was so categorically inclined to leave Jeddah. I first mentioned the declining safety level in the Kingdom, especially Jeddah, and second, my family had already left Jeddah so it would not be a major decision on my part to relocate to Qatar.

The next day I flew back to Jeddah and had only one idea on my mind and that was to make my potential list of business opportunities as solid as possible and to try to prioritize the full lists into my ten top choices.

When I returned to my office, my staff was extremely happy with the success of both the signing ceremony and the opportunity of having a new RE/MAX franchise in Qatar and for us in our Jeddah office to associate with on potential new joint real estate sales.

I left my office and drove home quickly so I could begin to finalize my list of business opportunities for the Al Jaidah family. I worked diligently for several hours on this important list, and then finally, around eight or nine p.m., I emailed the five brothers my final list of over fifty new business concepts.

In the morning, I received an email from Tariq, and he mentioned the brothers talked the night before and they were very impressed with the depth and strength of all the business concepts within the list, and especially with the first ten. He further mentioned that he will produce a draft employment contract and send it to me within twenty-four hours. I replied to his email stating that I would look forward to reviewing their company's draft job offer and I was happy that they liked my list. The next afternoon, I received their draft employment contract and I was ecstatic and quite overjoyed as it was very professionally prepared and the terms of employment far exceeded my present and existing contract.

The next morning, I replied to Tariq and mentioned that I had, in principle, accepted their draft contract for employment and I would add some subtle changes. Shortly after sending my provisional acceptance, I called my wife in Damascus and told her the good news which had taken place in the past 48 hours and that she should plan to return to Jeddah to help me prepare for my move to Doha.

I then prepared a short resignation letter that was presented to Mr. Bougary, the owner of RE/MAX Arabia, and mentioned that I would respect the clause of termination to be a thirty-day time period.

A few days later, I flew back to Doha to meet with the brothers and to sign my new contract. That evening in Doha, we enjoyed dinner at a nice Chinese restaurant, and it was very intriguing because at the end of the dinner, we were all given fortune cookies and each of their cookies all said the same and typical Chinese phrases and thoughts. I then opened my cookie and it stated: *"You are about to begin a new and fruitful venture."* We all laughed and thought that this was the best omen or sign that anyone could expect. I had kept that small paper for many years.

The next morning I returned back to Jeddah extremely happy and satisfied as my future appeared to be very bright and promising. I felt that now I could work in a field that I had always enjoyed, and that is new business development and franchising.

The next day my wife arrived at Jeddah from Damascus. We began the arduous task of packing. Earlier, I found many small round color stickers that I had placed on all items in our Jeddah villa. The red stickers were for the items to be sent to Qatar, the green was for the items to be shipped to Damascus, and anything without a sticker was to be sold in Jeddah. She agreed on almost all my suggestions.

We had hired one shipping company to handle the two shipments, and we found they were very qualified and quite professional as none of the items were mixed or damaged.

The following thirty days went by at a precipitous pace, yet everything was carefully packed and the remaining items had all been sold or simply given away.

First, Salma returned to Damascus and then I booked my flight to Doha in order to take up my new position as Senior Manager for Business Development.

When I finally landed in Doha from Jeddah, I spent the first two or three nights at the Doha Marriott Hotel as I had no accommodation or transportation. The next morning, I was picked from my hotel and taken to the office of the: Al Jaidah Brothers. I first met with Tariq as my new office would be just outside his large office. We met for a couple of hours discussing the future of my developing new franchise and business concepts. His multimedia company was in the same office building, so he took me upstairs to introduce me to his advertising and media team. That afternoon Tariq had planned multiple meetings with his brothers both in the office as well as a visit to each of their companies. The full knowledge of each of the brothers' occupations was paramount as was their office locations, so all future meetings could take place at any one of their offices.

Zeyad had called, and he suggested that he would pick me later that afternoon in order to show me a potential villa to possibly rent. This trip would also give me a chance to see other parts of Doha.

The villa was in an area quite close to the Al Jaidah Brothers office, and when we entered the villa, I liked it immediately. It had two large bedrooms and a nice combined living and dining area. The kitchen was very large and it had an extra room that was considered the maids' quarters. Also, the villa was fenced which provided a great deal of privacy.

Most importantly, the owner was a close friend to the five brothers so they were able to bargain with him to reduce the rent and negotiate the payment terms.

The villa was unfurnished, so for the next few weeks, I spent a great deal of time buying furnishings that were not included in my Jeddah shipment. I also started a major 'Green Environmental Campaign' by adding a large number of outdoor plants and a smaller number of indoor plants. When I first moved in, the only thing green was a handful of weeds growing in the garden. Within the first year, I had a marvelous green garden that was the envy of all my neighbors. This was also one of the best furnished 'bachelor's villas' in all of Doha because the majority of my single friends and married ones all lived in apartments and they never believed in adding any sizable interior or exterior improvements. To them, their apartment was simply a place to live for a short period of time while working and living in Qatar. For me, it was the exact opposite, I rented a sizable villa and I knew that I would be living and working in Qatar for at least five years so I felt it was very important to place my personal touches in my residence.

In addition, I had shipped many of our 'special pieces' of furniture that we had purchased while in Damascus and Jeddah. I was expecting my Jeddah shipment and in it were such items as: an old Damascene wood inlay game table with two inlay chairs, two antique clocks, many old Saudi antiques such as an old wood window and a wooden door, an old mixed mask collection from both Africa and Asia and some very nice and old framed maps of the Middle East and Palestine; etc. These had been an important part of our home furnishings both in Damascus as well as in our villa in Jeddah. It was also very nice as when my Jeddah shipment finally arrived in Doha, my wife was there, and she added her special interior design touches to the entire villa.

So all the major home furnishings such as my living room set, dining room table, kitchen appliances, and the outdoor furniture set of chairs, tables, BBQ and even a large outdoor bar needed to be purchased in Qatar.

The next very important purchase was my vehicle. I decided to purchase a new Chevrolet TrailBlazer, which is a 4x4. Earlier, I was told about the great camping and off-road ventures available in Qatar. During my five years in Qatar, I did a great deal of camping and discovering beautiful tranquil and untouched beaches.

The Inland Sea in Qatar

One area that I constantly visited was just a short drive south of Doha and was called by the English speakers: "The Inland Sea" or in Arabic: Khawr al Udayd.

This Inland Sea had only one major inlet to the Persian Gulf, and it separated Qatar from Saudi Arabia. My friends and I really enjoyed the off-road drive to get to this unique and beautiful beach area as it consisted of many long stretches of dry sand flats, and then once you got closer to the Inland Sea, you had to drive across major sand dunes. Each trip was a great experience and always contained a lot of adventure. Once we got to the edge of the water, we would set up our camp and enjoy a swim in the very warm and extremely salty water. The Inland Sea was much saltier than the Persian Gulf as the inland temperatures were much hotter and there was very little yearly rainfall.

Also, due to this high salinity and a major point that I enjoyed immensely: there were no sea snakes within the waters of the Inland Sea. Whereas in the Persian Gulf along the north and east shores of Qatar and the Gulf of Bahrain along Qatar's West coastline, you would occasionally observe sea snakes.

Actually, the name Doha has several meanings. One meaning of the word Doha is 'Forenoon' or 'the early hours'. I have read that another Arabic term *dohat*, meaning 'roundness' maybe a reference to the rounded bays surrounding Qatar's coastline. It is also a popular girl's name.

On several occasions, while snorkeling during the winter months in these coastal bays, I would come across these sea snakes. The first time I saw one, I thought it was an eel as it moved like an eel. During my twenty-two years swimming and snorkeling in the Red Sea, we would see countless eels, but never any sea snakes as the salinity of the Red Sea is much higher than the Persian Gulf or the Gulf of Bahrain. I have never liked snakes. Even today, I have a strong distrust and robust uneasiness for these reptiles. When I discovered that there were sea snakes in the coastal waters of Qatar, I became very cautious while swimming. I also discovered that the sea snake is ten times more venomous than the king cobra and this fact did not help my nervousness while swimming. On the positive side, the sea snake is very mild-tempered, reluctant to bite and they cannot open their mouths as wide as the terrestrial snake so it would be difficult for a sea snake to bite your arm or leg, instead they tend to bite your fingers when disturbed or agitated.

Due to the fact we were 'dune bashing' on each trip to the Inland Sea, I soon felt that I needed a more powerful vehicle, so I bought a new Chevrolet Tahoe Z 70. After I purchased this larger and more powerful eight-cylinder Tahoe 4 x 4, I gave my son Omar my one-year-old TrailBlazer. This Tahoe was one of the most enjoyable vehicles I have ever owned and driven. I also had it equipped with many special features such as a massive front 'bullbar'; a very special tuned exhaust system and I upgraded the front bucket seats which were re-installed with air-conditioning. The Tahoe handled the sand dunes much better than the TrailBlazer and was much more comfortable on the open highways within Qatar.

I enjoyed my lifestyle while living and working in Qatar as it was easy meeting new friends, and the social life was copious. I am still in contact with many of these friends and I make sure that each time I visit the States, I meet with those American friends residing in America. The other friends that live outside the States I am still in contact by email with each of them since I left Qatar.

The social life in Qatar was also a bright spot during my period there. In addition to the American Embassy, there were many foreign embassy functions to attend. Qatar being a much smaller country than Saudi Arabia, each embassy made it a point to invite a good portion of the foreign business community to their events. Saudi Arabia, on the other hand, had moved all of its foreign embassies to Riyadh, leaving Jeddah with only a scattering of foreign consulates.

In Doha, there were many concerts and cultural events. The Qatar Philharmonic Orchestra seemed to have a performance on a bimonthly basis, and there were many concerts performed around the city. Their music always contained a variety of Western and Middle Eastern works, thus making each concert very interesting.

The Doha Players was a small group of mainly Westerners that had a multitude of live theater performances throughout the five years that I lived in Doha. Actually, the group was formed in 1954 and was always the best social activity for many years. Unfortunately, in March 2005, one month before I moved to Doha, the Doha Players suffered a major bombing during one of its performances of Shakespeare's *Twelfth Night*. The show was brought to a heartbreaking end when a suicide bomber detonated his vehicle just outside the theater – injuring dozens and killing the show's director. The theater was destroyed by this bomb attack, but not the Doha Players' strong will and resolve to continue even without a theater to perform in. I remember seeing many of their performances at the American School or at the Sailing Club, or wherever they were able to find a suitable location, plus they would have a sold-out performance each night. The performances were not just for your entertainment but were more of a social scene to simply relax, meet new people, socialize, and network.

Another extremely entertaining Doha scene was attending the Comedy Club, which was hosted monthly at Ramada hotel. The Comedy Club would bring comedians from the UK, US, and Arab countries. Each show was always very, very entertaining and enjoyable.

During my tenure in Doha, the country opened the famous Museum of Islamic Art. This stunning building was designed by the renowned architect: I.M. Pei as he was coaxed out of retirement to design this splendid building. The Museum

Museum of Islamic Art

of Islamic Art is a combination of Islamic art from three continents dating from the seventh to the nineteenth century.

Its collection includes manuscripts, metalwork, ceramics, jewelry, woodwork, textiles, and glass. It is definitely one of the world's most complete collections of Islamic artifacts. I was very lucky to have been invited to the museum's grand opening, which was held in late 2008. I have always made sure that whenever I had my family or a special guest visiting Doha for the first time, I have them visit the museum. Today, it is considered to be one of the world's great museums.

I also discovered a very nice beach resort south of Doha called: Sealine Beach Resort that I would frequent either to spend the weekend or simply enjoying a great Friday BBQ with friends. It was always a pleasure to drive there and to relax, enjoy the fresh air and the clean waters of the gulf. My wife and I had celebrated many special occasions like my wife's birthday and several of our anniversaries at the Sealine Beach Resort. We were the first to have them use a fancy beachfront tent for our special occasions. They had many candles lined along the entrance of our tent, and even the chef, whom I knew very well, would personally serve each of our six or seven-course special diners.

During our stay at the Sealine Beach Resort, we would always have time to drive a short distance away for the resort to visit and enjoy the very special sand dunes, which are called the: 'Singing Sands'. There are very few beaches around the world in which you can enjoy these: 'Songs of the Dunes'. On only certain beaches, dry sand will make a singing, squeaking, whistling or screaming sound if a person scuffs or shuffles their feet with sufficient force. The phenomenon is not completely understood scientifically, but it has been found that only certain quartz sands will do this and only if the grains are very well-rounded and highly spherical.

Finally, I got back into sailing while I was living and working in Doha. A friend and I decided to take a one year course in Off-Shore Sailing and to receive our Coastal Skipper Certificate during our time in Doha. The course was very exciting and quite informative as we spent many hours at sea on a good size racing sailboat. After the successful completion of this certificated course, I was ready to buy my first large sailboat. At the time, there wasn't a wide selection of new or used sailboats in Doha, so I was traveling to Dubai on a regular basis to search for a sailboat. I did find a nice 32.3 Bénéteau, which was a French-manufactured fiberglass sailboat. This was truly a coastal cruiser and had a deep draft keel instead of the normal fin keel. The most important feature of this 32.3 sailboat was it had a wheel and not a standard tiller. I quickly became very accustomed to using the wheel even though our training sailboat had a tiller.

Another activity that I really enjoyed was seeing the old Al Koot Fort and wandering throughout the Souq al Waqif in the old downtown area of Doha. Actually, when I first arrived in Doha in 2005, the souqs renovation had not started, so I was one of the few foreigners that experienced the original Souq al Waqif and then shopped in it after

it's renovation. Originally, I was using the souq to purchase many hardware products that I could not find anywhere in Doha such as concrete nails, an electric drill, a fully fitted toolbox, etc. After they closed the souq for renovation in 2006, the contractor had placed all

Souq Al Waqif

the original coral stones in several massive mounds or piles outside the fort. After the contractor had installed the new infrastructure projects such as a new sewage system, drainage, and freshwater systems, they added state-of-the-art internet; Wi-Fi and electrical systems and maybe most importantly, additional parking for the expected crowd. Upon completing these massive projects, they soon rebuilt each stall and shop on its exact location and included the narrow and often windy alleyway in place.

I don't believe they ever allowed the use of neon lighting, so every time you walk along the old passageways, you feel like you are shopping and experiencing the souq as it was a hundred years earlier.

As a complete contrast to the Souq al Waqif, Doha had opened several new and unique shopping malls. My two favorites were the Villaggio Mall located near the new Aspire Academy and the City Center Mall Doha, which is located in the downtown or West Bay Area of Doha. The Villaggio Mall was very close to my home, so I was a regular visitor to this truly unique and distinctive mall. On many visits, you felt that you are in a small Italian hillside town and in other parts of the mall that you were on a gondola in Venice. This mall is large as it has over 200 stores, an ice rink and a good size food court.

On the other hand, the City Center Mall Doha is massive as it has five stories and over 370 stores, and truly, it is more of your 'typical city mall' than the Villaggio. I would frequent this City Center Mall as it had a large cinema and the movies seemed to be more up-to-date than the other cinemas in Doha.

While I was working and living in Doha, they started a massive residential and shopping area called the Pearl – Qatar. When I first visited the Pearl, it was mainly business-related. At that time, there was only a handful of restaurants opened and the majority of your walk was outdoors and the summer heat can be both searing and intense.

Finally, Qatar is noted for both its academic and sports excellence. In the area of Doha called Educational City, they have housed a great number of top international universities such as Carnegie Mellon University, Georgetown School of Foreign Service, Texas A&M, and Weill Cornel Medical College. I believe today, in total, there are over fourteen top colleges and universities existing in Qatar!

And when it comes to sports, Qatar is one of the leading countries in the Middle East in hosting international sporting events. To start, Qatar is hosting the 2022 FIFA World Cup, and in addition, they host yearly: the Qatar Tennis Open, Qatar Masters European Golf Tournament, many Motor GP races for motorcycling, and the H-1 Unlimited Hydroplane boat races.

So as you can see, Qatar offered me a multitude of activities to completely occupy my time for the five glorious years that I had spent in this fantastic country.

Qatar is a relatively 'new country', especially when you compare it with Syria, Palestine, or Lebanon. There was no evidence that the Romans had ever occupied the area. The earliest documented record mentioning any settlement in present-day Qatar was made in 1681 and the settlement was called: Al Bidda. In the documentation, the ruler at that time had built a fort in the confines of Al Bidda and the report had alluded to the etymology of the word: Al Bidda. This is interesting as Bidda is derived from the Arabic word badaa, meaning "to invent." When the previously uninhabited area first became populated, a settlement was essentially 'invented,' giving it its name. There were very few visits by Westerners to Al Bidda, but a German explorer who visited the Arabian Peninsula, created one of the first maps to depict the settlement in 1765. Then in 1801, David Seaton, a British political resident in Muscat, wrote the first English record of Al Bidda. He refers to the town as 'Bedih' and describes the geography and defensive structures in the area. He stated that the town had recently been settled by a Sudanese tribe, whom he considered to be pirates. Seaton attempted to bombard the town with his warship but returned to Muscat upon finding that the waters off the Al Bidda coast were too shallow to position his warship within striking distance.

And then in 1820, British surveyor R. H. Colebrook, who visited Al Bidda, remarked on the recent depopulation of the town. The same year, an agreement known as the General Maritime Treaty was signed between the East India Company and the sheikhs of several Persian Gulf settlements.

Bahrain became a party to the treaty, and it was assumed that Qatar, perceived as a dependency of Bahrain by the British, was also a party to it. Qatar, however, was not asked to fly the prescribed Trucial flag. As punishment for alleged piracy committed by the inhabitants of Al Bidda and breach of the treaty, an East India Company vessel bombarded the town in 1821. They razed the town, forcing between 300 and 400 natives to flee and temporarily take shelter on the islands between Qatar and the Trucial Coast.

Now, the Trucial States, also known as the Trucial Sheikhdoms, was the name the British government given to a group of tribal confederations in south-eastern Arabia which had been known as the "Pirate Coast." The name derived from the territories whose principal sheikhs had signed protective treaties (also known as truces), hence 'trucial' with the British government from 1820 until 1892. Doha was founded in the vicinity of Al Bidda sometime during the 1820s.

Between 1848 and 1850, the Al Thani family relocated from Fuwayrit to Doha. Fuwayrit was a small seaside village some 90 km north of Doha. These were very difficult times for all the families that lived in Doha and especially Wakrah, which was a small seaside village about 15 km south of Doha. As in 1867, many ships and troops were sent from Bahrain to assault the towns Al Wakrah and Doha over a series of disputes. Abu Dhabi joined on Bahrain's behalf due to the conception that Al Wakrah served as a refuge for fugitives from Oman. Later that year, the combined forces sacked the two Qatari towns with around 2,700 men in what would come to be known as the Qatari–Bahraini War. A British record later stated: "that the towns of Doha and Wakrah were, at the end of 1867 temporarily blotted out of existence, the houses being dismantled and the inhabitants deported."

Then in 1868, a landmark treaty was signed between Mohammed bin Thani and the British government, in which Qatar's independence from Bahrain was acknowledged and in which Mohammed bin Thani, was to be recognized as ruler of the Qatar Peninsula.

In December 1871, the Ottomans established a presence in the country with 100 of their troops occupying the Musallam fort in Doha. This was accepted by Mohammad bin Thani's son, Jassim Al Thani, who wished to protect Doha from Saudi incursions. The Ottomans held a passive role in Qatar's politics from the 1890s onwards.

Pearling had come to play a pivotal commercial role in Doha by the twentieth century. The population increased to around 12,000 inhabitants in the first half of the twentieth century due to the flourishing pearl trade.

Doha Coastline in 1904 with Many Pearl Boats

A British political resident noted that should the supply of pearls drop, Qatar would *"practically cease to exist"*. In 1907, the city accommodated 350 pearling boats with a combined crew size of 6,300 men. By this time, the average prices of pearls had more than doubled since 1877. The pearl market collapsed that year, forcing Jassim Al Thani to sell the country's pearl harvest at half its value. The aftermath of the collapse resulted in the establishment of the country's first customs house in Doha.

In April 1913, the Ottomans agreed to a British request that they withdraw all their troops from Qatar. Ottoman presence in the peninsula ceased, when in August 1915, the Ottoman fort in Al Bidda was evacuated shortly after the start of World War I. One year later,

Qatar agreed to be a British protectorate with Doha as its official capital under an official British Treaty.

Buildings at the time were simple dwellings of one or two rooms, built from mud, stone, and coral. Oil concessions in the 1920s and 1930s and subsequent oil drilling in 1939 heralded the beginning of slow economic and social progress in the country. However, revenues were somewhat diminished due to the devaluation of pearl trade in the Persian Gulf brought on by the introduction of the cultured pearl.

Doha in 1934

From the 1950s to 1970s, the population of Doha grew from around 14,000 inhabitants to over 83,000, with foreign immigrants constituting about two-thirds of the overall population.

Qatar remained an informal British protectorate until the treaties were revoked in 1971. Qatar officially declared its independence on September 3rd, 1971with Doha as its capital city. It is interesting to note that during 1971, both Bahrain on August 14th and the UAE on December 2nd had also declared their independence.

In 1983, the population of Qatar was only: 309,479, and a new hotel and conference center were developed at the north end of the Corniche. The 15-story Sheraton hotel structure in this center would serve as the tallest structure in Doha until the 1990s.

When I arrived in Qatar in April 2005, and when I left some five years later, I saw the major growth of both the country and the city of Doha. These were due especially to the enlargement of the West Bay district and the new Pearl Project.

Today, Doha is so different than when I first arrived, as the major downtown building was taking place at a frantic and accelerated pace from 2015 onward. On each return trip, I am utterly amazed at the progress and growth of both the city as well as the country.

The population of Doha is overwhelmingly composed of expatriates, with Qatari nationals forming a minority. I came across a population growth chart as this growth in the population was at its highest during my tenure in Qatar from 2005 until 2010:

Doha West Bay – Today

Year Population and percent increase:

Year:	Population:	+/ – % Increase
2004	339,847	+13.5%
2005	400,051	+17.7%
2010	796,947	+99.2%

Doha was included in Fortune's 15 "best new cities for business in 2011" and in 2019, Doha was in the top 10.

I had never realized this tremendous business opportunity when I first arrived in 2005, but since I worked for a group of five dynamic Qatari brothers, it soon became apparent that Doha was a special place to conduct business.

From my original list of fifty potential projects, I had narrowed my selection to only ten. During my five years of working for the Al Jaidah brothers, I was able to develop a good number of these top ten developments. And today, these same new businesses are still thriving and flourishing both in Qatar and within the other GCC countries.

The first business that I had introduced to the family was, of course, our RE/MAX real estate office. I helped locate and design our dynamic new office. We selected a very large office, so on the ground floor would be our real estate office with our realtors all working on the same floor and upstairs, we designed two large management offices for both the eldest brother Abdulatif and myself and a large meeting or conference room. In this manner, I was able to manage the real estate operation as well as develop additional new business opportunities for the Al Jaidah Brothers. The conference room also gave us a venue to hold our monthly Al Jaidah Brothers Board Meetings.

Since the RE/MAX business was operating well, I then had time to work on adding other new and dynamic business ventures to the family's business portfolio.

I visited my first Build-A-Bear Workshop® while in Las Vegas with my sister a couple of years prior to my work in Qatar. At the time, I said to her: "this would be a fantastic business opportunity in the Middle East." During those years, I maintained that idea, and now I had the chance to develop this franchise. I presented my BABW Business Plan during our next board meeting. Only one brother, Zeyad, had any knowledge of this franchise, as a matter of fact, the shop that he knew in the UK was an exact copy of BABW and was called: Bear Factory Workshop. *Build-A-Bear Workshop*® is the only company in the world that offers an interactive activity in *making* your own soft toys and custom teddy *bears*. Since the founding of the *Build-A-Bear Workshop*® over twenty years ago, *make*-your-own stuffed cuddly toy is a family experience. The board gave me the green light to begin negotiations with this US based franchise.

This was also the start of my multitude of international business trips for the Al Jaidah Brothers. On this first trip, both Zeyad and I traveled to the St. Louis area to meet with the owner and the franchise team at Build-A-Bear Workshop®. Within a very short period, we had signed a Master Franchise Agreement for the GCC and opened our first BABW store in Dubai. Today, there are the following BABW stores within the region: six in the UAE, three in Qatar, one in Bahrain, and one in Kuwait. The Bearquarters is located in Dubai. Today, this franchise continues to grow and expand within the entire GCC.

I then felt with the ongoing growth of commercial and residential buildings around Qatar, I personally sensed the country needed a professional and local property management company. So in 2005, Abdulatif and I created a new company called Badgeer Properties W.L.L. and this company would provide clients with quality property/facilities management services to the property owners and tenants alike in Qatar.

I followed these first three very successful new business undertakings with an additional three dynamic and new business ventures:

The first of this final group was Regus Al Jaidah Business Centers, in which we worked with the international brand: Regus. Regus is a multinational corporation that provides serviced offices, virtual offices, meeting rooms, and videoconferencing to clients on a contract basis. It is very successful in Qatar today.

Then I decided in Qatar, there was a strong need for a large Office Stationary store and it was to be a complement to our Regus Business Centers. I negotiated with the large American company called Office 1 and we soon formed a new company called Office 1 Gulf, which distributes: electronic equipment, cameras, office furniture including shelves and cupboards, pens, pencils, markers, staplers, paper, whiteboards and they also develop software solutions including mobile, retail and web applications, information technology, etc. This store is still at its original location on Salwa Road in Doha.

Finally, I thought to complement all our new companies, we needed a solid international human resources and recruitment company. I searched and found a great company called Kershaw Leonard, and they were willing to work with us in Doha. They had their home office in the UK and their branch office in Dubai so for them to expand to the lucrative and thriving Qatar market was ideal. Today, Kershaw Leonard still has an operation in both Dubai and Qatar.

I worked in Qatar a total of five great years for the Al Jaidah Brothers company, and during the five years, I felt that I helped to contribute, in a very small way, to the dynamic growth of Qatar's economy.

I had discovered that Qatar is by far the richest of the six GCC, as shown in the following 2017 data chart:

The Richest Economies in the GCC:

Rank	Country	GDP Per Capita
1	Qatar	$129,700.00
2	Kuwait	$71,300.00
3	United Arab Emirates	$67,700.00
4	Saudi Arabia	$54,100.00

One must note that Qatar has the smallest population within the entire GCC and has the highest GDP per capita at $129,700, which is the highest not only in the Middle East but also in the world

This wealth is due in fact that Qatar currently holds the world's third-largest Natural Gas Reserves. Only Russia and Iran have more proven gas reserves.

I was committed to the Al Jaidah family for only five years, and at the end of this period, I decided to return to Damascus as promised to my wife five years earlier.

At that time, Syria's country's GDP per capita was among the lowest in the Middle East, estimated to be $2,900. So I basically was leaving Qatar, which had the highest GDP per capita in the world to live and work in Syria which was among the poorest in the entire Middle East.

I totally enjoyed my five years living and working in Qatar, and I knew that my adjustment in Syria was going to be difficult yet, I did hold high hopes for a promising future.

Chapter Thirteen

My First Retirement

I moved back to Damascus in 2010 after completing five stimulating years of business development work in Doha, Qatar. I returned to beautiful Damascus and proclaimed that I was now "retired"…I have placed that word in quotation marks as I have always felt that no person should ever retire. I had always remembered my dad after he retired from his position of Yardmaster at New York Central Railroad he could not simply stay at home and do nothing. His first post-retirement job was working at Seville's local seasonal fruit and vegetable store. He really enjoyed working with the public, and he was a great salesperson at the grocery store. He had a knack of showing people how great the local corn was or how fresh and delicious the newest 'Beefsteak' tomatoes were that day. And after his morning duty, he would come home in the afternoon and tend his garden. I always remember he never brought any fruits or vegetables home from his day job as his garden's production was much better than what he was selling at work.

No pun intended, but I guess *"the apple doesn't fall far from the tree"*, so within the first month back in Damascus, I started planning for my first post-retirement job.

Throughout my life, I had many rich and varied work experiences, from teaching in schools to developing new business ventures, and from working in various upper management positions to working as a waiter. I had always thought that my work experiences were vast and diverse and most importantly: enjoyable.

I felt that I could have been called: *"A jack-of-all-trades and master-of-many"* instead of what most people would say: *"A jack-of-all-trades and a master-of-none."*

Whenever I would reflect on my many job positions, I always came to the same conclusion: "I truly enjoyed each and every profession." So retirement for me, like my dad, was out of the question. Why not find one more activity to work in? It would keep me young, right?

So that was my plan and mind-set upon departing Doha for Damascus in early 2010. While in Doha, I was working for five Qatari brothers, and I developed a strong personal bond with each of them. Also, while working in Doha, I found the time to master one of my favorite activities…to become more proficient and knowledgeable in the production of fine wines. Or in other words, become a true expert and connoisseur of fine wines within the framework and knowledge of truly understanding the cultivation and production of fine wines.

My first new business concept in Syria was to open a French-style vineyard, winery, and small boutique hotel somewhere in Syria. Two of the Qatar brothers would be my financial backers after I developed a Syrian Winery Business Plan. I worked feverishly and completed a Winery Business Plan in only a few weeks. I then submitted my professional Syrian Vineyard Business Plan to my financial backers. It was approved quickly.

Now there was only one last 'simple task' to complete: I had to find the large parcel of land for the vineyard, hotel, and winery.

Initially, my search encompassed all of Syria as I often found myself on the road for weeks on end. My search lasted for over six full months. I soon recognized that this was also a great way to rediscover this beautiful country. In my search, I stayed away from the major cities and concentrated in rural areas that had the potential of harvesting fruits and grapes. I also discovered that the Syrian "village people" were very down-to-earth, friendly, and extremely helpful during my entire travel.

I began my initial search in three small towns very close to Damascus. Bloudon, Saidnaya and Maaloula, all are within 30 to 60 kilometers from Damascus. Unfortunately, each of these towns did have a small, local grape production, but all the wine production was made from local grape varieties that were used primarily for consumption. Maaloula did have some of their local red wines on sale in several of the gift shops. I did purchase a bottle, and by far, it was too sweet for my pallet.

I continued my search in an area just 30 kilometers south of Homs as I was told there was an existing winery operating by a Jesuit priest called Father Francis who had come to Syria in 1966. In the immediate vicinity of the existing center and vineyard, there was the Syrian/ Lebanese Border Post, the old Hejaz Spur Railroad Line, and an old Hejaz Railroad Station in fairly good condition. So in my mind, I told myself that if I could find a suitable plot of land, it could have a dual purpose. It could be both a winery and a potential tourist area, being accessible to both Syrians and Lebanese visitors.

I discovered not only a very nice winery and vineyard as well as a small Community Help Center for all the local towns' people, both Christian and Muslim. Many of the villagers were suffering from various disabilities. This complex was called Al-Ard Center and had various small arts and crafts workshops in which the work was done by people with disabilities, providing an unprecedented resource in a society in which such people were usually hidden from view. Also, many of the local men would be hired to tend Father Francis's vast gardens and vineyards. I soon discovered that Father Francis was using only French vines and had a very good size vineyard and a solid production of wine. We became very good friends and he was very interested and curious to see the outcome of my search and eventual wine project. We remained very good friends up until his unfortunate and tragic assassination by extremists from the Al-Nusra Front at his community center in April 2014.

He was warned to leave by many as a fellow Jesuit priest called Father Paolo was kidnapped less than a year earlier by the Islamic State of Iraq and the Levant. Before Father Paolo's kidnapping, he had served for three decades at the Deir Mar Musa, a sixth-century monastery located near the town of Nabk. Deir Mar Musa was literally the Monastery of Saint Moses the Abyssinian, a monastic community of the Syriac Catholic Church, approximately 80 kilometers or fifty miles north of Damascus.

Father Francis had always said when he was warned: *No, I must stay to help the people of the area.* He was called by some, the *"Syrian Mother Teresa"* as he was helping the people of Syria for over fifty years.

I continued my search into the central region of Syria near the northern Lebanese border. I would spend the entire day driving, searching, and asking questions in each village. In the late afternoon, I would find a local small hotel usually of only one or two-star ratings. They were always clean and each had a great typical Syrian Breakfast. For me, this was a great way to meet the local Syrian people and for them to meet a true American who really loved their country.

This central region of Syria was abundant in great possible vineyard sites. Each potential land parcel had its advantages and disadvantages. I remember one of the most stunning and beautiful sites was a plot of land on a hillside in Central Syria. On the site, if you

Krak Des Chevaliers

looked south, you could see the beautiful Cedar Mountains of Lebanon. To the west, was a view of the Mediterranean Sea, and to the northwest was a view of the Krak des Chevaliers. The Krak des Chevalier is one of the most important and well preserved medieval castles in the world.

That afternoon I remember staying in a nice hotel called Al Wadi in the village of Meshtayeh just below the Krak des Chevaliers. They gave me a room with a balcony and a fantastic view of the castle. I had spent many hours on the balcony simply looking at the castle and its' changing appearance with the setting sun.

At night it was aglow with floodlights. In the morning, there was another fantastic view with the morning sun rising from the East casting great hues of gold and yellows across the ramparts. I now look forward to my return to the Al Wadi hotel as it was quite memorable!

On my next trip, I traveled up along the Syrian Western seacoast and visited the many small villages between Tartus and Latakia. Another beautiful parcel of land was in the mountains above the seaport city of Latakia, and again with beautiful sea views and mountain scenes. In the small mountain village of Salma, I discovered a new vineyard owned by a Lebanese family called Saadé. They too were using only French imported vines and had a very nice assortment of French Varietals such as Cabernet Sauvignon; Sauvignon blanc; Syrah; Merlot and a Chardonnay. I later learned that they exported all their grapes or juices to Lebanon and produced a great wine under the label: Domaine de Bargylus. The winery name in Lebanon is Château Marsyas and is located in the Beqaa Valley. I also discovered that the word Marsyas is originally a Greek name for the Beqaa Valley.

Also, in the north of Syria and in an area to the northwest of Aleppo was another great wine growing area located around the famous archeological site of Saint Simeon.

Saint Simeon holds a special place in my heart and especially now. I first visited Saint Simeon in November of 1975, wherein I discovered the history of this famous recluse monk as well as the details of the area. The story of Saint Simon is very interesting as first, his full name was Saint Simon Stylites the Elder and lived in the fourth century. I was told that monks in those days usually lived in caves to better concentrate on prayer and supplication. Saint Simon was a different hermit monk as wherever he tried to live, his followers would besiege him for questions and advice. He found it was said, an ancient 12 to 18-meter high pillar in the ruins of an old Roman city just thirty kilometers northwest of Aleppo. He then ascended to the top of the pillar wherein he lived on top of this two-meter wide pillar for thirty-seven years. His rationale was that "he was

The Column of Saint Simeon

closer to God on top of the pillar than in a cave or hut." Over time, he had developed quite a large following and upon his death, in 475 AD, he was buried with fame in Antioch, Turkey. Later, his followers built a very large Byzantine Church that surrounded his famous pillar. Saint Simon is now called *"The Dead Cities of Syria."* I later read that Saint Simon was declared a World Heritage Site by UNESCO in 2011. I was last there in December 2010 on my search for land and it had not changed too much from my first visit in 1975. I was brought to tears when I heard that the entire Saint Simon site was severely damaged in May of 2016 by unknown missile strikes.

So in 2010, I had high hopes that this could be the location of our new vineyard project, but the land prices were simply too high to make our vineyard project feasible.

I extended my search from Saint Simon to areas around the beautiful city of Aleppo. I knew there were one or two existing Syrian Vineyards in that immediate area, I discovered one, and it was called Cortas. Cortas was a bit disappointing as, at the time, they were not using any French or imported vines and their production winery was not professional enough.

After weeks of searching the Central and northern regions of Syria, I then decided to concentrate my search in the southern region of Syria. I knew this region had modest 'local' grape production and a local Syria wine and Araq called Al Rayan. Unfortunately, Al Rayan was noted for its Araq production and not for their wines. I also discovered another local wine production called Al Bazan Wine and Spirits. Here too, they were exclusively using the local grapes of the region, but with a local twist for grape delivery to their winery. In mid-September to early October, their winemaker would visit all the local grape producers to test the sugar content of their grapes. He would then set an appointment for each farmer to deliver their crop directly to the winery. At the winery, the grapes would be weighed and then processed using modern Italian machines. What impressed me the most of Al Bazan were the gigantic fermentation and holding tanks. The owner told me that these twenty-plus two-story tanks were constructed using the same local materials as they did many years ago during the Roman period. They were using volcanic rocks as the main construction material. This rock provided great insulation and maintained a constant temperature within these massive tanks. We developed a keen friendship and a strong working relationship not only for our new wine project but in the distribution and sales of his wines and Araq to the restaurants in Damascus.

The area was well known for its immense apple and various fruit production. Our search was near the city of: As Suwayda and at the lower slopes of: "Jabal al Druze" or also called "Jabal al Arab." *Jabal'* in Arabic means 'mountain'. I learned that the land was very rich in agriculture and had a high volcanic soil mix. Later, I discovered that this region, during the Roman period, supplied the Roman Empire with over forty (40%) percent of its' wine. Also, interesting enough, Emperor Philip was the first Arab Emperor of the Roman Empire, and he was also called by his nickname *"Philip the Arab."* I also discovered that one Jordanian Vineyard and Winery, St. George, was located just across the Syrian/Jordanian border. So this was even more encouraging for this location. I liked the location, as a guest coming from both Damascus and Amman could drive a short distance to our new vineyard and boutique hotel. Finally, the famous Roman Theater of Busra was just minutes away by car. I was very happy as this land site was going to be perfect for our new wine project. By this time, I had modified the original business plan to include not only the new vineyard and winery location but to encompass a small boutique hotel, a restaurant serving breakfast, lunch, and dinner, a small wine museum and twelve small cabins dispersed around the vineyard as our: 'Artist Colony'. Twelve months per year we would have artists staying with us and working in a quiet and discreet atmosphere. The artist would have their breakfast and dinner in our restaurant and we would send their lunch in a basket to their front door, so just in case the artist did not wish to be disturbed, they could hold off eating their lunch until they were truly ready.

So I negotiated the price and terms for the purchase of this large plot of land and had set a date for all investors to come for the signing ceremony.

Now, how was anyone to contemplate or expect to know that a small group of students in Daraa, by simply writing graffiti on a wall, would start one of the world's bloodiest civil wars? These unfortunate events in Daraa took place one week before our group of investors was to fly into Syria for the final purchase of the land for our winery and vineyard project.

Our planned meeting never took place and was simply held off for a week and then a month, etc. The project was, of course, placed on an 'indefinite hold' and still remains on hold at this time of my writing.

In conclusion, my first job after my retirement was now in shambles. The positives from this time and what I enjoyed the most was the opportunity to visit all of Syria prior to Syria's protracted civil war. I will long remember meeting so many interesting and friendly Syrian people in so many Syrian small towns and villages. These memories will never be erased.

The other positive that came out of my "first retirement job" was my great contacts with both Father Frances and Father Paolo as well as the owner of the Al Bazan Winery.

Actually, I discovered that the Al Bazan Wine and Araq were quite decent, rather pleasant, and very smooth to the pallet. So immediately after shelving the Wine and Vineyard project, I signed a contract with Al Bazan Wines and Spirits company to be the sole distributor for all hotels and restaurants in Damascus. Hence my second retirement job.

The wine that Al Bazan was producing was a solid, inexpensive, and locally produced and would have had a special position in the market in many restaurants and bars of Damascus. I had no trouble selling it to many bars and restaurants around the city.

At the onset of my sales and distribution, the Al Bazan Araq was unknown as most people had only heard of and preferred the other As Suwayda brand: *Al Rayan Araq*. I decided to take this challenge head-on, and I began to promote Araq Tasting Nights and very soon, my sales of Araq outpaced the wine sales. I found I was making solid money in a profession called 'sales' which I had detested before in all previous attempts. I discovered that sales can be fun only if you believe in your product.

I found that all good things may come to an end... and this was the case with my distributorship of the Al Bazan Araq and Wine. Very simply, the Syrian Civil War was beginning to escalate in the south of Syria and in Homs and Hama. The Al Bazan company was located in the south and so very soon, we could not receive enough Araq and wine to meet our demand in Damascus. The entire area to the southwest of Syria remained under rebel control until July of 2018.

Now, I must try going back to the Suwayda area to see what has happened to the Al Bazan Wines and Spirits company plus the owner and his family. And most importantly, what happened to the land that was so close to being purchased. It is also very interesting as now with the hostilities in the southern region of Syria abating, there have been two inquiries about my winery project in the past week. Who knows, I may update my Syrian Winery Business Plan and present it to another group of investors.

Then a short time after the wine projects, I met a great Syrian Businessman who was looking to expand his current Syrian telecommunications company. I had the necessary credentials to expand his company from a strict telecom company into new and diverse areas of trade and commerce. At Cypress Corporation, my job title was Vice President for Business Development, and it was a good fit for me and my previous positions.

For the first six to eight months, things were working very well as a team. I had developed many new areas of expansion, and this amounted to many business trips to the States. All-in-all, things were working out very well for all of us. But, once again, the Syrian Civil War reared its ugly head, car bombings intensified in Damascus and now the city was under aerial bombardment on a daily basis. The rockets and mortar shells were wreaking havoc on the population of the city and were emanating from the countryside just to the east of Damascus in the area called the Eastern Ghouta.

Dr. Maher and his family, fearing the fighting would intensify even more, left Syria for Dubai, as the stress and fear were getting too much for most of the prominent Syrian families. There was also the fear that the government was losing ground to the rebels, especially around the Damascus countryside.

Once Dr. Maher and his family left Syria, he suggested that I start working with a new company under the umbrella of Cypress Corporation called eSoft and ALC or Arabic Learning System. Again, I maintained the same business title as Vice President for Business Development, and my job was this time was to research and then contact international colleges and universities that either had or wanted to develop an Arabic language program.

I found this to be fascinating work and once again, felt that I excelled at my position. After I made initial contact with many major international colleges and universities, I then had to travel to the States and Europe to meet with each interested university such as Northeastern University, George Washington, and Georgetown. The concept of eSoft and ALS was very simple, we had already set up an online, live-training service so all the students wishing to add Arabic to their college educational transcripts and records were able to do their Arabic language training at their own pace, time, and at the Arabic language level that best suited to their current knowledge base. We completely did away with the standard classroom approach to a fully online experience. We were working towards our international accreditation and certification as the Syrian Civil War was escalating around us. The Damascus International Airport was closed as there were no flights into and out of the airport plus there was constant restlessness on the road to the airport with the resistance. So everyone was forced to travel overland to Beirut to use Beirut Rafic Hariri International Airport for all international flights.

The most important and damaging challenge we faced with eSoft was very simple, we could no longer find qualified Syrian web technicians to complete this project. Either they were inducted into the Syrian military, or they decided to leave Syria for a safer work environment. To this day, I still feel that the concept that eSoft brought forth would have been a tremendous success in all international markets.

Dr. Maher, the CEO of Cypress Corporation, hearing of our challenges at eSoft and the ever-increasing terrorist threats in the city, strongly suggested that my wife and I temporarily relocate to Amman, Jordan and I would continue to work for Cypress Corporation in business development, but in a safer location. My wife's mother and her two brothers were all living in Amman, so the transition from Damascus would be easy and trouble-free.

All-in-all, it was still a very arduous decision for my wife and me to contemplate and envision. She had always remembered her dad telling the story of when they left Palestine in April of 1948: "Don't worry, it won't be more than several weeks as the Arab army has vastly outmanned the Zionist." That was in 1948, and my lovely wife was imagining the same result some sixty-plus years later. My fears and worries were more materialistic. I thought of our home being ransacked or even destroyed by the rebel groups if they took over control of Damascus. We were also planning on leaving all our worldly possessions in our Damascus home and travel to another country with our possible return being unknown. It was a very daunting decision for both of us to make. Finally, in the end, we both agreed to lock our home securely and have a very trusted friend look after our household.

I still recall our trip to Beirut to catch our flight to Amman. When we left our house, all we could both image was that we may never return to Damascus.

Once we arrived at Amman, my wife's family did so many things for us as they were extremely compassionate for our plight. We arrived, and my wife's brother, in advance of our arrival had already purchased a furnished apartment for us to live. Plus a car was waiting in the parking area so we had transportation.

We both recall that everyone in her family was so kind and helpful.

Our transitory apartment was a walking distance to both her brothers' villas. It took no time for us to settle in and for me to begin work in Amman for the Cypress Corporation. Dr. Maher had signed a joint venture agreement with two Jordanian businessmen, and we had several projects. Paramount to these investors and partners was to develop a vehicle anti-theft system. Initially, my job was to source the hardware for this anti-theft system. Once more, I was doing business development and yet again, I was really enjoying my work. I was able to make a short-list of three international companies and then we decided, as a group, the top and most practical product. We then had to establish a new company that could sell, install and monitors each vehicle that had our anti-theft installed. This was challenging work as the cost of simply setting up several fixed workshops, numerous mobile workshop units, a computer program, installation teams, etc., was yet another overwhelming task.

Once that was all assigned and integrated financially, we had the formidable mission of introducing our new company to the Jordanian Police Department.

After weeks of presentations, it seemed that no topmost officers were willing to sign off the projects which needed permission. The biggest downfall was the fact that we'd learned that if a thief had stolen a car with our anti-theft tracking system installed, all they needed to do was to park the vehicle underground, thus making the electronic signals and tracking useless. There were also many financial risks that all the partners were not willing and ready to accommodate.

So all of a sudden, the project that we had been working on was halted and shortly thereafter terminated.

This corresponded to both my wife's and my displeasure in living in Amman. It was so different than life in Damascus. The people were not like the Syrian people we knew and loved in Syria. The way of life was different as you needed a car to get anywhere in Amman, whereas in Damascus, you could walk to 90% of your daily activities. On our small street in Damascus, you would find a greengrocer, my wife's hair salon, my barber, our pharmacy, a great men's clothing store, two restaurants, a pet store, etc. And in Damascus, a four-minute walk got you to the bank, the largest shopping street in all of Damascus, the butcher, and any other store that you required for the day.

Where in Amman, all the above was a long car drive away. The largest single factor for us both missing Syria was the tremendous difference in the cost of living. Jordan was so much more expensive than Syria, and yet, Syria was in the middle of a civil war. Gasoline for one's car was three times more expensive in Jordan than in Syria. All the groceries were more expensive. Even getting into Jordan, they charged an enormous entry tax. This then led Salma and me to reconsider living in Jordan or to head back to the place we loved…Syria.

It was a joint decision for us to return back to Damascus. Partially due to the fact that the company had closed its joint venture and that we both missed Damascus and never felt at home in Amman.

The only thing we had left behind in Jordan was our beloved dog, Ginger, who had been our family's trusted companion for eighteen years in Jeddah, Doha, Damascus, and now Amman. She too didn't enjoy Amman and simply died of old age while we were living in Amman.

On a positive note, while living in Amman, we bought a beautiful Siamese cat and I named him Marco Polo. Marco is still enjoying his life here in Damascus and is one smart cat.

Our flight back to Damascus was via Beirut Rafic Hariri International Airport, and we had our driver collect us and the three-hour drive seemed to take an eternity. We both wanted to get back home and to restart our life in beautiful Damascus. Thank goodness we found our Damascus house intact and we enjoyed our first night of sleep in Damascus.

When Dr. Maher heard about our return to Damascus, he immediately contacted me and asked if I could help in setting up his new office in Dubai and to look at new business opportunities for his company in the United Arab Emirates. I then again spent a great deal of time searching to see what might be a new and profitable business opportunity in Dubai. Interesting enough, the two initial areas of business development that I had researched and presented to Dr. Maher, he thought they were both great.

The first was for me to find a private Jet Aviation Company that either sells shares in the ownership of your private jet aircraft or are single flight dealers in which they supply the aircraft, and we simply supply the clients.

The second business concept involved the sale of luxurious yachts in the UAE. We both felt that both business models had merit and a great chance to succeed in the United Arab Emirates.

I then spent a lot of time in Damascus in the development and location of a private jet company. To my surprise, there were many operating internationally, and many of them were very interested in entering the lucrative Middle Eastern Markets.

I had coordinated my stateside meetings to coincide with various major business trips that Dr. Maher and his team were planning in the States. We attended the various telecom conventions in America, and then it was my time for our group to set off to visit the hugely profitable and large US jet leasing companies. The first was called NETJETS® out of Columbus, Ohio. We had a full tour of their facilities and a great lunch with the President of the company. Once we returned to Dubai, I followed up with many email messages to work out a deal with NetJets. Unfortunately, we never came to a long term commitment for various reasons. We followed up that great visit to Columbus with a smaller New York City Aircraft Chartering company which introduced all of us to the most bizarre and whacky business meeting any of us had ever attended.

I had set up this meeting in New York weeks in advance, and when we arrived, we were ushered into the conference room. There we sat for ten minutes with no one offering us coffee, tea or even a glass of water. Finally, the condescending and supercilious Jewish owner enters the room. He doesn't introduce himself and promptly sits at the head of the table in a pompous manner. He never shook hands with us and was as arrogant as any person we have ever met. Each of us reached for our business cards and gave them to this showy owner. This was the custom in all Arab meetings around the world to present your business card in a professional and polite manner. He never looked at one of the business cards and then he took out his own business card and literally throws it to each of us like he was dealing a deck of cards in a poker game.

He gave us a brief introduction to his company, and during that short overview, he was interrupted by three phone calls. Each call appeared to be prearranged by his secretary. It appeared to us sitting in that conference room that this was entirely a "staged performance" and he had absolutely no substance or interest in doing business with us in the Middle East. We exited that room as gracefully as possible, and I remember our group did not say a word to each other until we got outside the skyscraper. Then we all looked at each other and said: "What was that?" The four of us were in complete shock, NEVER in our lives had we been so disrespected and insulted by anyone, in any business, anywhere in the world. Needless to say, there was no thank you email sent to this SOB.

My search continued when we returned back to Dubai, and within a short period of time, I had secured a small aircraft rental company in Milan, Italy. I flew there and had several very positive meetings. When I returned back to Dubai, we had established a successful business relationship that lasted quite a few years.

After that launch, I concentrated on my second business concept that involved our company in the sales of luxurious yachts in the UAE. This was a much more straight forward venture that needed less financial input. I envisioned our company would simply represent the best international yacht builders and brokers that wished to enter the new and lucrative Dubai market. On my part, I was again completing a great deal of research into the most practical and advantageous yacht companies. I had compiled a master list of over twenty yacht brokers and manufacturers that wanted to work with us and enter the profitable UAE yacht market.

I then arranged a business trip to visit Europe's largest in-water yacht shows in Cannes, France.

Many of the yacht builders and agents I had contacted were going to be exhibiting in Cannes, so I had arranged appointments with the five top candidates. That year they had over 600 boats from two to sixty-five meters in length. Each of my meetings was very successful and in most, I scheduled an additional meeting in Dubai so each could have a better understanding of the UAE yacht market. This project was slow in developing mainly due to the lingering debt challenges Dubai was still facing since its 2009 Financial Debt Crisis.

In mid-2014, I was approached by a group of Canadian investors that wanted to use my franchise expertise and to form a Franchise Investment Group. We established the investment company a short time later with our headquarters in Ottawa. With a great deal of work and due diligence, we were able to initially sign MOU's with a group of seven new and exciting franchise brands. We continued building our brand into the year 2016 at which time I decided to leave the investment group and spend full time in Syria.

The Syrian Crisis was expanding at an alarming rate, and there was a great deal of fighting directly surrounding Damascus proper. My wife and I felt it was better for both of us to be in Damascus, first, to protect our home and second, to gain a true understanding of the reality of this conflict.

Russia has supported the Bashar al-Assad government of Syria since the beginning of the Syrian conflict in 2011: politically and with military aid, since the end of September 2015 through direct military involvement. The latter marked the first time since the end of the Cold War that Russia entered an armed conflict outside the borders of the former Soviet Union. For me, this was a major 'turning point' in the Syrian civil conflict.

Personally, for me, this direct Russian military involvement was the major turning point in the government's favor during this lengthy and prolonged conflict.

One of the final positions I held in Damascus, was that of an English Instructor at the French school or officially called Lycée Charles de Gaulle. A very good friend told me that the school was looking for an English instructor as in the past four months, they had four different English instructors and none had worked very well at the school. To be honest, initially, this potential job was not of keen interest as I hadn't been in a classroom for many years. I was now working and developing new franchises around the Middle East and Africa. My friend simply asked me: "Thomas, please just see the students and then you decide."

On my first visit to the school, I was simply observing several classes, and I remember saying to myself, "These students are really great and they deserve to have a proper English instructor!" I remembered the great words of Ralph Waldo Emerson: ***"The secret in education lies in respecting the student."*** I had always tried to keep that proverb in the forefront of my classroom teaching.

One week later, I found myself teaching English to the: sixth; seventh; eighth and ninth grades. When I first started, I found that the school's current English textbooks were not suitable and quite outdated. Over 95% of the material I gave to my students was self-made and often photocopied each morning. This consumed a great deal of my time, and I discovered for each hour of class time I was spending two to three hours of preparation time at home. This fact has reminded me of another great quotation by Mustafa Kemal Atatürk, founder of the Republic of Turkey: ***"A good teacher is like a candle – it consumes itself to light the way for others."***

I had enjoyed teaching at the French school for two and a half years. They were two and a half great years filled with tremendous enjoyment and fantastic memories. I often see my former students here in Damascus, and it is always a pleasure for me to converse with them. This has always reminded me of what the Dalai Lama once wrote: ***"When educating the minds of our youth, we must not forget to educate their hearts."***

I feel that I successfully achieved both.

The main reason I left the French school was that I needed to concentrate on completing this book and to have it published in a timely manner.

Finally, when I first decided to retire back in 2010, never did I imagine that I would have been involved in so many rewarding positions in such a short period of time.

Chapter Fourteen

Trying Times in Syria

I feel that my life in Damascus has seen some very trying times, well not 'some', but 'many' trying times.

You might say, maybe, that the two times I was shot at may register as being 'trying times' or maybe the truck bomb I encountered while playing tennis at the American School was also a trying experience or even the time I frantically raced for over 35 kilometers struggling to stay in front of three cars, and that was a trying encounter, but the most 'long-lasting trying time' occurred just after I moved to Damascus in 2010.

Hence the start of what I originally titled: 'The Trying Times in Damascus,' actually was not just Damascus, but all of Syria. And of all my past 'trying times' each had been short in duration compared to these eight-year-long conflict in beautiful Syria.

The civil descent and local protest in Daraa quickly plunged the entire country into a state-of-emergency. At first, the international news agencies related these actions to the Arab Spring, but this was totally different than what had taken place in Iraq; Tunis and Libya. In the beginning, it appeared to be many groups of ordinary civilians simply protesting over the governments' harsh crack-down in Daraa. Many of these initial street protests in other Syrian towns and cities grew in size and in magnitude as the initial weeks progressed into months and then years. Soon the innocent Syrian civilian protestors were bolstered by foreign terrorists who had completely different intentions and goals than of the original Daraa protestors. One large protest led to an even larger protest, and very soon, Syria was plunged into a bloody and lengthy crisis.

What we were initially facing in Damascus at the early stages of this crisis were many weekly car bombings, terrorist attacks, and a land grab from many of the various groups in their attempts to dislodge the President of Syria and his administration. Many cities in Syria, and not just Damascus, witnessed the rapid and escalating bloodshed.

Starting in late 2011 and during the entire following year, there was an ever-increasing amount of departures of the rich and influential Syrian families. They seemed ready from the onset of these hostilities to leave Syria as there were major concerns about the schools remaining open, and of course, the anxieties over the current economic situation in the entire country. The middle and upper-class Syrians were soon leaving Syria in waves. Unfortunately, this included many medical professionals, and after a very short period of time, it was difficult to find a trusted and renowned doctor to visit. Many of our friends had departed thinking that the hostilities would soon be ending and they would return to their homes in Damascus and other cities. Unfortunately, by early 2019 we see only a few of these families returning, as they had completely assimilated into their new country of residence. This has created a true 'brain-drain' within the entire country as many of these highly skilled professionals, especially doctors and technical workers were relocating in other countries that offered better opportunities.

Three-Year-Old Syrian Refugee Alan Kurdi

Soon following this initial exodus, many working-class Syrians were departing as their homes and jobs were being destroyed and factories were closing due to the intense fighting that was being witnessed in many towns and cities across Syria. These were the Syrians that were traveling to the west by any method and have been famously documented by many international news media outlets.

This shocking *image of a* young Syrian *boy* found lying face-down on a beach near a Turkish resort *showed the world the* tragic plight of these Syrian *refugees*. The Turkish photographer: won the: "Press Photo of the Year – 2016" for this stunning and most dynamic photo that placed the Syrian conflict at the forefront of international news.

The Syrian refugees had made an immediate impact on the world, especially in Western Europe. My biggest concern now since the major hostilities have subsided is the fact that these refugees may not return to their beautiful country to help rebuild this famous land. Like the initial group of upper-class Syrians, these middle and working-class Syrians have been integrated into many new countries around the world. I personally doubt that they would return as many have no homes to return to in Syria, and many have established themselves very well living abroad. Now for the remainder of the true Syrian refugee that are currently living in camps in the surrounding countries, they may simply try and wait until the true reconstruction begins in Syria so they too can have help and assist in rebuilding their homes and workplaces.

Now during the first year of fighting in many Syrian towns and cities, the government was forced to use more and more military actions to try to suppress and to quell the mounting protests. Also, with the increasing number of imported terrorists again, the government began using more and more military action. Very soon, the entire country was plunged into this civil conflict.

All across Damascus from late-2011 to mid-2012, there were constant car bombings, including a massive car bomb in Al Midan district and another next to the Central Bank in downtown Damascus. To help minimize these car bombing threats, the government quickly mobilized and began installing checkpoints at the most strategic parts within the city. Every car, taxi, bus, or van was thoroughly inspected at these well-manned checkpoints. Apparently, these checkpoints helped as the frequency of the bombings lessened. Plus my wife and I felt safer and more secure since the advent of these governmental checkpoints.

All major roads leading into and out of Damascus had checkpoints, thus trying to eliminate the import of explosives. In 2012, on a car trip into Lebanon, we encountered over nine checkpoints from our home in Damascus to the Syrian Border.

Soon with the diminishing number of Damascus car bombings, due to the advent of so many new checkpoints, the foreign resistance groups which were surrounding the capital soon began using other tactical warfare methods.

Our neighborhood in Damascus soon had rockets and mortar shells falling on a daily basis. You see, our neighborhood of Abu Roumaneh had been in the crosshairs of every terrorist group because less than 100 meters away from our front door, we have the military headquarters for both the Syrian Army and Syrian Air Force. And the Air Force Headquarters Main Building is eight stories high, thus making it a favored target for the resistance groups. From 2012 till early 2018, each resistance group was aiming at this preferred and important military compound. I am not sure if these resistance groups were simply poor shots or that their rocket and mortar systems were homemade and primitive, as it always appeared that the majority of their projectiles were missing their intended targets and simply hitting the many rooftops of our adjacent apartment buildings on our small street or the large Al Jahez Garden at the end of our street. My office is in front of our apartment and faces our street so any incoming rocket or mortar shell is quite well announced. Usually, the resistance would send one rocket at a time and I would go out to check if it had caused any casualties or damage in our neighborhood. So on this one particular occasion, I heard a rocket hit pretty close to our home so I quickly ran outside to survey the situation only to have a second rocket race past me fifty meters away from my head. That second one hit the roof just two buildings away on our street. I was

really getting worried as
the pattern has always
been one rocket per
attack. Within a few
seconds, a third raced
past me and appeared to
hit the Jahez Park at the
end of our street a few
meters from where I was

Goggle Map™ of Damascus

standing. I was now getting very worried as the only place for me to hide
to protect myself was behind a very small tree along our street. Within a
minute, the forth rocket raced over my head and hit a second roof about
100 meters from where I was standing.

By this time, I was petrified. What should I do? Should I try to
run back to the safety of my home or just say a short prayer? I will
always remember the high pitched whining sound a rocket makes when
it passes your head. Since this 'challenge', I have come to believe that
when it's time for you to die, there is only one person that knows it's
your time...and that is God.

Our daily life now consisted of hearing the multitude of sounds, first
of the incoming rockets, and then of the arriving mortar shells. The
homemade rockets were actually improvised or makeshift rockets and
they were called: 'Volcano's'. They were of various sizes, but normally
between 107 to 122 mm in size. Each had a large number of explosives
enclosed so they really created a large hole on impact. I can still remember
the sound of each rocket as it sounded more like a "whining" sound or
like a small "jet." Since the rocket was a straight line projectile, we were
never too worried that our apartment would be hit as we were living in
a garden apartment and we were 'protected' by the tall apartment house
adjacent to our house.

Now the mortar shells were a different type of projectile as they
would literally be shot upwards at a 60 degrees angle and come straight

down some distance away. Again, the resistance had crude homemade mortar shells and was actually rudimentary and quite simple. The resistance had commonly called their homespun mortar shells: 'Hell's Cannons'. Mortar shelling was much more common than rocket fire because I guess they were easier to make and much simpler to fire. Today in Damascus, virtually every street has a spall caused by the numerous mortar shells hitting the city. Our small street has at least six spalls, and the largest is just four meters from our front door. We were not at home when this particular mortar shell hit, but when we came home a bit later that day, we saw seven parked cars destroyed. Each with 20 to 30 shrapnel holes along the lower side of the impact area and all with their tires flattened. The explosive device penetrated each car no higher than sixty centimeters from ground level and the tires were in shreds. Two of the cars are still parked exactly where they were hit, unable to be moved. Thank God that nobody was near the blast site as they too would have been seriously injured. Again, when it is a person's time to die, there is only one 'person' that knows when it's your time.

Also daily, there were the many sounds of the outgoing shells that were caused by a large number of Syrian Artillery Guns or called: Howitzers. These large guns were being fired from the top of Qasioun Mountain, which overlooked the entire city of Damascus. These enormous weapons were daily pounding the Ghouta areas which surrounded Damascus and other nearby districts of the city which were under the opposition control. The Syrian military was using two sizes of the functional Artillery Guns so I developed the ability to differentiate the sound of the larger 152-millimeter guns from the smaller 130-millimeter sized guns. I coined these Howitzer noises to be the sounds of *"The Syrian Military Orchestra"* ...simply playing another routine symphony or composition for our entertainment!

Finally, a day would not be complete without the constant sounds of the Russian and Syrian Jets flying low overhead on their daily missions. The sound of each jet was difficult to differentiate as we had a lot of sound reverberations between the buildings, plus the jets were flying very fast and very low. If you were lucky and in an open space as the many jets flew over the city, you could tell the older Syrian Migs from the more sophisticated and newer Russian jets. Simply hearing or seeing the Syrian air superiority and strength gave many Syrian people a true feeling of "bitter confidence."

During any civil disturbance, one experiences many shortages, and during the seven years of Syrian hostilities, there was a multitude of important paucities that every household in Syria experienced.

In our area of Damascus, we were quite 'lucky' as we had our daily electric power cuts of 'only' three hours in the morning and again two or three hours in the afternoon. But in other areas that were close to the opposition groups, they were less fortunate. The power cuts were more numerous, and in many cases, there was no electrical power supplied at all. This suspension or cessation of electrical power was caused by four important factors: first, there was a real shortage in the capacity of the electrical generation all throughout Syria; second, the fuel needed to run the electricity generation plants were always in short supply; third, several of the electrical generating plants were under the control of the opposition fighters and fourth, the electrical network or grid in many towns and cities were simply destroyed by the constant bombing and fighting. So no electrical power could travel to the majority of these Syrian cities and villages. I found that I could live with the disruption of electricity as a matter of fact; I always remembered that we had more electrical power distribution through the duration of our Syrian Crises than many parts of Beirut and Lebanon.

Again, I discovered how resilient the Syrian people were during these times of hardships and shortages as it seemed at the very beginning of these daily and constant electricity cuts some businessman with great insight had imported a huge amount of LED light strips along with many 12 volt batteries plus the very important battery charger. Our electrician installed these LED light strips in the darkest and most important rooms, such as our kitchen, the pantry, and my inside bathroom which had no windows. These new LED strips were a real godsend so as soon as the government had turned off our electrical power, we would simply turn on our new and special LED Lights and they lasted almost till the end of the two or three-hour power cut. Many small business owners did the same for their shops and small stores. The larger stores, such as the supermarkets, restaurants, and malls, each had their own large generator just outside their place of business. Even the larger office buildings and certain large apartment buildings had their own generator. I also remember that in the small shopping area called Shaalan, which we would frequent often, had along both sidewalks a multitude of smaller generators each supplying power to that small store or pharmacy. One would need to weave between each generator and not brush against the hot exhaust pipes while dodging the other pedestrians. The odor emanating from them wasn't too bad as they were gas generators, but the diesel ones had created a strong odor that was quite repulsive. Finally, you would virtually require earplugs as the sound of each generator was deafening.

Personally, the main shortage and my highest priority were finding water. Our municipality water was in short supply, and in many cases, nonexistent. Everyone needs water for their daily needs, such as drinking, washing, and cleaning. In the beginning, you could find a private supply of water that was coming into the city by large water tankers. This was both costly and unreliable as their sources of well water were quite a distance from the heart of Damascus. The needs of the typical household kept increasing as no water was coming to one's home on a regular basis. The other challenge that these large water tankers caused was their large capacity which always far exceeded our own home water tank capacity. To combat this major challenge, I went out and purchased a small round inflatable swimming pool. So when the water truck had filled our existing water tank and the many plastic buckets placed around our garden, I would then simply take the trucks supply hose and fill my small plastic swimming pool with clean, fresh well water. Later, I would use a large plastic measuring cup to scoop up the water from our swimming pool and fill our numerous small 1½ liter plastic bottles. Still today I have a large amount of full plastic water bottles below each sink in our house.

During these trying and difficult times, people then sought to acquire more water during the governmental short allotted times of distribution. The Syrian people are very innovative and creative, so one by one, they began to add an exterior water pump to 'steal' water from the municipalities' daily ration and also from their neighbors. Every day you would see plumbers installing these illegal pumps and when the municipality water was turned on, each of these pumps was automaticity activated to increase the intake of the inexpensive government water to fill their own water tanks.

These water problems were augmented and widened once the resistance had taken control of Damascus's main water supply located at the Barada Water Springs some forty kilometers from Damascus. No longer were the water trucks allowed to fill well water near the Barada Springs, plus the opposition had controlled the main pumping station at the springs. There were rumors that the resistance had rigged explosive devices to the spring's main pump room, and they threatened to blow up the entire facility if the military tried to take control. They also stopped the pumps for days upon days. This tight grip on the city's water lifeline lasted for over a year. There was now no water coming into the city of Damascus. The Syrian government, sensing the imminent danger, quickly mobilized to find an immediate solution for this devastating problem. Damascus had at that time a population of over three million persons.

Many years ago, when the city of Damascus was expanding beyond its old city walls, the Damascus Municipality had great vision and insight. They had planned and established in each new residential area of Damascus that there would be certain land allocated for parks or simply green areas. In each planned park site, the Damascus Municipality would dig a water well and within the larger planned parks, they would dig multiple water wells so each park would be self-sufficient and independent for their water needs. The present government recognizing this new potential source of water for the now stranded Damascus civilian population began to run new water pipes from the water wells to the perimeter of each park. Along each perimeter fence, they then installed a long pipe and had added multiple water faucets so the population would simply bring an empty container and fill it up when required. I had in my home five large empty twenty-liter plastic 'Jerry Jugs' so each night I would drive to our closest green park to refill my Jerry Jugs. These five jugs fit perfectly in the trunk of my car. The park closest to our home, Jahez Park, had over twenty water faucets so the wait was never too long. It also became a meeting place for our community to socialize as you would usually see the same people day in and day out. You must have fun with some of these inopportune situations. Life is too short not to enjoy working positively around any adversity.

Now at the same time, there was a new business developing in which people would bring bottled spring water from Lebanon in large five-liter light plastic containers. This was ideal for your family's drinking needs, and after they were empty, you would use them at the park to refill with well water and to keep as an emergency and backup water source. In addition, they were much lighter than the twenty liters Jerry Jugs

Once the government was able to force a withdraw of these enemy combatants from the Barada Springs, life quickly went back to normal. Even though I had kept a supply of over thirty of these special five-liter plastic bottles filled with well water 'just in case' they were needed in the future.

One good point of conservation and environmental concern emerged from this water shortage as many people are still today using water-saving methods to conserve water. Many have continued to collect the water from the start of one's daily bath or shower as the water is usually cold from the faucet at the onset. So one can collect two or three bottles of the 1½ plastic water bottles each day and use that water from the start of our shower to flush our toilets throughout the day. Still today, I also have saved over fifty plastic bottles of well water, and they are still sitting under my bathroom sink, just in case we encounter another water shortage.

There were also other major shortages found throughout the Syrian civil conflict, such as in the supply of LPG (Propane) gas bottles. The majority of Damascus homes and restaurants all use this form of cooking in their kitchens so where there is a shortage, it was a major catastrophe. The reason for this particular shortage was simple as the only major LPG filling station was located outside the central city of Homs and that area experienced severe fighting for several years. This shortage of cooking gas was also seen to be the main reason why so many famous Damascene Bakeries went out of business and then closed. The most famous in Damascus was called: The Semiramees. The owner closed his bakery at the famous location and re-established his bakery in Cairo. He is yet to return to Damascus.

Gas and Diesel were always in very short supply resulting in long lines at every gas station. It became commonplace to have many stations closed for days-on-end. This was especially difficult for the many taxis plying the streets of each city, attempting to earn enough money to buy food and other necessities for their families. This important shortage was felt throughout the seven years of the Syrian conflict.

Finally, a very serious shortage quickly appeared at the onset of the hostilities, and that was in the important pharmaceutical industry. Pharmacy shelves were quickly emptied and the necessary and most important drugs were being smuggled in from neighboring Lebanon, thus resulting in extreme inflation and high prices. This pharmaceutical sector was especially hard hit as the majority of the Syrian drug factories were located in and around the northern city of Aleppo. Aleppo took the brunt of hostilities and damage. To date, reconstruction has not started. We are still finding shortages in 2019 and these are now due to the shortages of many of the raw materials needed in the pharmaceutical industry. This, in turn, has been caused by the multitude of sanctions placed on the Syrian government.

Domestic travel within Syria was quite limited due to the hostilities suddenly springing up in many cities and regions throughout the country. Sections of the main Damascus/Aleppo Highway were often closed for weeks on end. It appeared that the only region in which the main roads remained open were those in Latakia and Tartous all along the Mediterranean Sea Coast. These areas were never truly damaged like the cities: Aleppo, Hama, and Zabadani. In the early summer of 2012, during a lull in the fighting, my wife and I, with a close friend, drove from Damascus to the Syrian seacoast enjoying several days outside Damascus. We really enjoyed a great deal of fresh seafood at the various seafood restaurants along the beachfront. Also, the relief of not hearing any bombs or explosives was a major positive of this short vacation.

In October of 2011, I was lucky, as I had met a small group of Armenian friends living in Damascus that were planning a short trip to Armenia, and they asked me if I wanted to join them with their Armenian group traveling to Yerevan. We were very lucky as the Syrian Arab Airlines now called Syrian Air was still flying domestically as well as internationally. So with an uncertain future for international travel to and from Damascus and Aleppo, I accepted their offer. Plus, I had never been to Armenia so I could cross off one more country from my Bucket's List. We started on October 18th on Syrian Air with a small group of Armenians living and working in Damascus. We landed in Aleppo wherein we collected a larger group of Armenians living in and around Aleppo. In total, we had over seventy Armenians taking part in the tour and I was the only non-Armenian on the entire trip!

Our group returned back to Aleppo and then Damascus on October 25th.

Shortly after this Armenian trip, virtually all international travel was curtailed as the two main international airports in both Damascus and

Aleppo had been subjected to major fighting around each. This, in turn, caused virtually all international carriers to cease flying into and out of Syria. Also, our two Syrian airlines, the government-owned and operated: Syrian Air and the private airline called: Cham Wings had curtailed their operations due to the new warfare surrounding both airports and the major shortages of Jet Fuel. All members of our Armenian tour group felt very happy that we were able to fly to and from Yerevan before these challengers began eroding international air travel.

We saw international air travel into and out of Damascus decrease at an alarming rate by the end of 2011 to mid-late 2012.

For many wishing to travel outside of Damascus, the only connecting airlines were just available in Beirut, as the Syrian/Jordanian Border both at Dara and Nasib crossing had been closed due to the substantial fighting at both crossings. The Nasib crossing had just reopened to civilian and freight travel in early November 2018. We went across the Nasib crossing on November 5th to Amman in a taxi as no private Syrian cars were allowed at that time. The Nasib Syrian Border Crossing was a complete disaster with all the buildings in complete shambles. For the past six-plus years, each side had claimed it held the border thus making the fighting even more intense and this is very evident when one travels to the border area. Destroyed and wrecked trucks, buses, cars, and military vehicles were seen across the entire border area. All the Syrian government buildings were devastated and now only a few new portable cabins are being used for a passport, customs, and vehicle control and clearance. In mid-December 2018, the Syrian authorities allowed Syrian private vehicles to use the Nasib crossing so my wife and I decided to drive our car to Amman to enjoy New Year's Eve party. There was no improvement at all with the Nasib border area, as a matter of fact, it was getting worse because more Syrian vehicles were now using the crossing and more importantly, the number of Jordanian vehicles at the border had increased substantially. You would now see very long lines of up to two hundred empty Jordanian taxis crossing into Syria early morning.

Then in the early afternoon, the same Jordanian cars and taxis were exiting Syria traveling back to Jordan. But now, each returning car and taxi had an enormous amount of Syrian fresh fruits and fresh vegetables packed inside each.

Also, each car and taxi had filled his vehicle with Syrian Gas as the gasoline prices in Syria were dramatically lower than in Jordan. At that time, the liter of gas in Jordan was: .96 JD or about $ 1.35 USD per liter. In Syria, today the gas cost is only 225. Syrian Pounds per liter or $ 00.28 USD per liter at the current exchange rate. Over one US dollar lower than the Jordanian liter of gas. When one understands the economics, one then comprehends the reason why the Syrian/Jordanian Border at Nasib is so chaotic and crowded.

So for anyone, in mid to late 2012, wishing to leave Syria, the only opportunity was to travel overland from Damascus by car or taxi to Beirut. Beirut's Rafic Hariri International Airport was being stretched to its core due to the sheer number of Syrians using that small and undersized international airport.

Also, the drive overland from Damascus to Beirut had its own pitfalls. Not only was the cost prohibitive as the average taxi was charging $100. USD one-way, the weather often played a major factor especially in the winter months as the high pass you had to ascend, called the Dahr Al-Baidar Pass was usually closed due to snow accumulation. Beirut would experience heavy rain and Dahr Al-Baidar, due to its' height of 1,500 meters, would have a good deal of snow, so much so that the pass was often closed for hours to days at a time. The other obvious factors in making this 'simple' drive were the overly crowded immigration halls on both sides of the borders. But worse yet, once you entered Lebanon, you had to face the disrespectful and repugnant Lebanese drivers. And they seem to enhance this negative behavior once they spotted your car with Syrian license plates!

If you were lucky to overcome these major obstacles and your international flight was departing in the afternoon or early evening, you were in good shape. But many times, you had to spend the night in Beirut before catching your early morning flight. The hotel prices in Beirut were usually reasonable depending on the area and season that you chose to travel. What was really the most unfortunate and regrettable plight was the very high cost of dining or eating out in Lebanon, especially Beirut. And these were not simply 'seasonal' high prices, but permanently inflated prices.

Beirut International Airport, as I had mentioned, was small and overcrowded and simply was not capable of handling the additional amount of people departing or arriving. The initial entrance luggage screening had only two operational scanners and was always overcrowded and clogged. Once you passed this first delay, the next stop was the airline check-in counters. They were very busy yet manageable. We had always chosen to fly in Business or First-Class as those queues were much shorter and more controllable.

The final and major catastrophe at Beirut Airport was the long lines you always encountered at the passport control area. Usually, you get through this ordeal in less than an hour. But now, in many cases and especially during the holiday season, your wait could be up to four hours. And it is no different when one arrives at the airport. If you are unlucky to arrive just after a large jumbo aircraft, expect to wait between one to three hours at the Incoming Passport Control area. In early 2019 they enlarged many parts of the old delay areas throughout the airport, but still, it is a very small airport!

In late December 2019 I flew out of Beirut International airport and I have found major improvements in all areas within the airport. I must accept that the authorities had realized the severe 'challenges' facing their airport and have taken appropriate action.

Luckily, during mid to late 2018, traveling into and out of the Damascus International Airport had improved as the resistance groups fighting on the way and near Damascus International Airport were defeated. In all cases, the fighting has stopped completely. Thus the government decided to begin increasing their international flights from Damascus International Airport as most of the Syrian airports suspended their flights to Syria in 2012. You must remember that Syria has four airports, and at this time, Damascus International Airport is the only one handling

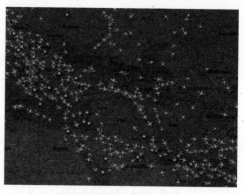

"Chaos Triangle"

international flights. The other three: Latakia, Qameshli, and Aleppo are usually accessible for domestic flights only and no international flights. By the start of 2019, Syria had only two functional airlines flying in and out of Damascus: Syrian Air and Cham Wings Airlines. Syrian Air is the country's flag carrier and obviously the oldest. Syrian Air had a fleet of eight commercial aircraft, six Airbuses and two ATRs. Only one A320–200 and one leased 15-year-old Airbus A340 in service by Syrian Air at the start of 2019. Cham Wings did have four operational A 320's within their fleet. The country also experienced restricted Air Space due to the category and is classified as a "War Zone." If you look at this photo, you can see how clear the airspace over Syria is even today. They even named it "Chaos Triangle" because it's not secure, and it prompted a rigid shift in commercial aviation routes, causing an approximate one-hour long flight to avoid the triangle.

These limited Syrian flights or the drive to Lebanon could be a hair raising experience, but many families and individuals still wanted to fly into Syria to see their relatives. These Syrians were willing to fly inside the chaotic zone just to spend a short time with their loved ones rather than talking to them over the phone or sending text messages.

By late 2018 and early 2019, both Syrian airlines began adding routes, so one could now fly in and out of Damascus International Airport to a few more popular international destinations instead of driving to Lebanon and using their airport. Unfortunately, in early 2019 and currently, the only available foreign airlines were from Iran and Iraq and they are very small airlines that make inconsistent and irregular flights to and from Damascus. So today, we don't have any major international carriers flying into and out of Damascus. This is mainly due to Syria having been classified as a "War Zone." So the list of international destinations is not very extensive. We are forced to use our two Syrian air carriers: Syrian Air and Cham Wings or drive to Beirut and use their overcrowded international airport.

During the seven years of the Syria conflict, the majority of the foreign embassies had closed and still remained closed until the beginning of 2019. In January of 2019, the United Arab Emirates announced the opening of their embassy here in Damascus, and we had all hoped and prayed that would be the start of all the embassies returning. But it is still the only foreign embassy to reopen in 2019; this has been a very slow and laborious task. There were only a handful of embassies that remained open during the entire Syrian Crises. The majority had closed in early to late 2012. The following embassies had remained open: Algerian; Armenian; Chinese; Czech Republic note: this was the only EU embassy to remain open and had an Ambassador during the entire conflict. They also had maintained the US Interests Section operating via the Government of the Czech Republic through its embassy in Damascus; India; Indonesia; Iran; Iraq; Philippines and of course the Russia. The Czech Republic Ambassador and their First Secretary were really a 'godsend' for my wife and me. They had always asked how we were doing and how we were getting along. I shall long remember how helpful and courteous their Ambassador and the two First Secretaries were in Damascus at the Czech Republic Embassy.

The old city of Damascus was saved from almost all of the serious and devastating bombardments and airstrikes. Yet, it had its fair share of rocket and mortar attacks, especially outside the old city walls in the mainly Christian areas of Bab Touma. Many people had lost their lives, but nothing on the scale of the destruction of the old city of Aleppo.

Unfortunately for the old city of Damascus at the initial onset of the hostilities, there were many car and suicide bombings in and near the old city. The government quickly acted and installed many checkpoints within the areas surrounding the old city thus cutting back on these types of destructive attacks. At the height or apex of the resistance fighting in and around the city of Damascus, the opposition had reached extremely close to the old city and was mainly situated within the famous "Ghouta" which is the green agricultural belt that used to surround the entire capital. Over many years, much of this prime green and lush area called the Ghouta, which made Damascus so famous, has been turned into residential and industrial areas. This Ghouta region was a prime area for the resistance and opposition to hide and thus swell in number leading to their constant attacks of mortars and rockets which rained down on virtually every district of Damascus for many of the seven years of hostilities.

In late 2017 and early 2018, the Syrian government, with the help and assistance of the Russian military, had a dedicated military strategy to rid the areas of all hostile powers and opposition groups. Cease Fire Agreements were set in place in which all enemy forces were bused out of the area and were relocated in the Northern Province of Idlib. True peace in and around Damascus was soon realized and things began returning back to 'normal'. I placed normal in quotation marks as nothing can be the same after seven long years of fighting in any country.

My wife's family had a beautiful parcel of land within the Ghouta, and everyone that had visited this farm had called it: '*The Garden of Paradise*'. Before the civil war had started, friends and family would visit this "farm" each weekend to enjoy a traditional Syrian barbecue in a truly tranquil and peaceful atmosphere.

I last saw the 'farm' in late 2012. After the 'liberation' of all the areas around Damascus in 2018 and early 2019, we had sent some people to survey the farm, and what they found was nothing but total and utter devastation and destruction. There were very little living items found at the farm as over one thousand trees were cut; all animals killed or eaten; not one flower remained. The California style house was totally destroyed; there was no longer a green grass area and many of the water fountains were destroyed. To our amazement, the swimming pool was littered with hundreds of empty artillery shell casings.

The family had spent a lot of time restoring their own vintage vehicles that had many family memories attached. The oldest was a 1956 Chevrolet Bel Air four-door sedan, which the family traveled to Bagdad in 1964 and it had tremendous sentimental value, especially for my wife.

The other restored car that had great sentimental value was a 1975 Green Peugeot model 505. This was the last car that my wife's father had driven and was meticulously restored.

This car was simply stolen by someone…nobody ever knew and still today remains a mystery. The final vehicle was an old model Peugeot Tarpaulin Pick-up Truck. That too is missing.

This farm will probably never be repaired as it would be very costly and time-consuming to even try to bring it back to its' original beauty and splendor.

Damascus has really changed since the start of the crises back in 2011. The peace and tranquility that Damascus had always been best known for had quickly evaporated, starting with these horrible actions back in early 2011.

Finally, what I really enjoyed was the simple fact that I had the opportunity to visit many parts of Syria prior to the country's Syrian Crises. I will long remember meeting so many friendly people in so many beautiful Syrian towns and villages.

Chapter Fifteen

My Love of Travel

In the words of Saint Augustine: *"The world is a book and those who do not travel read only one page."* I feel that my life has been full of travel adventures that no other person could understand or image. I trust that you will enjoy my many unique and interesting journeys.

In the words of the late Anthony Bourdain, he summarizes travel in the clearest manner that made more sense to me over my many years of travel: *"Travel isn't always pretty. It isn't always comfortable. Sometimes it hurts; it even breaks your heart. But that's okay. The journey changes you; it should change you. It leaves marks on your memory, on your consciousness, on your heart, and on your body. You take something with you. Hopefully, you leave something good behind."*

Traveling has always been in my blood and has been my main passion since I was a very, young boy.

I believe my love for travel initially started when I first began collecting stamps and First Day Issue Covers. I had joined a philatelic club in my elementary school, and many of the stamps I traded were from foreign countries. The names of these countries would cause my mind to wander and make me dream of these distant and unknown lands. I always had a small international map by my side to locate these foreign and remote nations. Also, my aunt Louise knew that I had a keen interest in stamp collecting so

First Day Issue Cover

she enrolled me to receive the US Post Office: First Day Issue Covers. Several times a month I would welcome these specially designed envelopes, bearing newly issued postage stamps which were postmarked on the first day that those stamps were placed on sale by the Post Office.

Many of these fantastic envelopes had nice drawings of the site or the event on the left side and then, of course, the new stamp on the right side. I had two nice stamp albums; one for domestic stamps and the other for foreign stamps. In addition, my aunt gave me a special folder for my covers. Today, I am still an avid philatelist, as I currently have over forty-five stamp albums.

I began my travels with my mom and dad during our many summer holidays on the New York Central Railroad. My dad worked as a Yard Master on the railroad, and each summer, he would receive free family railroad tickets anywhere along with the extensive New York Central network. This included as far East as Boston and as far west as St Louis. Buffalo was always our departure city. My dad simply loved American Baseball and I fondly remember him checking the summer baseball schedule for all the home games of each city along with the full New York Central Railroad system. He would then plan our travel dates to coincide with his favorite baseball team's home schedule.

The New York Central Main Train Station in Buffalo was a real artistic building and was built in an art deco style in 1929 and was 17 stories tall. This was one of the country's busiest train stations for fifty years and was always the main station we would depart from our many summer vacations.

Each summer we would travel in a different direction…one year we would travel east, and that would include a ride on a very famous and legendary train called: The

Buffalo Central Train Station

"Empire State Express." Our first stop was in Albany so we could change trains to Boston for a Red Sox home game and then down to New York City for any of the Yankees, Giants, or Dodgers home games. My dad especially enjoyed the New York Giants home games as they were playing in the large

The New York Giants –
Polo Grounds

stadium called the Polo Grounds up until 1957. At the end of the 1957 season, both the New York Giants and the Brooklyn Dodgers moved to California.

Then after 1954, we would add Baltimore to see the Orioles play as previously they had been located in St Louis as the St Louis Browns. We had seen them playing in St Louis along with the St. Louis Cardinals in previous years. Finally, we would take in a game or two in Washington DC to see the Nationals/Senators.

In an alternating summer, our trip took us west, and we would use either the famous "Lake Shore Limited" or the "Cleveland Limited" train and our first stop was in Cleveland to see an Indians game. These special trains were New York Central new luxury trains and were a limited express which was a type of express train service that stops at a limited number of cities in comparison to other express services on the same or similar routes. On every flagship train, each had its own special train Drumhead on the end of the last carriage. I found a great collection of the various train drumheads within the National Railroad Museum in Green Bay, Wisconsin.

Then it was onto Detroit to see a Tigers game. The Detroit Tigers were my dad's favorite team in all of American Baseball. If the schedule permitted, we would travel to Chicago to take in either a Cubs or White Sox game, and then finally, we'd take the train down to St. Louis to catch either a Browns or Cardinals game. In 1951, we missed one of the most unusual games in American Baseball only by one day. It seemed the famous owner of the St. Louis Browns, Bill Veeck, played a famous and notorious stunt in St. Louis when on August 19, 1951, he ordered Brown's manager, Zack Taylor, to send Eddie Gaedel, a 3-foot 7-inch, 65-pound midget, to bat as a pinch hitter. When Gaedel stepped to the plate, he was wearing a Browns child's uniform with the number: 1/8. With no strike zone to speak of, Gaedel walked on four straight pitches, as he was ordered not to swing at any pitch. The stunt infuriated American League President at the time: Will Harridge, who voided the midget's contract the next day.

Personally, one of the most embarrassing travel memories I ever had throughout all my summer family travels took place in Chicago when I was nine or ten years old. My parents, in their efforts to save money in our hotel room expenses, had always requested a baby's crib for me to sleep in as the hotel cribs were free and a roll-a-way bed had a certain charge added to our room. That morning I had woken up earlier than my parents and at the room's window was a window cleaner who was staring at me. I guess he was looking at the biggest 'baby' he had ever seen in a crib. I remember trying to hide under the crib's small blanket to no avail. I was totally embarrassed and mortified. When my parents awoke, I told them of my humiliating experience, and they simply said: "Tommy, don't worry...!" How could I not worry? This man was probably telling his coworkers of this entertaining and hilarious sight of a very big boy sleeping in a baby's crib. He and his coworkers must have been laughing the entire day.

In the mid-fifties, we discovered there was a precipitous decline in the domestic train service. It became evident that the train's on-time departures, as well as their extremely late arrival times, were getting worse-and-worse. In addition, the train carriages were in a steadily declining state of disrepair and maintenance. We also had found that our own safety was in jeopardy as many of the original and main city train stations were now in poorer and more rundown sections of the inner city.

Finally, the crime rates were increasing in all these areas. My dad and I also found the same increased crime level when we went to a Buffalo baseball stadium to watch a game. One afternoon while walking to Buffalo Bison Stadium to watch a baseball game, my dad was robbed at knifepoint in broad daylight. I know that was one of the last baseball games we ever attended together.

I had always enjoyed traveling by train with my parents, yet now things were changing and for the worse. The summer of 1955 marked the end of our family's summer train excursions.

At the beginning of summer in 1956, my mom had decided in less than one week that we should drive to California. Impulsive traveling was always my mom's way of life, and this time, she outdid herself.

All-in-all, my mom had organized our two-week trip from Western New York to Southern California and the return two-week journey in less than seven days.

After her surprise announcement, she had completed the following: she purchased a brand new 1956 Buick Special four door hardtop; had persuaded my Uncle Eddie who had one glass eye and his wife Aunt Jenney to join us; convinced my eldest sister to bring their oldest son, my nephew, Dickey, to Orchard Park so he could travel with us on this cross-country road trip and finally, she went to the main office of the AAA (American Automobile Association) to have them

1956 Buick Special

prepare their famous TripTiks Road Maps for our imminent departure. These TripTiks maps were a series of paper maps that indicated the route to follow. The suggested highways were usually marked with a dark green felt-tipped marker pen, to help the driver while confirming his directions. Also, my brother Don was only sixteen years old, and he only had a temporary drivers-permit. Therefore, the only 'real drivers' we had on this trip were my mom and my Uncle Eddie with his glass eye. The six of us then set off for California.

Remember, in 1956, there were no GPS; no online hotel bookings; no internet; no Goggle maps; no computers; no mobile phones and no digital cameras.

To this day, I cherish those memories of that trip.

It is like the great scholar, traveler, and explorer Ibn Battuta once wrote: *"Traveling – it leaves you speechless, then turns you into a storyteller."*

Today, that first trip to California still stands out in my childhood memories as one of the best vacations I have ever enjoyed. I saw for the first time: Mount Rushmore; Las Vegas; Disneyland and the Grand Canyon. These four places were the highlights of my first cross-country car trip.

I grew up in Orchard Park, New York, and all through my young life, I'd been watching cars and large trailer trucks driving along US Highway 20 outside my bedroom window. US 20 originated in Boston and ended in the state of Oregon within a mile of the Pacific Ocean. It is considered: "the longest highway in the US" as it connects New England to the Pacific Northwest and covers over 3,365 miles or approximately 5,415 kilometers.

At the end of our street was Baines Truck Gas Stations directly on US 20 and as a child, it was always a place I would visit on my bicycle. This was the beginning of my: 'Imaginary World of Travel' I would see those large 18 wheelers with a multitude of different state license plates and dream that someday I would visit each state.

After this first cross-country trip, we began exploring and visiting many locations within the States with my mom. My dad was never interested in sitting that long in the car, so the majority of our trips were only my mom and me.

One of the most terrifying and yet unique US trips I had ever made was during the early summer of 1958. At the time, I was only thirteen years old and I was working as a dishwasher at the Orchard Downs, an upscale restaurant in Orchard Park. After the school year was completed, I worked full time at the restaurant. One night the bartender told me that he was driving out west to the Grand Teton National Park in Wyoming within the next few days for a summer job as camp consular. Grand Teton was just south of the more famous Yellowstone National Park. He then said that he needed someone to share the driving as he was planning to drive non-stop to the park. I guess he thought that I was old enough to drive as he asked me if I would like to join him on this journey. Without hesitation, I said yes.

I remember when I got home, I went directly to my parents' bedroom and woke them up and told them that I was planning to go to California in two days. They were both tired and sleepy as they said: "Good Tommy, have a nice trip."

The next day, I asked my mother if I could use her suitcase and she said yes, of course, but why? I reminded her of my planned trip to California. Oh yes, for sure…My parents never believed that I was traveling until the next morning when the bartender drove up to our house to pick me up. They came out to meet this young man and they had the most baffled look. They really did not believe that I would decide to travel in such a hasty and impulsive manner.

We backed out of the driveway, and we waved goodbye. That was when I discovered that his car was a stick-shift transmission. My only practice in driving occurred when I came home after work and late at night. I would take the keys to my mom's car and simply drive the car back and forth on our long driveway. Some weeks later, I gained the courage to back it out onto the street and drive a short distance. Each late-night experience helped me gain knowledge of driving and develop my own confidence. Up until this journey, I'd never driven a stick-shift vehicle.

Once we left, he quickly noticed that I was intently watching him shifting gears. He asked me what was wrong, and I was honest and told him that I had never driven a stick-shift car. No problem he said I will teach you.

I also noticed that he did not have a map, and so I asked him why? He explained that US Highway 20 would take us close to the Grand Teton National Park, so all we needed to do was pay attention and stay on US 20.

US Highway 20 – Sign Board

When he was driving, he asked if I would be the 'navigator' and vice-versa while I was driving. I said of course, as I felt that I was a good navigator. I have always had a solid sense of direction.

He drove for over ten hours, and then he asked me if I could take over so he could rest. It was an open stretch of highway so he pulled over to the side of the road. We switched positions and I immediately stalled the car as I forgot about using the clutch. He was very calm, but I was upset with myself as I could not get the knack of using the clutch. I prayed that once 'we' got the car in fourth or

US Highway 20 – Typical View in Nebraska

top gear that I would not need to slow the car down in order to down-shift. I must admit that he never got any solid sleep while I was driving.

I believed we traveled over 2,000 miles and forty hours of continuous driving. Of course, we stopped for both gas, food, and coffee. We drove through Yellowstone National Park, and then we headed south to the Grand Teton National Park.

Then came that fateful moment…we arrived at the entrance of Grand Teton National Park. He was turning right into the park, and I was about to be deposited in an open area on an unknown American Highway ready to begin hitchhiking my way towards Southern California.

I understand that today it is very dangerous and unsafe to hitchhike in America. At that time in 1958, it was more common to hitchhike, and many people felt sorry for the poor hitchhiker.

I got my first hitch in about an hour, and this driver took me into the state of Utah. From there, it was another ride or two to Las Vegas and then many more rides were necessary to get to Southern California. As I got closer to my sister's home in Santa Ana, we stopped and I was able to call her so she would know that I was getting closer. I finally made it to her front door completely exhausted, dehydrated, and extremely hungry.

I enjoyed Southern California to the utmost for almost a month, and then it was time to return to New York. My sister dropped me off along a new California interstate highway, which was very close to her house. I still recall the feeling of uncertainty as I was not expecting such a strong feeling of remorse and insecurity. This time, my hitchhiking was different as when I left home as I had a ride for over seventy percent of my journey. Now, I was at the starting point of my return and I was hitchhiking all the way. My sister waited until I found my first ride and then I was back on the road again. This time, my return hitchhiking adventure would take me to new highs and phenomenal lows.

Firstly, the weather I encountered along my journey home was very hot, humid, and simply stifling. The route I had selected was along Route 66, and it passed through the states of Arizona, New Mexico, and Texas. This was now the end of July and definitely was not the best time for someone to try to catch a hitch in 100° F weather. I discovered that people were simply not interested in stopping for anyone. Plus, many of my rides had simply dropped me off in the middle of nowhere as they were traveling to some small side road that led to their small hamlet or rural small town. In addition, once I arrived at the Texas border, it seemed like the weather conditions changed from hot to very hot and with severe thunderstorms. What a combination.

Texas is also where I encountered my first pervert. I was picked up in an old Texas licensed pick-up truck, and I tossed my small suitcase in the back. This man immediately appeared to be a true and wholesome degenerate. He kept asking me: "Where are you from?" "Why are you hitchhiking?" "How old are you?" Then he started talking about his daughter at his farm and that she would love to meet me... OK, enough is enough...A short time later, he was slowing down and he appeared to be planning to turn, left so as he was slowing and turning. I quickly opened my door and jumped out, plus I did not forget to grab my suitcase. All I wanted to do is to get out of that place.

I immediately started to thumb-a-ride. Thank goodness, I was very lucky as only a few cars had passed before someone had stopped. This time, it was an older couple and they were driving to the next town which was larger. They dropped me off at a small diner so I had something to eat and time to clear my mind from that incident of the perverted and immoral farmer.

It was now getting dark, and I got another short ride but this time the driver dropped me off in what appeared to be: in the middle of nowhere. What was also very frightening was that on the immediate horizon were big black thunder clouds and I could see severe lightning.

Summer Thunderstorm

I was in for a good old fashion Texas Summer Thunderstorm. Luckily for me, a short distance down the road was a bridge and overpass, so I quickly walked towards it.

I had never witnessed a storm approaching at such a fast speed and with so much intensity. I simply sat on my small suitcase under the viaduct and 'waited-out' this massive Texas thunderstorm. The rain was so intense that many cars simply stopped under my bridge to wait out the deluge. As quick as this cloudburst appeared, it had finished equally fast.

A short time later, another Texan had stopped and asked me how far I was going? I told him New York, and he said in a strong Texas accent: "Great, get in son, as I am going to New York City." What a clear stroke of luck. He was also planning to drive straight through as he was catching a flight to Europe from JFK Airport in two days. This last ride was very interesting as we talked about many subjects and at each gas and food stop, he would take a swig of bourbon from his concealed flask. Finally, while I was sleeping, we were driving in Western Pennsylvanian and he passed the interchange that would have taken me to Buffalo. When I woke up, we were very close to Philadelphia which is in Eastern Pennsylvanian and much further from my destination of Buffalo. He felt very bad, so much so, that he drove to the airport in Philadelphia and purchased a one-way air ticket to Buffalo. For me, it was a grand way to finish my hitchhiking adventure.

As Tim Cahill once wrote: *"A journey is best measured in friends, rather than miles."* I have met a great number of friends during my countless journeys throughout my life, and this Texan was probably my first.

If I were going to include all my unique and interesting American Travels, this chapter would balloon to over a thousand pages.

At one time, many years ago, I had counted that I had traveled over twenty-seven times on one-way cross-country trips in America, and the myriad of these journeys had matchless experiences.

Finally, a few years ago, there was a very funny incident while driving cross-country in America. I was driving from Green Bay Wisconsin to Minneapolis, Minnesota and the motorway went from a four-lane divided highway suddenly into a two-lane road. The speed limit went from seventy miles per hour to fifty miles per hour in a very short distance. Before I could substantially slow down, there was a police car approaching me from the other side of this small road. I didn't realize that nowadays, police cars have their radar active for all oncoming vehicles. I checked my rear-view mirror and yes, indeed, the police car made an abrupt U-turn and was fast approaching with his lights glaring and siren blaring. I immediately pulled over and the officer approached my rent-a-car and asked me, "How fast do you think you were traveling?" I told him I did not know as I was not paying attention to my speed as I was just on the interstate. He said: "He clocked me at seventy-seven miles an hour." "Please, could I have your driver's license and car registration?" The registration was in the name of the rent-a-car company and my only valid license was from the State of Qatar. He took both and then a few minutes later came back and said that he was only going to issue me a warning. I thanked him and took the warning. He then asked: "Sir, I have only one question. Which state in America is: Qatar?" Oh boy...I had a real winner, and this was a true story!

Domestic travel in America has always been a true pleasure, and on each and every trip there, I have had many memorable experiences. I have visited all fifty states and it is very difficult to judge my favorite as each state has its own splendor and uniqueness. As Matthew Karsten once wrote: *"The truth is every place in the world has something of interest."*

Through the years, I found out that if you talk to the majority of Americans about 'international travel' they would mention their trips to either Mexico or Canada. To me, international travel is exactly what it implies: 'worldwide travel' or 'global travel'. International travel is what I profoundly and intensely love.

From my first trip to Europe back in 1967 to my last trip to Ajman, in the United Arab Emirates only a few months ago, I passionately enjoyed traveling. This Christmas and New Year's 2019, and I was in Southern California.

A couple of years ago, I counted the number of countries that I have visited, and it surprised me that this number exceeded one hundred countries. The number of countries was fairly easy to calculate as the world is supposed to have only: 195 countries and that is as of 2019.

Now one small dilemma occurred as I was compiling my list of countries. I had visited all the regions and provinces of Yugoslavia in 1973, and at that time, it was simply one country under the leadership of Marshal Tito. Today, the area of Yugoslavia has been split into seven different countries. These are: Serbia, Croatia, Bosnia & Herzegovina, Macedonia, Slovenia, Kosovo, and Montenegro. Do I count these seven as one (Yugoslavia) or seven?

Finally, in concluding this chapter, I wanted to mention the number of 'continents' that I had visited in my lifetime. This subject simply opened a vast trove of questions. Just how many continents are there? Which continents were included?

In the US, we are taught that there are seven continents, Asia, Africa, North America, South America, Antarctica, Europe, and Australia/ Oceania.

Yet, if you look at the Olympic Flag, it has five rings for the following five continents and they are Africa, the Americas, Oceania, Asia, and Europe.

I guess the Olympic Committee never had included Antarctica as it is uninhabited and irrelevant

The Olympic Flag

to the Olympics. I also found the practice of dividing the Americas into two continents is not universal and is definitely not relevant to the Olympic flag.

To add a new perspective, I have met several well-traveled individuals who say there are only five continents. As they combine: North and South America into the "Americas" and they even go as far as combining Europe and Asia into: "Eurasia."

So what I finally concluded concerning the number of continents is that it all came down to how a person defines 'continent'. According to the Oxford English Dictionary, the first time the word 'continent' was used in print, in 1559, it was thus: "Continent is a portion of the Earth, which is not parted by the seas asunder." This Oxford definition in itself brings up a new set of questions.

Is the Middle East part of the continent of Asia, Europe, or Eurasia? Like "orient", the terms "near east", "middle east" and "far east" are descriptive terms and official definitions probably don't exist. Again, according to the Oxford English Dictionary: 'Near East' is said to be: "A region comprising the countries of the eastern Mediterranean, sometimes also including those of the Balkan peninsula, south-west Asia, or North Africa. With the 'Middle East States' lying between the Near and Far East, especially between: Egypt and Iran and the countries between them."

Then the: "Far East" would be: "The extreme eastern regions of the Old World, especially including China and Japan."

On a final subject, some people tend to agree that 'North America' collectively refers to Greenland, Canada, the US, Mexico, and Central America. Their line stops in Colombia. Is Hawaii considered part of Oceania, a group of islands in the South Pacific or North America?

In conclusion, I feel that what I was taught in school in America was that there are seven continents. I have visited four of the seven. With Australia/Oceania, South America, and Antarctica being the only three I have not visited.

Finally, I have often been asked which cities and countries are my favorites and that I would love to revisit? The answer is best defined by region or continent.

Please note, I have left out any Middle Eastern country and city as I have visited each country and the majority of cities of the Middle East on multiple occasions. It would not be fair to try and compare Syria and Damascus to any city or country in Asia. As hands down, these two would rank number one not only in Asia but in the world.

In Asia, I would say that the Maldives would be my top country as it has the most relaxing and beautiful beach resorts in the world. The seawater is crystal clear that you'd think it is artificial. The city would be Bandar Seri Begawan, this tiny yet flashy capital of the Sultanate of Brunei, is on the island of Borneo and has many elegant mosques; striking Islamic architecture; a great five-star resort property and the home of the infamous Proboscis Monkey.

In Europe, the country would be Spain as it is so diverse; it has great food and contains some of Europe's greatest tourist sites. The European city is Prague and is my favorite because it has one of Europe's best historic centers; it is a great 'walking capital' and the city is extremely picturesque. I will be there in May and June of 2020, enjoying the renowned Prague Music Festival as I have already booked my flight and have my hotel reserved.

In Africa, the country is South Africa. I have been to South Africa three times and would return in a heartbeat. This country simply has so much to see and do that you cannot get the true taste in merely a few visits. I simply adore the wildlife, the Garden Route to include both Plettenburg Bay and Knysna and the majestic seascapes. The city would be Cape Town for its great wineries in the Stellenbosch area, Table Mountain, the Victoria & Albert Waterfront to all the great seafood restaurants.

Finally, in North America, the top country is Costa Rica, as I feel it is one of the safest countries in the world and has no standing army; I simply love the visits to its many rain forests, and the country has boundless plants and animal biodiversity. My top city, without a doubt, is San Francisco, as it has access to the greatest California Wineries. I still love to catch a ride on their cable cars. For great food, I always enjoy the famous Fisherman's Wharf.

I am not sure you saw similar comparisons of my two most favorite cities? To me, both Cape Town and San Francisco are 'sister cities' as they have so much in common.

I feel that there are two sayings that truly sum up my vast experience in traveling throughout the world.

The first is: *"I am not the same, having seen the moon shine on the other side of the world."* Written by: Mary Anne Radmacher

And the second is by one of my favorite authors John Steinbeck as he wrote: *"People don't take trips, trips take people."*

I have gained insurmountable pleasure, and copiousness by simply doing what I enjoy most...traveling the world!

Chapter Sixteen

"My Bucket's List"

I have been developing my own "Bucket List" ever since I saw the movie starring Jack Nicholson and Morgan Freeman in 2007. The movie was actually a comedy/drama and was about Billionaire Edward Cole (Jack Nicholson), who is the owner of a hospital and car mechanic Carter Chambers (Morgan Freeman). They are complete strangers until chance lands them in the same hospital room.

Movie the Bucket List

Jack Nicholson can't believe that in his own hospital, the administration had placed him in a semiprivate room and he was sharing it with Morgan Freeman. The men find they have two things in common: a need to come to terms with who they are and what they have done with their lives and a desire to complete a list of things they want to see and experience before they die. Actually, Morgan Freeman explains the concept of making his Bucket List as he had many places he wanted to see before he "kicks the bucket." Against their doctor's advice, the men leave the hospital and set out on the journey of a lifetime.

They travel in style as Jack Nicholson is very wealthy and owns an executive private jet. So the movie shows them crossing off places and experiences that they had just accomplished.

In the past, prior to seeing the movie, I had always made a list of destinations and countries that I had continually dreamed and imagined to visit, but at my start, I was calling that list my: "Dream List." Soon after enjoying this movie, I changed my title to "Bucket List." Actually,

I had so many places and things to do on my Dream List that I finally made two lists: the first is my Bucket List of Cities and Countries, and the second is my Bucket List of Experiences, specific things to see. Of course, both lists comprised of things I must see and do prior to my own death.

As the famous author, Sandra Lake once wrote: *"With age, comes wisdom. With travel, comes understanding."* This maxim is so true especially when one is creating your own bucket's lists as with travel, I truly believe I will come to an understanding as Sandra Lake states.

I have just discovered, in one of my old hanging files in my office, a very 'special list' of things to: "See in America." This very old list had started many years ago. So many odd places that in fact, today, I have no clue about the reasons why I had placed so many locations on this "See in American List." This list contains a total of 51 places for me to see. Just now, I have crossed off the ones that I had visited. So now, this list contains only 22 remaining places and locations. That list now includes such places as The Grand Old Opry in Nashville to the Volcanoes National Park in Hawaii. Today, I have no idea or reasons for placing The Grand Old Opry on this old list, because I have never enjoyed and still do not enjoy Country Music. Another strange attraction was the Iowa State Fair. Why that was on my original list, I might never know!

It was ironic as the last city that I had crossed off my current Bucket List of Cities and Countries was Salalah, in Oman, as I visited that beautiful area to celebrate my seventy-second birthday in September of 2017. I actually stayed forty kilometers East of Salalah as the city of Salalah had nothing special to see and do except to utilize the airport for my arrival and departure. The small city I stayed in was called: Mirbat and was a very famous and legendary city. Plus, it was very close to the tropical forest which makes this area so unique and famous. I stayed at the Mirbat Marriott Resort which was extremely remote and directly on the Indian Ocean. I had informed the Marriott Management Team, prior to my arrival, that I required a nice quiet room as I was planning to start a good deal of writing on this third book. They really went out of their way to accommodate my needs as I was booked in the enormous Presidential Suite which had two large balconies both facing the Indian Ocean; a good size work desk and a very comfortable chair. In addition, they soon realized I enjoyed a massive amount of green tea on an hourly basis so the housekeeping department had placed a great assortment of various green and specialized tea bags in my suite. This suite was very, very conducive to writing. I began my stay with less than ten pages completed in the entire book and when I left, I had completed over forty pages of the main manuscript. More importantly, though, I had completely reorganized all my chapter titles. That one single task took a great deal of time and effort and I have stayed on message ever since those few days on the Indian Ocean.

Also, the beach area in front of the resort was quite extensive, thus making it great for long relaxing walks. Several days I took the afternoon off to visit both the old city of Mirbat and more importantly, the famous tropical rain forest. This area, I discovered, is the only area in the Arabian Peninsula to host a tropical rain forest. This was due to its unique topography. The Indian Ocean, along this portion of the Omani Coast Line, hosts a strong monsoon season. It also has a very high mountain range just a few kilometers inland from the seacoast. So when the torrential monsoon rains begin, the majority of the downpours all hit these high mountains thus making the entire mountainside green and lush.

My visit to Mirbat was just after the monsoon season had ended, so the entire area was a very beautiful and picturesque tropical forest. There were lakes with small paddle pleasure boats; many picnic areas; restaurants; many tropical birds

The Empty Quarter

and everything in the entire locale was green. The other amazing finding is that on the rear side of these tall Omani Mountains is the start of the famous: Empty Quarter of the Arabian Peninsula. The region is almost empty of human beings due to the extreme heat, scarcity of rain, lack of both vegetation and water, hence, in Arabic, it is called: 'Ar Rub al Khali' which means the 'Empty Quarter'. It is also known as the 'Great Sandy Desert'. This desert area also accounts for over a quarter of the total landmass of Saudi Arabia and is among the largest continuous deserts in the world.

I have always enjoyed the saying from Gustave Flaubert, the French novelist: *"Travel makes one modest. You see what a tiny place you occupy in the world."*

I discovered that the old city of Mirbat was very famous because in 1970, the SAS (Special Air Service) was called in to defeat a large group of communist-backed rebels that were threatening the pro-Western Sultan and Western oil supplies from Oman. Their other tasks were to bolster the Sultan's army, save Dhofar and the Straits of Hormuz and keep the Omani Oil flowing. Then in 1972, a small regiment of only eight SAS soldiers and a handful of Omani and Arab fighters had decisively defeated over 200+ communist rebels at the Battle of Mirbat thus beginning the end of the long rebellion. The fighting mainly took place around the old Mirbat Castle and it was said the rebels thought they would win an easy victory as the SAS were armed with just their personal weapons, one mortar, a Browning machine gun and a single Second World War 25-pounder gun. The insuring battle raged on for hours and finally, the call for help from the SAS resulted in several Strikemasters aircraft arriving on multiple strafing runs. The communist rebels finally fled leaving behind many of their dead and wounded. It was later indicated that half the communist force was killed or wounded. The final toll was two SAS, six Arab soldiers and an Omani gunner dead, plus one Arab wounded. As this was a very covert British action in Oman, this battle was never spoken of or reported in any UK

Newspapers. In total, the SAS had lost twelve men during the entire six-year Omani War. The war finally ended in 1976.

So my stay at the Mirbat Marriott Resort was very rewarding and really gratifying, and I had intentions of returning, but unfortunately, in October 2018, I had read that the Marriott had dropped their management contract for this property. I was also planning to have our next "Webber Family Reunion" at this great Marriott property.

On my original "Dream List", I was very actively crossing off countries and sights such as South Africa; Victory Falls in Zambia; Hawaii; Japan; Hong Kong; Singapore; Philippines; The Napa Valley Wine Train; etc.

On my new and current Bucket Lists, in addition to Salalah, I have already crossed off: Borneo, Brunei, India, Sri Lanka, Maldives, Armenia, Georgia, Agadir, etc. I am a very active Bucket List follower and wish to see all the countries on my current list prior to my own time to "Kick the Bucket."

On my Bucket List of: "Countries and Cities to See" it seems to be very straight forward as I have had these ten countries on my list for quite a long time.

The first country, #1, I have listed is really not a country at all but an island state of Tanzania called Zanzibar. It is actually an archipelago of islands and Zanzibar is the largest island within the archipelago and lies within the Indian Ocean. I have always been fascinated by simply the name: Zanzibar. It has always stirred my imagination and my strong desire to visit this famous island. Some years ago, I had taken our family on an African safari and we included both Kenya and Tanzania, but unfortunately, Zanzibar was too far from our planned safari itinerary. Also, in Jeddah, there was a Kenyan pilot who worked for Saudia Airlines who had a bar in his apartment called: 'The Zanzibar'. He had visited Zanzibar many times and had told me many magical and stimulating stories of his own travels to Zanzibar.

On the island of Zanzibar, I want to see the old city called Stone City and enjoy the pristine beaches all along the sandy coastline. In addition, many kinds of spices such as Cinnamon, Cloves, and Nutmeg are grown on the many Spice Plantations of the island. You can also see many different and endemic species of rare Monkeys and even some giant Tortoises. Unfortunately, Zanzibar has still eluded my visit.

Country number #2 and #3 are very straight forward and have been on my Country List for many years, and they are Russia and China. In Russia, I would love to visit the following cities: St. Petersburg and Moscow. In St. Petersburg I would visit the world-famous Hermitage Museum as I have heard so much about this treasure chest of art and culture. It is also the second-largest art museum in the world and includes the largest collection of paintings in the world. The collections occupy a large complex of six historic buildings along the Palace Embankment, including the Winter Palace, a former residence of Russian emperors. My first visit to Russia must take place either in the spring or summer as I know I cannot handle the cold weather of the Russian Winters.

China, I had visited many years ago, but only on a short day tour from Hong Kong to the mainland. To me, that is not considered: "seeing China" in my humble opinion. I have always been fascinated by the sheer magnitude of the 'differences' of China to any other country. My interest was accelerated after I had completed reading Gavin Menzies's book titled: *1421 – The Year China Discovered America.*

This was one of the few books I simply could not put down as I completed it in record time. The book first describes China during the Ming Dynasty, and the first chapter described China up to the year 1421 when four great flotillas or armada's sailed from Beijing to all corners of the world, including North America. The book also describes in great detail the voyages of these four massive fleets. I must see China prove that the story of this book was true within China. Let me mention one very strange experience that took place while I was reading this book: *1421*, I was vacationing in Napa Valley California during the time I was reading this interesting book. After a full day in Napa Valley, starting with an early morning hot air balloon ride and then several wine vineyards tasting room visits, I retired to my Napa Valley Marriott Hotel. I had decided to have a simple dinner of soup and salad in the bar/lounge. I ordered a Caesar Salad and as I usually ask the waiter: "What country was Caesar Salad originated in?" He did not know so I then asked him to ask the chef. He came back a few minutes later and said that the chief claimed the country was Mexico! I said, "Correct", and I asked what nationality the chef was, and he replied Mexican. I asked if I could speak to him as 99 out of 100 chefs do not know the answer to my questions as to the origins of Caesar Salad. A few minutes later, the chef comes to the bar and introduces himself and I saw standing in front of me a Chinese looking person. I apologized and said that I was sorry and that the waiter said he was from Mexico. He replied: "Yes, sir, I am from Mexico. But you look like you are from China or Asia? I was born in Mexico as were my parents; grandparents and great grandparents." I asked him exactly where in Mexico he was from and I presented a cocktail napkin and had him draw a map of Mexico. He drew a map. I still have the same cocktail napkin today, and it was exactly like the map in the book where the Chinese had deposited a group of settlers 600 years prior. I asked him further if others in his village had slanted eyes and he said yes sir. One last question I asked: do you know of the famous green and black Chinese Lacquered Boxes? And he said again, "Yes sir, they are made in my village today!" Now was this simply a strange coincidence or was this book: *1421 – The Year China Discovered America* actually full of true facts? After this extremely bizarre and weird episode in Napa Valley, I truly believe in the power of divine chance or fate! China, I can't wait to visit you!

The next country on my Bucket List of: "Countries to See", #4 would actually be the island group called: French Polynesia in the Pacific and is actually an: "Overseas Country" and is under the full financially assistance of the French authority. There are many islands and atolls within this vast island group, but the four that I would like to see and visit are the following:

Firstly, Bora Bora, this has always been on my Bucket List, but you never want to travel so far only to see one island, so that was the main reason for including the full island group called French Polynesia and only three of the seven main islands.

Bora Bora still ranks number one for me to visit in French Polynesia as it has very beautiful blue and turquoise water; great resorts that many have luxury bungalows 'over the water' and a lot to see within the water. I had moved Bora Bora up to my number #4 place on my list mainly because of the hotel bungalows in the water, as we had the same luxury accommodations in the Maldives, and I still remember how great they were even today. Today, I also enjoy snorkeling and Bora Bora appears to be the best place to truly enjoy that aquatic sport. The island is surrounded by a lagoon and a barrier reef and in the center of the island are the remnants of an extinct volcano rising to two peaks. What more reason does one need? One of the other motives I had placed Bora Bora on my list is because of its name. To me, Bora Bora is very exotic and mysterious creating a very unique and enigmatic environment. It is also known as the "Pearl of the Pacific" as well as the "Most Beautiful Place on Earth" by others and that in itself has maintained my keen interest in seeing Bora Bora.

Now, if one starts with the island of Bora Bora, you should next include and visit the island of Tahiti. Again, the name Tahiti is so legendary; tropical and remote. Actually, Tahiti would be your best and the only island to land in from abroad as it is the largest and the airport has the most international air connections in all of French Polynesia. Then you would simply connect on a flight to Bora Bora and the other islands from Tahiti. I feel that Tahiti is far more touristic than the other two islands as it has the largest population, the only major international airport and the largest assortment of resorts to select.

Now my third island within French Polynesian is extraordinary, and it would be Rangiroa. Mainly because it is widely known as the second-largest atoll in the world and is over 80 km in length and a width ranging from 5 to 32 km.

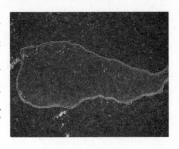

Rangiroa Atoll – French Polynesia

Once again, my holiday in the Maldives made me a true lover of atolls. There are other reasons such as I have heard there are numerous vineyards, which are unique in the world, all located on the edge of the lagoon and produce not one harvest, but two harvests per year. The main winery is in the heart of the small village of Avatoru. All the grapes are brought to the winery by boat, so I can't wait to visit this Polynesian Winery. The other reason is the famous 'Blue Lagoon,' which is a smaller lagoon formed on the southwestern edge of Rangiroa. Its shallow waters heighten and accentuate the bright blue color of the water. Also, there are the local Pink Sands making up the many sandbars around the Blue Lagoon. What more reasons does one need to discover these three islands of French Polynesia?

Tarsier

Now, my number #5 country on my Bucket List is another island: Madagascar. Being a Zoology major at university, I really developed a love for two different mammals one is the Tarsier, and the other is the Lemur.

Several years ago, I saw while visiting Bohol, a Tarsier in the wild while traveling in the Philippines:

The other mammal is the famous Lemur. The species of Lemur that I really like is the Ring-Tailed Lemur and again is only found on the island... Madagascar.

Ring-Tailed Lemur

Where in the world is the best place to see the Lemur in the wild more than Madagascar? As all of the lemurs are endemic to the island, which means, they can only be found in Madagascar and nowhere else on earth. Also, their descendants underwent dwarfing and evolved into species that are unique to Madagascar.

Also, I would love to see Madagascar as it is the fourth largest island in the world. I want to see it's beautiful and unique landscapes, distinctive nature with certain species of trees that can only be found on the island of Madagascar.

My next country, number #6 on my Bucket List is Nepal and Nepal has been on my Country List the longest of all. I have always been intrigued by the fact that Nepal contains Mount Everest, the world's highest mountain and many more of the top ten world's tallest mountains. Mind you, I am not a trekker yet I have placed Nepal on my list because of the following: Nepal contains a nice mix of both Buddhist and Hindu temples and I have always enjoyed visiting and seeing the architecture of these special religious temples. Next, it would be for Sightseeing, as Nepal has some of the greatest views of nature than almost any other country. Next, the fresh air would be a pleasure. Finally, I would like to visit the capital Kathmandu because back in 1978, I had a potential teaching position available there, but I had chosen Iran instead. From what I have been reading since the devastating earthquake in 2015, Kathmandu has rebuilt many of its temples and its infrastructure. Yet, when a country experiences over 9,000 deaths, it does take some time to totally recover. Nerveless, Nepal remains number #6 on my Countries' Bucket List.

My next country on my list #7 is actually three adjoining countries in East Asia. They are Vietnam, Laos, and Cambodia. I see no advantage to visit only one of these three countries in East Asia list on my Country Bucket List as a combined number #7, as once you have traveled that far it would be best to concentrate one visit in all three countries.

Of the three, Vietnam would be my first country to visit of the trio. While I was attending dental school from 1966 to 1968, I was enlisted in the US Navy and was commissioned as an Ensign JG officer. When I decided to leave dental school in 1968, I had already served as a junior officer for over two years and when I dropped out of dental school, my expectations were great that I would be enlisted full time in our US Navy. Remember this was the height of the Vietnam War so I felt that I would be going to 'fight for my country' in Vietnam within weeks or maximum months. My first wife and I kept expecting my deployment letter from the Navy and then that day finally arrived as I received a certified letter from the Navy. I remember after the postman had delivered the letter, I collected it and then decided to wait and enjoy a few hours of 'freedom' from the impending news contained within. I finally opened the envelope and read out loud the news to my wife and baby Thomas…The letter stated: "You have been honorably discharged from the US Navy…" Wow…what great news…no Vietnam for Mr. Thomas L Webber.

Well to this day, I still want to visit Vietnam and, of course, I know that it has changed dramatically since the late sixties and that massive war.

I had heard and read about Vietnam's famous China Beach made prominent as a US Military R&R location. I would love to visit China Beach today. Also, a must-see location is the beautiful Hoang Beach and Caves. It appears on every tourist page this very stunning area of Vietnam. I still remember the many photographs of those magnificent rocks rising from the blue turquoise waters of Hoang Beach.

Also, my trip to Vietnam would include the following two cities. First, the old capital of South Vietnam then called: Saigon and now called: Ho Chi Minh City. They are worth visiting as there are still colonial structures and traditional Vietnam buildings to discover among the tall and new skyscrapers. I want to see the famous second city in Vietnam called: Hanoi. The primary site I would like to see in this large city would be the famous 'Hanoi Hilton' an old prison used originally by the French colonists in French Indochina and then used during the Vietnam War to house our POWs.

In addition, a visit to Vietnam would not be complete without a tour of the countryside as it must be very active with agriculture and farming and I feel it would offer some real "Kodak Moments."

After my visit to Vietnam, I will plan to visit both Cambodia and Laos, wherein you find much less overall devastation from the Vietnam War some fifty plus years ago. In both of these countries, I would visit the many Buddhist temples and shrines. I would love to visit the most famous temple complex in Cambodia called Angkor Wat Archeological Park. I do believe it is now a World Heritage Site by the UNESCO.

The main site I would love to see in Laos is actually an entire village called: Luang Prabang. The entire city has been a UNESCO World Heritage Site since the mid-1990s. It is made up of over thirty Buddhist temples, and shrines and all are in the traditional Laotian style and architecture. It appears to be a 'must-see' historical site.

The next country on my list is number #8 and is also in Asia, but quite far removed from all major cities. It would be Mongolia and especially the capital Ulaanbaatar. Mongolia was added to my list only seven to eight years ago as I had met the Mongolia Ambassador at Large for Egypt and the Levant on a business trip to Jordan. My brother-in-law, who lives in Amman Jordan, is the "Honorary Mongolian Ambassador" for Jordan, and me had met the ambassador several times while the ambassador was visiting Amman. He had enlightened me about the sheer beauty of his country and that in effect was the main reason I had recently added Mongolia to my Countries Bucket List.

I had seen many pictures of the unique and unusual Mongolia 'tent houses' or as they are called: 'ger' by the Mongolians. You even see them now in the capital city, so instead of seeing tall apartment buildings, the families are still living in these unusual round tent houses.

Mongolian Tents or Ger

The history of Mongolia is diverse as it was 'founded' by Genghis Khan around 1,200 and was visited by Marco Polo some years later. I really want to visit the north and west, as the Ambassador claims it is as beautiful as Switzerland as there are numerous mountains and rivers to discover. I know I will visit Mongolia in the summer months as during the winter, the temperatures can reach $- 50^0$ C.

Following Mongolia, I would have to place Tasmania as the ninth 'country' to visit on my Bucket List of Cities and Countries. While Tasmania is officially not a country, but simply an "Island State of Australia", I have always placed Tasmania on this Bucket List as it doesn't fit on my second Bucket List of Experiences.

So why did I place Tasmania on my list? Well, I have two different reasons: firstly, it is because of one animal called the Tasmanian devil. While studying Zoology in college, I have always been intrigued by a special class of mammals called Marsupials or officially called: Marsupialia. This small and unusual infraclass of mammals includes kangaroos, wallabies, koalas, opossums, wombats, and the Tasmanian devils. Today, the only place one can see the Tasmanian devil in the wild is in Tasmania. Unfortunately, it has become extinct many years ago on the mainland of Australia. And since the late 1990s, the devil facial tumor disease (DFTD) has drastically reduced the devil population on the island and now threatens the survival of the entire species. The Tasmanian devil has been placed on the endangered list in 2008, so maybe in the very near future, they too will become extinct on the entire island of Tasmania.

The Tasmanian devil is the size of a small dog and has become the largest carnivorous marsupial in the world since the extinction of the Tasmanian tiger or called a thylacine back in 1933 again on the mainland of Australia. It will not attack humans and usually avoids conflicts thus, its name may be an error or inaccuracy. This mistakenness or erroneousness was enhanced by

Taz

the movie comic called Looney Tunes as they introduced 'Taz' as a vicious and nasty Tasmanian devil in their cartoon series.

The second reason I want to visit Tasmania is that I was told a lot about this country by a close Syrian friend while we were living in Jeddah. He had a house and family living there and told me of the many interesting things to do, see, and eat while visiting the capital Hobart.

He knew I did not eat meat, so he told me about the fresh and delicious seafood available throughout the island such as Oysters, Salmon, and Crayfish. He mentioned that there were many restaurants from simply a takeaway to some great five-star restaurants available.

He also knew that I was very much into sailing, and he reminded me of the famous and annual Rolex Sydney to Hobart Yacht Race, which is one of the most difficult yacht races in the world. It starts on Boxer Day, which is December 26th, in Sydney. I have been keeping up with the results of this race for many years so to see it live would be 'mind-boggling'. This famous race started in 1945 and the winning yacht took over 6 days and 14 hours to complete the race. Now with the newest and fastest Maxi boats, it takes only 1 day and 9 hours for the fastest line-to-line honors. These new Maxi yachts are all 100 feet or 30.5 meters in length and they all reach an astonishing speed during the race.

He also said there was something called "The Taste of Tasmania" which follows that famous race again in Hobart at the famous Battery Point. It initially started simply as a place that the various crews that had completed this grueling yacht race could find something to eat and discover the culinary expertise of Tasmanian Food. Today, it has been expanded from the original 22 stands to over 100 in 2018. I have already checked and found that there will be a new Marriott Luxury Collection Hotel opening in December 2019, and since I have been a Platinum Rewards Member now called Titanium Rewards Member of the new Bonvoy Rewards program, my stay will cost a nominal amount as I have accumulated many, many points with Marriott!

Now, my final country on my Bucket List of Cities and Countries is Cuba. I have included Cuba on my list because for so many decades, it was inaccessible to Americans and then there was a relaxing of tensions under the Obama Administration, but now we may have increased the difficulty of visiting Cuba under the current administration in Washington.

Anyway, I will see Cuba before I 'kick the bucket' and one of the first sights to see after the many sights of Havana would be to take the Hersey Train to Hersey Town. I saw a documentary on Hersey Town many years ago, and I was very impressed with the original concept and the visionary and creative spirit of Melton Hersey. Now I understand it is being refurbished and the Hersey Train is still running daily all the way to Matanzas.

I just read about a very historic, strong cultural and a very nature-loving city called: Trinidad, Cuba. This must be seen as I love a city that combines the above as well as has some of the most pristine beaches in all of Cuba.

The other major reason to visit Cuba is to see the house of Ernest Hemingway in Havana, which is called Finca Vigía. I have been a lover of his works and also the places he lived and drank for the past forty-plus years.

This fascination began in December 1971, while I was touring Europe and living in Madrid. It was a small pension on Calle del Príncipal just a few meters off of the Plaza de Santa Ana, and I used to frequent an old tapas/bar called Cerveceria Alemana. I soon discovered that this bar was the favorite bar of none other than Ernest Hemingway. There were many old black & white photos

Cerveceria Alemana

of him enjoying his favorite drink and food with many famous people. In all the photos, he always appeared to be surrounded by many people and he was always smiling. The sheer ambiance of this famous bar made each visit extremely enjoyable for me.

The next favorite bar of Ernest Hemingway that I had visited is called Harry's Bar near the famous Gritti Palace Hotel in Venice. My wife and I were staying at the other Luxury Collection Hotel of Sheraton called the Hotel Danieli and I wanted to visit The Gritti Palace Hotel to compare the two hotels so we walked along the canal to the hotel. After our visit and dinner at the Gritti Palace, we took a slow walk back to our hotel and we stumbled on the famous Harry's Bar. Again, one gets a sense of esteem while enjoying a drink knowing that many years earlier, Ernest Hemingway was enjoying his favorite drink at the same bar.

My next encounter with an Ernest Hemingway property was on my solo trip to Key West in June 2010. I visited the beautiful Hemingway Home and Museum and really enjoyed that particular visit.

So now one knows my intention of visiting Havana. Simply to experience one additional Ernest Hemingway hide-a-way on the beautiful island of Cuba.

Finally, the above ten countries are all that I have listed and enclosed on my first list and which is titled: 'My Bucket List of Cities and Countries'.

The second and final List that I have compiled is called: 'My Bucket List of Places to See and Experiences', and this list contains ten specific things; places and areas to see and experience.

This Bucket List was forever changing, but now I have kept the ten up-to-date with all selections remaining intact.

My number #1 and the top experience for me to view and experience has remained the same for many years, and it is for me to see and view

The Northern Lights – Aurora Borealis

the Northern Lights or also called the Aurora Borealis. I have always dreamed about viewing the Northern Lights first hand and this was enhanced by loving them for many years. All I need to do now is to simply close my eyes and I see the Aurora Borealis quite vividly.

But by having the Northern Lights on my Bucket List and it being number one, simply seeing them in my 'mind's eye' just doesn't cut it and does not justify me completing this wish to see them first hand. In my research, I found that one must find a location north of the Arctic Circle, and that is easily accessible to travel to. I reduced my search to number one: Norway and number two, the small towns and villages on the Lofoten Islands or any of the surrounding islands in the area. In addition to the Lofoten Islands, the following three small towns would be a solid choice to select in order to really see the Northern Lights in the clearest skies and least populated areas. I would first stay in a Norwegian town called: Alta as it is known as "The Town of the Northern Lights" as well as boasting having the first Northern Lights Observatory. Next, I would select: Tromsø as it is known as: "The Capitan of the Arctic" and offers such adventures as dog sledding, reindeer sledding, camping, all under the Northern Lights. And finally, I would choose Bodø, as it has a domestic/international airport and the flights only take 90 minutes directly from Oslo. Bodø Airport was also famous for the stationing of the Lockheed Martin U-2 spy aircraft in 1958. On 1 May 1960, a U-2 piloted by Gary Powers was headed to Bodø from Pakistan but was shot down over Russia, causing the U-2 Crisis of 1960.

Number #2 on this special list is titled: International Train Rides. This broad title includes the following three special and unique train routes. Firstly, the "Orient Express" followed by the Trans-Canadian Railroad and finishing with a ride on the Trans-Siberian Railroad. These three international railroads have been on my list since the inception of this Bucket List. The reason why these are listed number two on my list is that from my early childhood through my early teens, international train travel has been paramount in my dreams and desires.

The Orient Express has really held top billing as long as I remember as it was the world's most famous and luxurious long-distance international train ride and one of the oldest and the most glamorous of all. Today there is no 'original' Orient Express, but a private company that uses the original cars

Orient Express

from the 1920s and 1930s on all their routes. I plan to take their *Orient Express* from London to Venice as soon as I can.

The next special and unique train route was called the Trans-Canadian Railroad and now is called "the Canadian." I would take this train from Toronto to Vancouver as the travel time is only: four nights and three days. It only stops in four cities along the way. They do offer a very special first-class service called 'Prestige Class' and it appears to be extremely luxurious and maybe even better than the original Orient Express. With this Prestige Class, your stateroom has a double 'Murphy Bed', a private shower with full washroom, plus a full window and in-cabin flat-screen monitor with video selection, etc. The stateroom transforms into a great 'day room' with a large L shaped sofa that faces the enormous window to view the majestic Canadian scenery from Toronto to Vancouver. Included in the ticket price of this Prestige Class of travel is your full all-inclusive program which includes: three meals per day which are all: included with priority reservations in the dining car and a Pre-dining appetizer service with an all-inclusive beverages; snacks; unlimited drinks both alcoholic and non-alcoholic; your own personal Concierge, turndown service and enhanced amenities; access to a Complementary coffee, tea, fruit and cookies in the lounge car; access to the Skyline car; access and reserved seating in the Panorama car; a reserved seating in the Park and Dome cars.

You can clearly see that this Prestige Class Service is very much like staying at any top five-star international hotel on wheels while traveling across the most beautiful Canadian landscape.

This special train route has always impressed me from a teenager because of the very beautiful scenery you see from the train. It is supposed to be simply 'breathtaking' and now, after learning about this special first-class service, my desire to travel on this special train has increased dramatically. The final international train ride that I must take is the Trans-Siberian Railroad as from the original movie called Doctor Zhivago back in 1965; I have always had a deep desire to travel on this specific Russian railroad. I am not even sure there were scenes in the movie using the Trans-Siberian Railroad, but I know there were train scenes with very cold and wintery conditions outside the compartments.

Let me regress, while starting this particular chapter, I felt it would be one of the easiest chapters to finish and to complete in record time. I found out the exact opposite while enjoying the writing and completing this chapter, I found that I spent enormous time researching each country, city, sight, and experience prior to starting my writing. In addition, I was spending a great deal of time downloading each specific photo to be used within this important chapter. I found that my research was consuming over seventy percent of my time and energy. I also discovered that I was completing this chapter at a very slow pace, which was good because I did a lot of fact-findings on each entry on both my two Bucket Lists. This was never more prevalent than working on my third famous railroad, the Trans-Siberian Railroad.

I was originally planning to take this famous train from its starting point: Moscow on to its final destination: Vladivostok on the Pacific Ocean, which would have been a six-day journey. What disappointing facts I discovered during my research. There were no private toilets in your first-class compartment and no shower facilities on the train. It then became obvious that I would change my original plan concerning the Trans-Siberian Railroad and instead of taking the full duration of six days, I would take the entire ride for only one or two days maximum. I have checked the three classes available for travel on the Trans-Siberian Railroad and I feel strongly that the First Class travel would be necessary as each first-class compartment would only have two bunk beds in each compartment instead of the usual four in second class and an open compartment with all complement of bunk beds in third class. Unfortunately, in both the first and second class of travel, all the toilets and washrooms are not in your compartment, but at both ends of each first and second class carriage.

I have always enjoyed train rides since a youngster, and that enthusiasm and interest has not decreased over the years, but now in my old age, I must realize that I can only absorb train travel first-class necessities and the Trans-Siberian Railroad offers only a bare minimum of comfort and relaxation than my first two train routes.

Number #3 is for me to experience a Category Four or Five Hurricane. I still remember while growing up and watching the devastation of many famous American Hurricanes on our black & white television sets such names as Audrey in 1957 to Camille in 1969. They had left a strong imprint in my mind. And for me now to simply try and experience a devastating hurricane, first hand, is extremely important. I also had the opportunity to "feel" a characteristic and representative hurricane in an exhibit at the MOSI or called: Museum of Science and Industry in Tampa, Florida. In the museum, they had this special room that simulated the wind and noise of a Category One Hurricane; then it switched to a Category Two and then a Category Three followed by a Category Four and finally a Category Five Hurricane. The difference between a Category One Hurricane to a Category Four or Five Hurricane was enormous. The room came equipped with a handrail so you could hold on to withstand the typical and characteristic winds encountered during the five categories of hurricanes. Plus the sounds are still clearly retained and decipherable today in my mind!

I came very close to completing this hurricane experience as I landed in Tampa Bay International Airport on October 9th, 2018. I was traveling from Washington Dulles Airport to Tampa Bay. It was at the exact same time and day that Hurricane Michael was

Track of Hurricane Michael in October 2018

advancing in the Gulf of Mexico and was very close to the Western Coast of Florida. The Clearwater and Tampa Bay region of Florida was spared a direct hit from Michael, yet the tidal surges; high waves and gusty winds were evident. The next morning after my arrival, my first son Thomas had decided to drive me along the Western Coast of Western Florida from Clearwater down to Fort De Soto. We took many photos of the storm surge; the strong winds plus the huge waves that were battering the Florida coast from Hurricane Michael. The following weather photo clearly shows how close Hurricane Michael came to Tampa Florida, exactly the same day of my arrival.

Mind you, I am still not crossing off this experience, because I was not in the direct path of a Category 4 or 5 hurricane. I must wait for another hurricane experience that would bring that specific hurricane in my direct path.

Well, number #4 is a very interesting hotel that I have wanted to stay in since it opened in 2017. It is called:

The Walled Off Hotel

"*The Walled Off Hotel*" in the occupied West Bank Palestinian city of

Bethlehem. Of course, it is a play on the name of the lavish Waldorf Astoria Hotel in New York City.

It is also noted to have: *"the worst view of any hotel in the world"* The hotel was built four meters from the Israeli West Bank Wall and this offbeat boutique hotel was designed by the acclaimed and controversial street artist 'Banksy'. The hotel has scores of exhibits that show the everyday troubles of the

Mural in the Walled Off Hotel

Palestinian People and what they are experiencing in the Occupied Territory of Palestine. For example, there is one suite that has a large mural over the bed that shows a Palestinian boy fighting an Israeli Military person, and they are fighting with pillows with the feathers flying every which way.

To me, this is a very unique and special hotel that well deserves a visit in the very near future.

Next on my list and #5 is the famous Cappadocia Caves in south-central Turkey. This 'underground cave city' has always been on my list as I had seen many years ago a documentary on the area, and it was described as the only *"moonscape region"* on earth. There are hot air balloon rides so you can get a tremendous overview of the entire area and to see the famous 'Fairy chimneys' which dot the area. Many of the hotels in this region do offer 'cave type rooms' for the guest to sleep in and experience. For me, this would not be an option as I know that I would be extremely claustrophobic in just thinking of spending a night in a closed and claustrophobic environment. Nevertheless, one can see and experience this unusual landscape in a more conventional standard room experience.

Number #6 on my places to see and experience would be the Ancient City of Kursh in Sudan. Having seen all the wonders of Egypt, I have now added the ancient Kingdom of Kush, which is along the Nile River Valley in Sudan. This ancient Kingdom of Nubia dates back to 8000 BC or the Late Bronze Age and flourished for many years. Several black Nubian Kings had actually conquered Egypt and set up the Egyptian 25th ruling dynasty there. Now, much of the Nubian architectural treasures were

Pyramids of Meroe or Called the "Northern Cemetery"

lost with the construction of the Aswan Dam and the creation of the vast Lake Nasser. Yet today, in Sudan, you can see over 200 pyramids and many temple complexes dating back to this most famous Nubian times.

I believe there are more remaining pyramids in Sudan than in all of Egypt. I especially want to see and walk around the Pyramids of Meroe, which are also called: "The Northern Cemetery" in Sudan.

Number #7 on my Bucket List is another island that is located off both the Yemeni and Somalia Coast in the Arabian Sea called: Socotra Island. This is again a very unusual geographic area that beckons my strong travel interest to see and explore. Even more unusual Socotra Island could be considered part of Africa or Asia as it is about 240 km from Somalia and over 340 Km from the Arabian Peninsula. This is maybe the reason why many scientists have called Socotra Island: *"the most alien-looking place on earth."*

What Socotra Island has been over 700 special endemic species of plants and animals that are only found on this particular island, nowhere else on earth. Biologists have coined this special island as: *"Jewel of biodiversity in the Arabian Sea."* People have also described Socotra Island as: *"remote and ecologically unique,"* and these are some of the main reasons why Socotra Island is on this important list.

My desire to see Socotra Island was increased when I first visited the new Aspire Park in 2006 within the Aspire Zone and adjacent to the famous Aspire Academy in Doha. This park had many species of trees from Socotra Island, and each tree was well labeled as to its name, place of origin, etc. I particularly remember the following special trees from Socotra Island located within Aspire Park:

Socotra Island – "Dragon Blood Tree"

Not only these two trees are found on Socotra Island, but many species of plants are also found on this island and the other smaller islands within the archipelago. All have a rich fauna, including several endemic species of birds, such as the Socotra starling, the Socotra sunbird, and the Socotra warbler. Many of these bird species are today endangered by killing by non-native feral cats.

As with many isolated islands, bats are the only endemic mammals native to Socotra. The island does have a few reptiles such as skinks, legless lizards, and one special species of chameleon. There are also many invertebrates only found on the island, such as several spiders, including a special tarantula and three species of freshwater crabs. The idea of having freshwater crabs, I find, is very

Socotra Island – "Cucumber Tree"

strange and odd as the island is considered a tropical, desert climate with very little rainfall per year.

Finally, I would really like to snorkel along the coast of Socotra as their coral reefs are diverse, again with many endemic species.

I have also read about the series of caves with many inscriptions, drawings, and archeological objects left by sailors from the first century BC till the sixth century AD. They discovered that most of the text used is written in the Indian Brāhmī script which is one of the oldest known writing systems of Ancient India. I really must see these interesting caves.

At this time, a visit to Socotra Island may be next to impossible if not one of the most difficult places to visit due to the ongoing Yemeni Civil War. Prior to the onset of this long and ugly war, you had two options of getting from the mainland of Yemen to Socotra Island. There were flights from Sana'a and Aden International Airports directly to the island's small airport. Today, many of the flights to and from Socotra have been canceled. There was also a cargo ship service from Mukalla directly to the main Socotra Seaport just five km from Hadibu. Unfortunately, the journey takes two to three days, and the service is used mostly for cargo and not for passengers.

In 2018, Socotra was occupied by both the UAE and Saudi Arabian Armed Forces creating many challenges for the people and possibly for the many rare and endangered plants and animals. They did supply some much-needed medical aid and supplies.

Now number #8 on my See and Experience List will be the unbelievable and beautiful area called: "Heaven's Gate Mountain" from the Tianmenshan Mountain Cableway in Tianmen Shan, China. This Cableway is the longest in the world and is over 7,455 m long, which is well over 7 km in total length. It starts from the city of Zhangjiajie and climbs to the top of the highest mountain in this Tianmenshan National Forest Park. Along the way, pass over 40 shorter mountain peaks and you see both the unique "Heaven's Gate Cave" and the "Heaven Ladder." The "Heaven's Gate Cave" is exceptional as it is a mammoth cave that measures 130 meters in height and 50 meters in width. This site can be visited, but unfortunately, it has 999 stairs to climb to the base of this distinctive and religious sight. This will be best seen by me from the car of the cableway. The "Heaven Ladder" is a twisting mountain road that has 99 turns and is considered the most amazing mountain road in the world.

At the peak, you can tour the famous "Hanging Garden" also called the Bonsai Garden. There are also many additional sights to experience within this extremely special National Forest Park. For me, simply seeing the photos of this Tianmenshan Mountain Cableway makes us want to immediately book my flight to China.

Tianmenshan Mountain Cableway

Number #9 on my experiences and sights to see and experience Bucket List is the extremely interesting Skeleton Coast in Namibia on the South-Western coast of Africa. It was first described by early Portuguese sailors as: *"Gate to Hell"*, to the *"End of the Earth"* and finally: *"One of the most untouched places in Africa."* What I also want to see are the hundreds of shipwrecks along its long 500 km coast and many animal skeletons.

Namibia Skeleton Coast – Shipwreck

Very few places on earth you have a desert meets the sea, yet along large portions of the Skeleton Coast, this is very common. Where in the world would you see lions and hyenas stalking seals on the water's edge? A lot of other African wildlife are also seen along the coast from elephants; leopards; cheetahs; giraffes to Oryx all are visible along the remarkable and extraordinary Skeleton Coast.

Even though this Skeleton Coast is hostile, isolated, and remote, it still offers safari's, charter flights, and base camps for one to relax and enjoy the sheer untouched beauty of this most unusual seacoast in the world.

This now leads me to my final selection on this most important and most interesting Bucket List. I have always wanted to experience feelings, sounds, and sensations of visiting Rio Carnival.

Actually, the two major cities in Brazil, San Paulo, and Rio de Janeiro have worked out a schedule to have the major Samba School parades on two different nights, so one could literally see the San Paulo parade on Friday and Saturday, and then you could fly to Rio to see and experience their Samba School parade on Sunday or Monday. The Rio and San Paulo Carnivals are actually both six-day parties with the two most important days being those two nights with the huge professional Samba Schools parade. Well, either both cities and simply just a stay in Rio for their spectacular six-day parades would be enough for me to delete this experience from my Bucket List. I will make that decision when I come close to my final scheduling of this final experience.

Actually, I had listed seeing and experiencing the Mardi Gras in New Orleans on my original list, but I changed it to the Rio Carnival because I have never been to any country in South America and the Rio Carnival is considered the "biggest carnival in the world" with its two million visitors per day in attendance. Whereas the Mardi Gras in New Orleans is considered the "The Greatest Free Show on Earth", and is a spectacular treat of the senses. I will still keep my final selection of the Rio Carnival as my number ten selection because I will see and discover a new continent and experience a more raucous crowd of over two million people.

Mind you, this Bucket List is not static as it will never be completed. Mainly because as soon as one experience or sight is achieved, I will be replacing it with a new and more exciting experience or a special place to see.

While I was working on completing this chapter, I came across a very, very interesting online article that was written in early March 2019 and its title was: "10 Countries NOT to put on your Bucket List."

I found this list to be very interesting and decided to share the list within this appropriate chapter of my book.

Number #1:   **North Korea** – and the rationale was: we have no US Embassy presence in the country, and all tours must include a full tour package.

Number #2:   **Kingdom of Saudi Arabia** – and the rationale was: major visit visa problems, and each application has less than a 50% chance of being accepted! **Note:** I have been carrying a Saudi Arabia Business Visa for the past six years. In 2018, I renewed it for an additional 1,825 days. It is very interesting to know the rationale for issuing a visa in days. We all should know that the Saudis are still using the Hijri Calendar, or also called the Islamic Calendar and therefor March 1st, 2019, in the Gregorian calendar relates to the 24th of Jumada Al Akhirah 1440 in the Hijri Calendar. Each month in the Hijri Calendar is about 11 days shorter than the relative month in the Gregorian calendar. There again, one Hijri Calendar year is approximately 354.36 Gregorian calendar days. Finally, my Five Year Saudi Business Visa of 1,825 days is exactly 365 days in the Gregorian calendar and in the Hijri Calendar, the five years is only 1,771.80 days or approximately 10.6 days per year. So literary, if one uses the Hijri Calendar, he would be gaining 54 days over the five year visa period.

Number #3:   **Iran** – and the rationale was again: we have no US Embassy presence in the country; all tours must be a group tour package, etc.

Number #4:   **Cuba** – and the logic was: you will always have a very difficult time obtaining the visit visa. Note: Cuba is on my Bucket List, and I will do anything possible to obtain a visa. I thrive on surpassing large and difficult obstacles.

Number #5: **Syria** – and the logic was: getting a Syrian tourist visa is almost impossible. Note: I have been living in Syria on and off since 1975, and now, I possess a Syrian Residence Card, thus making it legal to stay and live in Syria. We have been trying to obtain a Visit Visa for my two sons and for two friends who want to visit and see Damascus again. I will agree with the author of this article on this point as obtaining a Syrian tourist visa is a very difficult task at this time.

Number #6: **Somalia** – and the reasoning was: the continued existence of Somali Pirates. I had thought that the pirate problems were a thing of the past, but I guess I am wrong.

Number #7: **Central African Republic** – and again the rationale was: we have no US Embassy presence in the country; borders of this landlocked country are dangerous, etc.

Number #8: **Angola** – and the rationale was: that simply to get the visa application, there are far too many fees to pay and there is no guarantee that you will receive your visa in a timely manner.

Number #9: **Libya** – and again the rationale was: we have no US Embassy presence in Libya since 2014, and there are too many armed militias running the country plus manning checkpoints throughout the various major cities.

Number #10: **Algeria** – and the rationale was: that simply to obtain the visit visa, you must pay a large amount in advance for your: hotel; prepaid tours; domestic travel; etc. Plus it is not a "travel-friendly country."

Remember, this was published in March 2019 and it reflected the popular views in America at that time.

Chapter Seventeen

My True Friends

My only True Lifelong Friend, of course, is my lovely and devoted wife, Salma. Through all of the good and bad times we have experienced, she has always been steadfast in her support and at my side throughout our forty-three plus years. Whenever I was under the weather, she had her concoction of: "ginger and honey" hot drink that always seemed to be the correct and fastest remedy for my illness.

I really believe in the words of David Tyson, the Canadian rock music producer and songwriter who wrote something that is so true with our own friendship: *"True friendship comes when the silence between two people is comfortable."*

She has always been there for me…One is very lucky when you find your true friend in your wife and at the same time, your friend being extremely beautiful and intelligent. I have always described Salma *"Like a great French Red Wine, she is getting better with age."*

I can still remember the night I met Salma and how close I came from not attending that party. As I said before, Damascus in late 1975 was not the magnet for single foreign females. To this day I wonder what would have happened if I didn't attend that party? Would Steve have met her and started dating her or what? I soon discovered that I was not just falling in love I discovered that I was gaining a true and good friend.

If I go back to my years in high school, I found that I had only one "true friend" and that was Jim Laks. Jimmy and I were always the 'total opposites'. In high school, I was the "Tallest Senior" and Jim was the "Shortest Senior"; he was a bit chubby, and I was very skinny; his family was quite wealthy wherein my family was strictly middle class; I had a part-time job throughout high school and Jim did not need to work. Yet, we did have many similarities such as we both had a love for 'fine clothes'. Many days Jim and I would skip school and go downtown Buffalo to buy a new "Gant" shirt or a new sweater. Clothes became a passion for both of us as they continue today with me.

Another similarity was our love for alcohol. I was one of the few classmates in all four of our high school years that had a part-time job. I was a dishwasher at the Orchard Downs restaurant, and I would usually get off from work at 11:00 p.m. Jim and a few of our friends would wait for me outside the back door of the Downs and then we would walk to our only liquor store: McNeil's Liquor Store. You see, I looked a lot like my older brother Don and when I would walk in the owner always thought I was Don. Don was four years older than I so this worked for quite a few years and it continued even after Don graduated from high school and joined the army. I guess that old man McNeil never kept up with my family.

I would always buy Seagram's 7 Crown Canadian Whiskey, as it was smooth, not too expensive and we liked the name. Jim and a few friends and I would take the bottle behind the old Orchard Park Water Tower and simply take a swig and then pass it on... We would all try to gulp it down as 'cool as possible' as no one wanted to show the others that we could not handle this straight bourbon without coughing or choking. Then, a few weeks later, we decided to modify our drinking habits and become more 'sophisticated'. I would still buy the Seagram's 7 Crown and the others would go to the grocery store to buy a large bottle or two of 7 – Up. Back to the old water tower, but this time we would each take one swig of the 7-Crown and then we would wash that down with a mouthful of 7 – Up! Thus we had invented our own and special 'mixed drink'. Seagram's 7 Crown was both Jim's and my favorite drink for many years.

So too were our similarities when it came to adventure. Many times, after I left work, Jim would pass by, and we would both head to his father's car dealership and literally "borrow" one of his dad's used cars that were on the lot. Usually, they were the smallest cars, for what reason I don't recall...Maybe it was that we would not stand out while driving a stolen vehicle or that they required less gas on our Friday Night Drives. I do recall one week when we decided to 'borrow' a Nash Metropolitan, a very small and dangerous car. It was unsafe as it had very small tires and a very short wheelbase. That night in the Metropolitan, Jim was driving a bit too fast as we were on our way up to the local Ski Resorts. We rounded a sharp corner and the car rolled over and we landed upside down. Instead of fear or distress, we both began laughing so hard that I almost peed in my pants. No one was hurt, so we simply climbed out and then proceeded to push the Metropolitan up-right. First to one side and then we righted the little car. All the time laughing and joking at what had just happened. The car started and we simply drove off and continued on our way. We really never paid much attention to the scratches on one side and on the top until we returned the Metropolitan to the used car lot. I guess that next Monday morning there must have been some confusion as no one could have explained how that car got scratches on one side and on the top.

Another similarity that Jim and I shared was our love for sports cars. We were the only two seniors that were driving sports cars in high school. As a senior, Jim had his dad buy him an Austin Healy Sprite. I saved my money working as a dishwasher at the Orchard Downs restaurant, and my mom contributed half the amount and I

1959 Black Austin Healey 100 – 6

bought my first car. It was a black 1959 Austin Healey 100–6.

The 100 stood for the car's top speed in mph. As a matter of fact, it was the first 'affordable' sports car that could reach that speed. I really loved that car and drove it all throughout high school and then on to California until my first year in junior college. While in high school, Jim and I would often race after school and on the weekends. Never once did either of us have an accident or cause an accident during our high school senior year. We both knew our sports cars' potential and always respected that point.

Jim and I both had average grades in high school, never the top nor the bottom…simply average. All our fellow students were applying to top colleges, I had decided to apply to the Erie County Technical College and study hotel and restaurant management. After my acceptance, I found my heart was not really into that major. Jim had never really thought too much about college nor had a clue as to which college he wanted to attend. His parents wanted him to attend the University of Buffalo as his two elder brothers had done before him, but I guess Jim simply did not want to spend the time at university.

After our high school graduation, I had received a letter from my sister, who was living in Southern California, and she had invited me to come to California and attend Santa Ana Junior College and live with them. She also felt that I would be able to get a part-time job working as a waiter in one of the many restaurants near her house and the college.

I talked to Jim about joining me in California; we could drive out there together, attend this junior college together and enjoy the Golden State with the most beautiful bikini-clad girls in the world together. He jumped on the idea, and all he needed to do was to try to convince his parents to accept this new adventure. That was an easy task as they knew he did not want to attend the University of Buffalo so in their minds, some junior college in California was better than no college for Jimmy.

So for the entire month of July and into the first week of August, we both prepared ourselves for our journey to beautiful Southern California and to view the world's most spectacular California Sunsets. I bought a luggage rack for the back of the Austin Healy and we then packed our bags, kissed our parents' goodbye and set off in my Austin Healey sports car to continue our education in the "*Golden State*": California. It was the last adventure we ever had together.

We drove throughout the day and shared the driving along the way. Our first night's stop was Rolla, Missouri, as we were very tired. We found a nice small motel on Highway 66 right next to the Missouri School of Mines and Metallurgy. We were on the road for over 14 hours; drove many miles through five states and had a very good time. After we checked in the motel and had dinner, we walked around the university campus. Classes had not started, but there were a few students on campus for their summer program. I remember we met several students like us freshmen, and after talking with them, they thought that Jimmy and I were both a bit: 'off our rockers'. We still had a long drive to California ahead of us and we only knew the name of our new junior college, nothing more and were driving a small sports car. Crazy New Yorkers.

We both had a good night's sleep, and early the next morning, we were on Highway 66 again headed West. Jimmy was really a great friend and a solid driver. I never questioned his decisions but his only negative that I discovered on our trip was that he didn't know how to read a road map. While he was at the wheel, there was no problem as I have always been a competent map reader, but the challenges came when I was driving and we came to a major new junction; traffic circle or intersection. Where do I go, Jimmy? Complete silence, so I would pull over to the side of the road and take the map to make an accurate and suitable decision. This happened so many times one could not imagine.

We made it to our second night stop in Amarillo, Texas, from Missouri, through Oklahoma into the panhandle of Texas in a very quick time as the speed limits were much higher in 1962 than today. I remember our first impression of Texas was that all the men were wearing Texas ten-gallon cowboy hats. Near our hotel, there was a Texan Steakhouse and we indulged in two large steaks with all the trimmings. Yes, I was consuming meat in those days. All the motels and restaurants were reasonable and low priced, but we were two young high school students and all prices seemed very expensive.

The last night on the road, we made it to Holbrook, Arizona. My memory serves me right that my biggest remembrance was of the high temperatures as this travel was completed in the heart of the summer, during the month of August. All along the trip, but especially from Texas to Arizona, the temperatures were scorching. Since we were in a convertible, I believe, we had the top down throughout the majority of this long-distance trip. Needless to say, when we finally entered California, we had a nice facial and arms suntan/sunburn.

The last leg seemed to have taken the longest because we were both anticipating our entrance to California, and it seemed like the miles were going by so slowly. I do remember we were traveling at high speed and within the second hour after entering California, we were stopped by a California Highway Patrol Car. I think he really felt sorry for the two young boys in an open-top sports car with New York license plates. He gave us a real break, as no ticket was issued but he reminded us of the current speed limit and told us to drive safely...We did heed his advice and drove the remainder of the way under the posted speed limit.

When we finally arrived at my sister's house, they had all gone on vacation so the house key was at the neighbor's house. Jim and I spent the next ten days in pure heaven as we had a very nice three-bedroom house to stay in and no adult supervision and no one to tell us what to do, when to sleep, or where to go. I was able to buy beer and wine, even though the legal drinking age was 18 and I was still only 17 years old, but I looked much older so I would confidently go into a liquor store and simply select the beer or wine and act like I was above the legal age. I was never denied a purchase as I guess I developed a certain swagger or self-assertiveness while entering all liquor stores.

With our wild consumption of the beer and wine, we went berserk several times and those nights we really trashed my sister's house. Many nights we simply phoned a telephone number at random and started talking nonsense. We annoyed many people during our wild days and night. We often drove down to the beautiful beach areas in Newport Beach which were a few miles away from our home in Santa Ana. We found that the California myths were not really myths... they were all true. Gorgeous tanned girls in the skimpiest bikinis all enjoying the white sandy beaches. Many guys surfing and the sound of the Beach Boys resonated over the entire beach. And those tall palm trees and beautiful sunsets... we were both in paradise.

When Jim and I finally sobered up, we decided to try to locate Santa Ana Junior College. We knew we needed to collect all the registration documents and other pertinent entrance information. Jimmy had selected business as his major, and I selected Pre-Dental. A decision that I would regret in the coming years...

Jimmy never attended college, and yet he became a very successful businessman at an early age. He had built, from scratch, Western New York's largest imported car dealership in a matter of only a few years, all before he reached the age of 21. Unfortunately, Jim died in a horrible car accident just two and a half years after he left Southern California. He lost control of his small yet very fast sports car and he wrapped the car around a tree...He died instantly along with his passenger. When I received the news, I was devastated and was ready to drive home and abandon that semester at school. I had many phone calls to his parents and they insisted that I did not leave school as that would be what Jim would have wanted. It was hard for me to comprehend this loss for many years to come. I kept thinking after his death: "Only if I tried harder to convince him to start junior college with me...or to start working in California and not to go home"...Who knows one's fate? Unfortunately, Jim was one of our first classmates to die from our Class of 1962.

This was such a waste of a bright and ambitious young business mind. And Jimmy was my first loss of a 'true friend' from high school.

I had always enjoyed the words from Washington Irving and how he described my friendship today of Jim Laks: ***"Sweet is the memory of*** *distant friends! Like the mellow rays of the departing sun, it falls tenderly, yet sadly, on the heart."*

Now, during one's undergraduate college and university study, one usually acquires 'friends', which I did, but for me, really no "true friends" were developed.

This changed when I attended Dental School at the University of Buffalo. On our first day of classes at the University of Buffalo Dental School, none of the students were talking to one another as absolutely no one knew anyone.

It was so true what C.S. Lewis, the Irish-born scholar, novelist, and author wrote many years ago about friendship and especially the day I meet Tom: *"Friendship is born at that moment when one person says to another, What! You too? I thought I was the only one."*

A lot of the new Freshman students we coming to Buffalo from New York City, so the atmosphere was quiet and subdued. New conversations with students were hard to come by as many seemed a bit too apprehensive and nervous. And all on the surface gave the impression of being very egoistical, a bit rude and discourteous. Hey, I don't need this… I was walking around the room and then suddenly I saw a fellow student standing by himself and a bit lonely. We started talking and I then found out that he was from the Buffalo area and more importantly, he was Polish. That was great as my mom was 100% Polish. Tom instantly became a friend in this vast multitude of impolite "foreigners." From that initial meeting, Tom and I have remained close and dear friends, even though we only see each other once every two or three years. When we do see each other, it is like we had never been apart. He and I never developed a friendship with any of the New York City classmates; this too helped create a long-lasting bond.

It is hard to find a person "right off the bat" that you can talk to and confide in, but Tom was that friend from the onset. It became a habit for us to study together and usually at my parents' house. My parents really liked Tom as he was very polite and well-mannered. I liked him as he very accepting, and I do not remember any time that we had argued or had words and remember we have known each other for over fifty years.

Tom is one of my only friends that has known both of my wives. He wasn't too close to Diane as he felt she was distracting me from my studies, and maybe this was a true reflection, as my grades did suffer somewhat after she came to live in Buffalo. He was the best man at our wedding and was also one of the first to visit the hospital to see our newborn son. Tom did complete his dental school and went on to be a very successful dentist in a small town south of Buffalo. We did lose our close friends for a period of time when Diane, Thomas II and I, left Buffalo for Southern California. But on each trip that I would make to visit my parents, Tom and I always found time to meet and to "catch up on old times."

After I divorced my first wife, Diane, and married Salma, on our honeymoon, we got together with Dr. Tom and his new wife in Springville, New York. Tom was married then and the four of us really got along very well and we do to this day. Salma and I had two boys and Tom and his wife had two beautiful girls and exactly the same age as our two sons. We often discussed and joked over the idea of them marring. We would usually spend our summer holidays in the States and of course, we would always see Tom and his family. The last time I saw Tom was in 2018 while I was visiting my brother and sister in Western New York. Tom drove up from Springville and he came to my hotel in the Niagara Falls area and we had a great lunch in the hotel's restaurant/bar and we talked for over nine hours. He is not into the electronic age, as a matter of fact, he did post a letter to me that had a small electric wire protruding from the top…it was his example of "Electric Mail."

My friendship with Dr. Tom is a great example that one does not need to see your "true friend" on a daily or weekly base in order to maintain a friendship. I consider Tom as my "Long Distance True Friend."

Another "Long Distance True Friend" is Jerry Johnson. Jerry is a true friend and probably my only true friend that I see less often than any of my other true friends.

In the words of Diana Corte: *"There is magic in long-distance friendships. They let you relate to other human beings in a way that goes beyond being physically together and is often more profound."*

I first met Jerry when I attended an Optimist International Club meeting in San Diego, and he was the President or Vice President of that San Diego chapter. The Optimist Clubs were mainly concentrating on Community Service Programs especially relating to youth programs, recognizing the local youth and identifying youth's efforts in arts, sports, and academics. They develop leadership and fellowship in the youth of that community.

I attended the Optimist International Club meeting as I believe I was representing the Young Optimist Club on the campus of San Diego State University. I remember I was to give an update on our university chapter as well as to receive an award for my overall academic excellence plus my acceptance to nine out of nine US Dental Schools. This was a first for our chapter of the Young Optimist Club at San Diego State University.

Jerry and I talked for quite a while after the meeting, and we slowly became friends. We have remained friends, though two marriages each and for over 53 years. Jerry is my only true friend that I had known before I attended dental school and I still know him today.

He helped see me off on my way to Buffalo to attend dental school as well as welcome me back to San Diego after I had left dental school.

Jerry was in Insurance Sales, and we remained solid friends while Diane and I were living in San Diego. Several years later, Diane, Thomas II, and I went to Europe and lived there in a VW Camper for almost one year. We left and Jerry was there giving us a fond farewell and wished us a safe trip. We returned a year later and Jerry was still there ready to welcome us back "home." By this time, he had given up selling insurance and was in buying and selling cars both in Los Angeles and San Diego County. Jerry was in auto sales and made all of his sales of cars through the various car auctions located in L.A. County. Jerry introduced me to buying and selling of used cars. I had no plans for work so I was listening to Jerry with great enthusiasm. He was a registered car broker with his auction number and a small handheld auction signboard. I joined him one day at the L.A. car auction and I was very impressed with the business scene and Jerry's skill and ability in identifying a good deal. At that time, each auction broker used what everyone called the: "auction bible" and that was actually a book called: *The Kelley Blue Book* for the true value of each used car. *The Blue Book* had all makes of cars plus everything from the car millage; general condition and additions like a/c; power windows; etc. That day Jerry bought one or two cars that he said would resell quite quickly. They did and I know he made a lot of money on those two transactions. I asked Jerry if I could join him next week so I could purchase one car. That following week, I got together my initial investment for my next trip to the car auction. I had a very modest initial investment of only $1,000. USD, but you must remember this was 1972 and many car prices were in that starting range, especially at a car auction, as many cars sold for much less.

Our plan was as follows: I would purchase a car, with Jerry's own professional input; I would fix up and clean the car, place an advertisement in the local newspaper, and then try to sell that same car. I had preset three business objectives for myself with my new found work in buying and selling cars: 1) I would try to sell that vehicle within two or three weeks of its purchase; 2) the full selling price received would then be completely reinvested in my next car purchase and 3) I should make a 'modest' profit on each vehicle. I soon discovered that there was to be substantial money made by this proven method of sales and real fun doing it.

The first car I purchased at the auction was a white 1964 Mercedes 190 D, and I paid $1,000. USD for it. This was a very low price as the idea of purchasing a "diesel" car at the auction was virtually unheard of in those days. I drove the car for a few weeks' cleaned and waxed it and then sold the same Mercedes for $3,000 USD. I still remember the older couple that purchased it, they were living in L.A; in their late sixties and had just returned from Europe where they had seen many similar Mercedes Benz Diesels. They gave me a check on the same day and after I cashed the check, I then took that same amount and returned to the auction with Jerry. This time to buy a slightly newer car and at a price of no more than $3,000.

This second auction car was again purchased for a low auction price as it was a 1969 Datsun (now called Nissan), light blue, station wagon. You see, the Japanese manufacturer was quite new in the California market so again, I bought it slightly under my full cash amount. Again I drove it for a few weeks, polished it and again sold it for a nice profit.

The third car I had purchased at the auction was a real 'steal' as Jerry informed me and a true: 'sleeper' in auction terminology. It was a 1970 maroon, Porsche 911 Targa, in spotless and immaculate condition and with very low mileage. The Targa model was and still is my most favorite Porsche model ever produced as it has a fully detachable roof, with a large Chrome 'roll-bar' behind the open top. Most importantly, I bought it for $6,000. USD, and that's why it was considered a real giveaway. The car's *Kelley's Blue Book* value was over $9,000 USD for only six thousand, it was a real bargain. Again, I was very lucky as on that day at the auction not too many buyers were looking at this splendid Porsche Sports Car. As the bidding started at one thousand dollars, I was determined that Jerry's number was held high in a quick and firm manner. And at six thousand dollars, Jerry's small handheld auction signboard was the last remaining held up high. Jerry and I knew that we got a real bargain as on our way out to see the car again, we were offered $7,000, on the spot, and for the same car, we had just paid $6,000! No, thank you was my spirited answer.

The sale of this car was unique and still, to this day unforgettable! The method of my selling this Porsche was exactly like the other two cars, I drove it for a week or two, ensuring that it was in perfect running condition and then I placed a newspaper advertisement in the L.A. Times. I had also placed my selling price at $12,000. The first day the advertisement ran was a Thursday morning edition and that day I received many calls. That evening I received a call from Dallas Texas and

Porsche Targa

the man with a very strong Texas accent asked: "Are you the owner of that 'Porsche'?" I said blissfully: "Yes, sir"! He then asked me for the color and then confirmed that he wanted to see it. He then said he would fly into Orange County Airport now called: John Wayne International Airport on Saturday at noon in his private jet and if I could meet him there. "Yes, of course" was my stunned answer, "I will see you at the airport on Saturday at noon." Was this guy for real or what? I remember that Diane thought that this was a joke or a con, but nevertheless, I was willing to give this Texan the benefit of my trust... That Friday and Saturday morning, I made sure that the car was spotless and perfect. Diana drove our friend's car and I drove the Porsche to the private airplane arrivals area at the Orange County Airport. At exactly noon, here arrives a beautiful twin-engine private jet and outcomes this big burly man with a "Ten Gallon Texas Hat" along with a gorgeous blond 'bombshell' with an extremely short mini skirt. They walked over to the car and I simply tossed him the keys... and said enjoy. I helped him adjust the seats and mirrors and told him the 'Porsche' had a full gas tank. I then asked him: "What time will you be back?" He grinned and said: "four o'clock." He drove off with the most unforgettable sight...this large Texan with a ten-gallon Texas Hat with his girlfriend's blond hair fluttering in the breeze... both sticking out of the top; of a beautiful Porsche Targa, heading out to enjoy Southern California.

Diane thought I was nuts and questioned my sanity… "You just gave your key to a total stranger!" I guess I have always been a person that believed: "The glass was always half full" instead of Diane: "saying that same glass was half empty!" type of person. I told her that "Anyone that would fly his own jet from Dallas Texas to Southern California deserves to be trusted." Exactly at four o'clock, he drove back into the car park grinning from ear-to-ear and drove the Porsche near his aircraft. He hops out and then tosses the keys back to me! And said: "Sonny, what price are you asking for this 'Porsche'?" I told him only twelve thousand dollars. He then took out his checkbook and wrote me a check for twelve thousand dollars. Now the surprise continued, as he then said: "We have a small problem", I immediately thought he was going to tell me to hold on to the check for a while or something like that, but instead he said: "Please keep the 'Porsche' for the next month or so as I am taking my girlfriend to 'Europe' and I won't need it until I return." I then stammered and said: "Oh, oh okay…"

Diane, Thomas, and I then stood there in total shock and bewilderment as he entered his private jet, sat in the pilot's seat cockpit and started his twin engines and began slowly rolling away from his jets parking space. We stayed there for another three or four minutes waiting for his plane's takeoff…All three of us were watching and waving goodbye. The first thing I did when I got home was to call Jerry Johnson to tell him what just transpired. He was very happy and told me that he never had that much of good luck in reselling any of his own vehicles and you could feel in his voice there was no envy, but pure joy and delight for my success. Another great sign of a true friend.

What a predicament! What to do for one month? Should I

"Hap-Pea" and "Pea-Wee"

simply park it off the street and purchase another car or do something crazy? I selected the latter, of course, and in two days, we were packed and off to tour California in style. We drove up Pacific Coast Highway One through some of the most science roads the state had to offer, our first stop was Buelton the home of the renowned Pea Soup Anderson's famous restaurant. This time, as always, we had their legendary Split Pea Soup and we sat below their famous poster of both "Hap-pea" and "Pea-wee."

Thomas was really happy looking at these two small 'chef's' splitting each pea with a mallet, and I believe a chisel. The next stop was Solvang, The popular Danish Capital of America. That night we elected to spend the night in the well-known hotel in the region called: The Madonna Inn. Now nothing to do with today's famous signer that bears the same name. Each room within the Madonna has a unique and different décor… from a "Rock Room" atmosphere to a bright pink decorated room with a big four-poster bed in an overly pink-colored: "Pink Room." I believe our bathroom had a "Waterfall Shower" that Thomas simply loved. The next morning we continued north along the Old Coast Highway One, not California 101, but Highway One! Just prior to the highway entering the famous Big Sur area, we stopped at the magnificent Hearst Castle. This was built by the famous and extremely wealthy newspaper millionaire William Randolph Hearst. We really enjoyed the huge outdoor swimming pool called: The Neptune Pool.

After our visit and tour of the Hearst Castle, Highway One takes you along the Pacific coast in an area called: Big Sur, which has the most beautiful scenery of any place in

California Condor

America! Unquestionably and hands down the most beautiful. As you

have for many miles, a curving and twisting road, all many feet above sheer cliffs that plummet down to the Pacific Ocean. And in the Pacific, you see countless Sea Otters and Seals playing in the ocean. We decided to spend more time along this picturesque stretch of highway so we stopped at the Big Sur Inn and were very lucky to find a room at the Inn has only twelve rooms. Another unique feature of the Big Sur Inn, back then, was they would rent you a 'hollowed-out log' for. 25 cents per night for anyone who was hiking or low on cash. Our room was very rustic and I even remember the front door had panels of wood that had a separation of a centimeter or two between each wood panel. Not the greatest door for one's love of privacy. We had a very early dinner as the restaurant closed relatively early as they rarely have guests driving the Coast Highway One at night. That entire stay was one very special night in a very special place in America. We were also very lucky as the weather was fantastic as we kept the Porsche's Targa top off throughout the entire trip. After we left the Big Sur Inn, we continued heading north along Coast Highway and we stopped many times along the way simply to gaze at the sea life below and then we spotted a large California condor above us.

This is one of the largest North American flying birds and is easy to spot as it has a wing-span of 9 to 10 feet! So Big Sur offers breathtaking views of the great Pacific Ocean on the left side while admiring the thick green forest on the right side. Never a dull moment on California Highway 1 in the Big Sur area of Central California.

Our next stop was the renowned city of Monetary famous for the setting of John Steinbeck's novel: *Cannery Row* and its famous Monetary Fisherman's Wharf. On our way to San Francisco, we passed through some very solid agricultural land, which is recognized as 'The World's Capital for Artichoke's.' This is located in a city called Castroville. There is also another: world's Capital for Garlic' and this is a bit further north and closer to San Francisco in a town called: Gilroy.

We then enjoyed three nights in my most favorite American city: San Francisco. One can never say enough about this truly legendary '*City by the Bay*'; with its old cable cars, the Golden Gate Bridge, and of course, the celebrated Fisherman's Wharf.

After that four day excursion in San Francisco, we then headed East on Interstate 80 to Lake Tahoe and to both great gambling towns called: Stateline and Reno. Reno is known as: "*The Biggest Little City in the World!*" We also spent a lot of time at Squaw Valley, where they had the Winter Olympics in 1960. We were also lucky as the Aerial Tram Way was open, and we all rode up to the top. Then we headed south through the old California Gold Rush country. This area had a rich but short history as the gold ran out and the miners all went elsewhere! Nevertheless, the scenery is still very beautiful and the area still has a couple of famous sites that can still be visited and toured. We did pan for gold at the famous 'Sutter's Mill' and had lunch in a town called: Calaveras, famous for the book authored by Mark Twain, titled: *The Celebrated Jumping Frog of Calaveras County.*

The next day I wanted to show my son, Thomas II the Ancient Bristlecone Pine Trees, which are the "Oldest Living Things on Earth" and they preceded the California Giant Redwood Trees by about two or three hundred years...

We hadn't been to Death Valley, so why not drive across it in the Porsche Targa? This was still such a fascinating place to tour, all with our Targa roof stored away. Then I decided to visit a place completely the opposite of Death Valley.... so I drove to Palm Springs. After one night there, it was time to head back to Southern California. Then I told my wife: "We must decide what do we do next?"

Ancient Bristlecone Pine

There was a fairly straightforward answer to my question: It was essential to stop driving the Porsche and to buy another replacement car. Why? Well, what would I do if the Porsche had a small accident or someone had stolen it? So I locked it securely and then called my friend Jerry Johnson.

Jerry came to our rescue once again, as he suggested we drive to the L.A. Car Auction next week. This time, for me rules were a bit different, instead of buying my next car for twelve thousand dollars, I went back to my original

1970 Datsun 240 Z

price of six thousand and started looking for another car and preferably another sports car at that amount. Jerry wasn't planning on buying a car on this trip, so his full attention would be to help me find a solid replacement for the Porsche 911. We got to the auction early so we could study each car that was going up for auction. Jerry was so talented and he seemed to have memorized that Blue Book cover-to-cover. We had identified three cars and we were going to bid on each and the one that sold for my six thousand or under was going to be my next car. The first two went for well above our target of $6,000. USD and then came our third, a burnt orange 1970 Datsun 240 Z sports car. We both kept our fingers crossed and by the end of the bidding, I had it for $5,900. USD and I drove it home with the dealer's license plates.

It was really unique yet very unusual as now I had two of the most popular foreign sports cars on the American market, and I could drive both to determine my preference before I gave up the Porsche in a week's time. I really enjoyed driving both and at the time, I was to deliver the Porsche. Hands down the Porsche, with its German engineering and craftsmanship, was far superior to the Japanese manufactured Datsun 240 Z.

The Texan had arranged to have the "Porsche" trucked from Costa Mesa to Dallas. So now I was driving only one car. Our personal lives were really changing and changing fast. The following three month period was a very hectic and life-changing experience for my family and I. Diane and I had our differences, major differences and I felt the only and best answer was to settle our marriage in a civil divorce. I felt that it would be best for Thomas and now, as I look back at this period of my life, it was the best for Thomas and for both Diane and me. Our divorce was very sane and rational, especially for Thomas as he was fast approaching five so he had time to settle in with his life minus his father's constant presence. Again, Jerry was a very stabilizing force for me especially with the fact of me not seeing Thomas each day of the week. We all survived and I will always thank Jerry for being there especially for me.

I had decided to go back to San Diego State and obtain my California Lifetime Teacher's Certificate. Diane had found a full-time job, and Thomas was attending school. That next year, I had found my first teaching job up in Irvine so I left the San Diego area and began to see Thomas less-and-less. After that full year teaching at a middle school, and being awarded "Teacher of the Year", I decided to take a year off to complete writing my first two books. Jerry and I saw each other on my trips back to San Diego, as the editor of the first book was living near San Diego and after my grueling hours with the editor, I would always find time to see Thomas and Jerry and his family. This carried on for over six months and then I had decided to move to Damascus, Syria. Jerry was again there for me, as I had a lot of personal items that I could not take with me to Syria. Jerry was willing to place all my boxes and cartons in his already overcrowded garage. I remember him saying: "Thomas, don't worry about anything as they will be here for you when you return home from Damascus." Little did we both realize that day would never arrive.

After I married Salma in 1976, we planned our honeymoon first to the UK and France and then to the States. Southern California was always our final destination, both to see my sister and her family and also to see Jerry and his family. The minute we came by Jerry's house, it was like that one year started to disappear. It was like I had never left, but I had a new and beautiful wife, and I was still planning to live in Damascus…Salma hasn't really seen Jerry a lot since our honeymoon. But I was able to see Jerry and catch up on old times on each of my business and personal trips to San Diego. We have managed to stay in contact first via letter writing and now with emails, Whatsapp, and Skype. I saw Jerry and his new wife in October 2018 during my last trip to the States. Now, Jerry is well known in the San Diego Real Estate Market and goes by the name: "The 'Loan' Ranger."

Now, when most people think about a true friend, one always thinks this person as a 'longtime friend' right? Well, there was one really true friend that entered my life for a very short period of time, and his name was Sheikh Ahmed Kassim Darwish, whom I had the pleasure to meet during my work in Doha, Qatar.

To this day, Sheikh Ahmed was one of the strangest and most bizarre friendships I have ever known or ever encountered. He turned out to be such a close and confidential friend in such a short period of time.

In May of 2007, I went to Jeddah to visit my grandson Yusuf in Jeddah. During that visit, I decided to have my Annual Medical Checkup at United Doctors Hospital in Jeddah as I had been seeing the same doctor in the same hospital for many years. This year, there was a real unexpected outcome to one part of my medical results…my PSA or Prostate Specific Antigen was tested at 54 ng/mL… In the past, most doctors considered PSA levels of 4.0 ng/mL at my age and lower as normal. Therefore, if a man had a PSA level above 4.0 ng/mL, doctors would often recommend a prostate biopsy to determine whether the prostate was malignant; cancerous; benign, or free of cancer. Men with prostate cancer often have PSA levels higher than four, although cancer is a possibility at any PSA level. Well, 54 was well 'off-the-charts' and my doctor, for many years in Jeddah, recommended that I do a retest once I arrive back in Doha as they had found that the calibration of certain PSA testing machines occasionally varies.

Immediately upon my return to Doha in late May, I had my prostate level retested at the best hospital in Doha, and the new test results proved to be all the more damaging than my Jeddah test results as my PSA level was now 61 ng/mL. All I could think about was: "What am I going to do with this cancer-like symptom?" Directly after my Doha test results, I contacted my wife in Damascus and informed her of this shocking and upsetting news. She began planning to come to Doha to be by my side as soon as she could make her reservations for travel.

That next evening, I was invited to an Italian Embassy's Reception for their National Day or also called: Foundation Day Celebrations held in one of the top five-star hotels in Doha. I didn't feel like attending this function, but at the last minute, I decided to attend this gathering, as I thought it would: "be good to get my mind off this horrible subject of cancer."

Vividly, I still remember just after the receptions' cocktail hour, the majority of the guests swarmed to the dining area of the adjoining reception room to enjoy the Italian dinner feast. When I finally arrived at the reception, there appeared to be no free chairs available. I walked and walked, and finally, at the rear of the ballroom, I found one empty seat at the most distant table in the room. I politely asked if that single chair was taken, and the Qatari gentleman who was seated next to the empty chair said: "It was and feel free to sit down young man." That chance meeting I had at the Italian Embassy's National Day Reception in Doha has changed my life forever.

Sitting next to me was Sheikh Ahmed Kassim Darwish and his Japanese wife and young and attractive daughter. The table was the furthest from the front of the ballroom, as they also arrived a bit late. I quickly found Sheikh Ahmed to be a very friendly man, and as I later learned that the head of one of the top three richest Qatari Business Families.

I then discovered that Sheikh Ahmed's older brother's daughter was married to the eldest brother of the Al Jaidah Brothers family. This was the family I was working for in Doha, so we did have a starting point in our casual 'table talk'.

Through the course of that evening's dinner, one conversation led to another, and I found this Sheikh Ahmed was extremely likable and enormously intelligent. We discussed his daughter who was planning to spend her next four years in Japan earning her Bachelor's Degree in Japanese. OK, her mom was Japanese, but for a teenager who just graduated from an Arabic High School in Doha Qatar to enter a Japanese university was unheard of, in my humble opinion.

Sheikh Ahmed and I were engrossed in conversation for the majority of the evening. And to this day, I have no recollection of how the subject of prostate cancer originally came up between us. We all know the subject of cancer or any disease is not the desired topic at any dinner table and should never be discussed, especially with a total stranger. I told him of my worries and the current levels of my PSA testing. He was keenly interested in my plight as he had his prostate removed a year before, and his PSA was 'only' around: 10 ng/mL at that time. My level was now 61 ng/mL, so he knowingly took a strong interest in this American's major health problem.

He asked if I had a copy of the last two medical tests and then gave me his business card. He said: "Webber (a name he had always called me from this first meeting till his passing), please send me a fax of all the pages of your last two PSA Test results. Once I receive them, I will immediately forward them to my doctor in Bangkok, Thailand, where I had my prostate removed a year earlier."

The next morning Sheikh Ahmed had six-page fax waiting for him on his private fax machine. He called me and confirmed that indeed he had received the six pages and that he had already forwarded them to his doctor in Bangkok. That same afternoon Sheikh Ahmed called me the second time and said: "Webber, my doctor in Thailand wants to see you immediately!" What is this? In less than 24 hours, after meeting Sheikh Ahmed, he's telling me I must go to Bangkok to see his doctor at once.

Now, what had also occurred that same morning, was very interesting as my brother-in-law, who was then a doctor working at the Cleveland Clinic, had heard of my prostrate challenges from my wife, so he, in turn, asked me to send by fax all my test results and records to: "The Leading Prostate Surgeon in America" who also worked at the Cleveland Clinic and a close friend of Dr. Zeyad, my brother-in-law. I thought, sure, two opinions on the same important subject are better than one, and it would not hurt, right?

By now, things were working at a very fast pace, and I had realized I didn't discuss this entire matter with my employers, the five Al Jaidah brothers. So that next afternoon, we all met and I explained the entire situation and they were all very concerned and worried. Of course, they all knew and had great trust and a strong belief in Sheikh Ahmed, yet they still suggested I call the States to get that all-important "second opinion."

Next, I checked with my wife in Damascus to see if she had booked her flight, and she confirmed that indeed she was scheduled to arrive the next afternoon to Doha. I then checked with Qatar Airways for the availability of their flights to Bangkok over the next two to three days.

That late afternoon my brother-in-law called and confirmed that he had arranged a specific time in two days for me to call his doctor at Cleveland Clinic. Also, Sheikh Ahmed called me from Abu Dhabi to see if I had booked my flight to Bangkok. I explained the entire situation and said I would make my decision after I spoke to this specialist in America. I sensed from his voice and tone that he was a bit upset over this second opinion 'nonsense' as he called it. I immediately called Abu Latif Al Jaidah and asked him to call Sheikh Ahmed to make sure he fully understood my concerns and the reasoning and logic behind my wanting a second opinion. Abu Latif was, of course, married to Sheikh Ahmed's sister. I did not want Sheikh Ahmed to be upset as he had already done so much for me, and just knowing me for less than forty-eight hours. It appeared that Abu Latif's phone call had smoothed things over with Sheikh Ahmed as nothing more was ever spoken with Sheikh Ahmed of my second opinion wishes.

Two days later, I called the doctor at the Cleveland Clinic. The first thing he asked me: "Do you have US medical insurance?" I replied: "No, I don't, but don't worry about that as money was not an issue." He then proceeded to ridicule the PSA testing machines used in the Middle East as that was virtually 'impossible' to have such a high test result. He then spoke of the "worse-case-scenario" and that was to have my malignant prostate gland completely removed. Then he said that since you do not have US medical insurance, I will begin quoting prices: the new PSA Test and Ultrasound would cost so much… I interrupted him and said, "Doctor, do not concern yourself over the cost, as my life is more important than dollars and cents", he continued with the cost of the operation; the Anesthesiologist; the after-care cost…and again, I interrupted him and told him: "Money is not a concern and please do not mention prices again." His very next words were: "…now the cost of the room would be…" I finally said, "Doctor, thank you very much" and I hung up on him.

I immediately called Qatar Airways and made my booking for my wife and me to Bangkok with an open return, now, that I discovered my "second opinion" was useless. I then contacted the Marriott website to book my room reservation in Bangkok. I found a nice property called the JW Marriott Hotel, and it was on one of the main streets in Bangkok called Sukhumvit Road. I booked it for my arrival date and for them to have the hotel car pick my wife and me from the airport. I had reserved my room for only five days knowing I could always extend if that was necessary.

Then I called Sheikh Ahmed to inform him of my Qatar Airways departure date to Bangkok with my wife and of my Marriott hotel details. I asked if he could then make a tentative appointment with his doctor in Bangkok. I also asked him for all details as to both the hospital's name, address, phone numbers, and the doctor's name. He then informed me of the very good news that my JW Marriott Hotel was a walking distance to the Bumrungrad International American Hospital. About twenty minutes later, he confirmed my appointment with his doctor for 9:00 a.m. two days from then and gave me all contact numbers, directions, etc. I thanked him emphatically and told him that I would keep him informed of all progress in Bangkok.

My wife arrived in Doha from Damascus that next afternoon, and we had a nice dinner to discuss in detail what had transpired over the past two weeks. We also discussed that this was going to be our second trip to Thailand as in 1996, we had a family trip to Bangkok and we visited the entire North of Thailand. I still remembered that when we booked that trip's itinerary, our agent was surprised that we hadn't selected the famous Thai beach areas in the south of the country. I told him: "You know we have some great beaches in Jeddah so why should I see the same beautiful beaches in Thailand?" Plus, I felt it would be an immense 'educational experience' for my two sons to visit the renowned northern cities of Thailand. That decision turned out to be a very wise choice as we really enjoyed the cities of Chiang Mai, Chiang Saen, and Chiang Rai, and the legendary area called the "Golden Triangle" and finally the well-known Seven Hillside Tribes of Thailand. It was a very enlightening experience, not just for our sons, but for my wife and me as well. And what topped it off was our friends who had selected Phuket and the beach areas of the south had five days of rain! Not one drop of rain fell during our sojourn in the north.

The next day, Salma and I had a morning departure on Qatar Airways to Bangkok, and the flight took only seven hours as we arrived in Bangkok late afternoon or early evening. The Thai visa and arrival procedures were very fast and proficient and as we later found out everything in Thailand works professionally and flawlessly. When we had completed our passport control, I looked for the luggage area and I thought I saw Sheikh Ahmed there. I looked again and that person was gone. I did not give it another thought as I knew that Sheikh Ahmed was still in Abu Dhabi on business. The hotel's driver and car were waiting for us and we found ourselves back in Bangkok not as a tourist this time but on a far more serious mission or undertaking.

The JW Marriott Hotel was very nice, and Salma and I settled into our room and enjoyed a light dinner in the hotel's special Executive Lounge. I set the alarm for 7:00 a.m. so we would not be rushed. That next morning, while we were preparing, the phone rang at 8:00 a.m. The voice at the other end of the phone shouted: "Webber, where are you?" I said, "Who is this?" And he said: "This is Ahmed, where are you?" "Ahmed what are you doing in Bangkok and Ahmed, my appointment is not until 9:00!" "No, come now as the doctor is already in his office." "OK, we will leave the hotel shortly…" It took only ten or fifteen minutes to reach the Bumrungrad Hospital from our hotel. When we arrived in front of the hospital, we both thought it was a mistake as it looked like a shopping mall or a five-star hotel, so we had to ask where the hospital was. Right here, sir.

As when we entered, we still thought that this could not be a hospital as it resembled a hotel. We were immediately greeted by a friendly girl who whisked us off to the VIP desk. A few seconds at the desk to confirm that I was Thomas L. Webber, and then immediately, she escorted us to the doctor's office a couple of floors above the entrance. I asked her on the way: "Are you sure this is Bumrungrad Hospital?" She asked, "Why?" I said as we just passed a food court and I have never been inside a hospital with a food court. In addition, there were no 'typical hospital odors' associated with this hospital. We got to the doctor's floor and this area had only doctors' offices. To our astonishment, sitting by the doctor's office door was none other than Sheikh Ahmed. "What are you doing here, Sheikh Ahmed?" He ignored that question and quickly opened the doctor's door and said: "I want to introduce you to my doctor?" Introductions were made and then Sheikh Ahmed excused himself and said: "Webber, I will wait for you outside."

I felt that the doctor knew that Salma and I were still in a state of shock and bewilderment over the appearance of Sheikh Ahmed, so he explained that Mr. Ahmed was a very good friend and also a recent patient of his. I then proceeded to take out all my reports and test results, and the doctor quickly said: "They will not be needed as all your documents had already been scanned into the hospital's patient computer system!" OK…I also discovered that during my entire stay and my multiple visits to the Bumrungrad Hospital, I had received only one small slip of paper and that was my Visa Card's tiny paper receipt given to me on my departure. This hospital was truly: "Paperless", everything, and I mean everything, was forwarded by the hospital's internet service.

What I also discovered and admired was that there was no mention of the cost of this or that…The doctor knew that I had a major prostate problem, so he took care of that important issue first and then decided on the various pathways to resolve the high PSA level. He had arranged for many tests that morning and at each testing station, there was no waiting or delays. Bumrungrad American Hospital was completely and totally a very organized and structured hospital. To this day, I have never been to a hospital-like Bumrungrad Hospital. Some have come close, but no hospital has equaled the systematized approach we discovered at the Bumrungrad Hospital. After the initial set of tests that morning, I returned to the doctor's office and he told me that I should come back at 4:00 p.m. that same afternoon as he will have the majority of the test results. As we were leaving his office, Ahmed was waiting outside the door and only then I realized that I had never introduced Salma to Sheikh Ahmed. I suggested that we have lunch, but Sheikh Ahmed apologized as he had to see another doctor and to complete some important work at the hospital.

Salma and I discovered a great 'local restaurant' directly across from our JW Marriott Hotel. To this day, I can still remember the fantastic taste of those glass noodles and fresh shrimp.

We ate there often for the remainder of our stay in Bangkok… This lunch gave Salma and me a chance to catch up on all the events that led us to Thailand and to my friendship with Sheikh Ahmed. From

Glass Noodles and Fresh Shrimp

Jeddah, where initially I discovered my 'challenge' to Doha with my encounter with Sheikh Ahmed and his family and now Bangkok with this discovery of such an innovative hospital

We returned to the hospital at precisely 4:00 p.m. and once again, found Sheikh Ahmed waiting for us outside the doctor's door. We went inside and found the test results. They were not very encouraging as they found multiple small tumors within the prostate; there was extreme swelling of the prostate itself, and my PSA registered at 48.0 ng/mL. Then the doctor gave us certain statistics; the first being that a man of my age with a PSA of over 10 ng/mL there is a 50 to 60% chance that it is cancerous. Second, since they discovered my prostate was greatly enlarged, this may have been one of the contributing factors for such a high PSA. He then asked if I wanted a biopsy and he explained in great detail about this painful and upsetting procedure. I knew that I wanted to find out if I had cancer or not, and by doing nothing, we were never going to know the truth. So I agreed…The doctor suggested that we do the prostate biopsy operation two days from then at 8:00 a.m. In that way, the lab could determine if these small tumor-like growths were malignant or benign. I said we will see you in two days' time.

We then left the doctor's office, and still outside waiting for us was Sheikh Ahmed! He suggested that he takes us both out to dinner that evening and then to enjoy some great jazz music at a local hotel. He said:

"This way, we can get our minds off the subject even for a short period of time."

When Salma and I returned to the hotel, we both felt it may be best to bring our two sons to Bangkok just to be on the safe side. We called them, and they both agreed. I went to the travel agency and arranged for Omar to fly in from Jeddah to Doha and Ramsey to fly from Abu Dhabi to Doha so they can both fly together to Bangkok on the same Qatar Airways flight and all within the next two days.

It was a really nice dinner with Sheikh Ahmed, as it was my first opportunity to sit with him without his family. We found that he was really interesting, quite intelligent, and had a nice positive view of life. After dinner, we went to the Sheraton Lounge as that night they were playing great jazz music. When we entered the lounge, it appeared that everyone knew Ahmed. There were so many greetings that it took us almost ten minutes to make it to 'his special table'. He had also invited the doctor, which gave me a different perspective of his personality and a few other friends were at our table. All-in-all it was a very enjoyable evening and gave me a greater insight into this special friend Sheikh Ahmed.

The next day there were no appointments at the hospital, so Salma and I set off to be a: "typical tourist." We decided to take a half-day: "Bangkok Canal Tour," as we hadn't taken that tour on our first visit to Bangkok, some eleven years earlier. The tour was very interesting as we could see many areas normally not seen on an average tour. There were so many small canals that we traveled upon with only residential homes on these canals. Small canals led to larger canals and all were used years earlier as basic modes of transport. We now discovered and knew why Bangkok, in the nineteenth century, was called: "The Venice of the East."

Well, the day arrived for the prostate biopsy procedure, and to be honest, I was very nervous inside but carried a strong façade and concealed my worries behind a smile. I did not want my wife or sons to worry about me. I found that I was anxious for two completely different reasons: firstly and obvious reason: I may have cancer, and that was my biggest worry by far and secondly, I knew that the biopsy procedure was quite painful and quite uncomfortable. First, cancer was a big worry and during the two days prior to the operation, I was thinking and trying to remember if anyone in my immediate family had cancer or had ever died from cancer. I could not remember anyone of my relatives dying from any type of cancer. This was a true relief, but still, I could be number one.

The second reason for my worry was the thought of the intense pain and that I knew it was going to be real. I have always had a very low threshold for pain, especially for this particular procedure, as I knew they would shoot these big thick needles into you prostrate from your rectum to extract the suspected tissue. The night before, I was reading on a website that some 75% of all primary prostate biopsies are all negative and again, over 90% do not find cancer with the first attempt. So why should I subject my body to this severe pain if it has such a low discovery rate? I came very close to calling the doctor to cancel this procedure.

So the night before the operation, I opted to call Sheikh Ahmed for his opinion, and his reply was very simple: "Webber, have it done so you will have peace-of-mind for the future." He was right, again... So we arrived at the hospital a half-hour ahead of schedule as there were some preparatory procedures, etc. to complete before the pain would commence. The operation took less than half an hour as all they were doing were sending these large probes into the areas of the suspected prostate tumors. Ugh...The pain was excruciating as each large metal needle felt like it was going through my entire body. "When will they stop?" A minute after these thoughts, the doctor said: "We have finished"...This operational procedure was the most painful than anything I had ever felt or experienced in my entire life.

My recovery time was short, and I left the hospital by mid-afternoon. Now our biggest challenge was waiting for the hospital to inform us of their biopsy results and diagnoses. The doctor said it would take two days.

Our two sons arrived that early evening, and we all had dinner at the hotels New York Steakhouse. So the next day while waiting for the final test results, our boys had the opportunity to meet Sheikh Ahmed and we went out again as: "Typical American Tourist." This time to the famous Jatujak Market, where one can buy any kind of exotic animals and see a real live 'Cock Fight' just around the corner.

Monday came faster than I had anticipated, and my doctor's appointment was set for 9:00 a.m. As soon as I saw the doctor's face, I knew the results were negative as I now believed he would make a horrible poker player. I was right; the biopsy results were all negative. So there was an immediate sense of relief and at the same time, a strong sense of concern. What caused my PSA to be so elevated? Did I really have prostate cancer and simply the biopsy missed the tumors, as I had read in so many reports? Why was my prostate so enlarged? What do we do now? No one, including my doctor, seemed to have answers to these concerns…

What he said next has stayed in my memory since then: Mr. Webber, you have three options and the decision will be up to you and you only. Option one: We can do nothing and keep your prostate gland in place… all you must do is to take daily prostate pills to control the PSA and do a follow-up exam every six months. Option two: We can remove the outer layer of the prostate as that is where cancer usually spreads from and we must hope that it is completely removed or there could be some health-related repercussions Or Option three: surgically remove the entire prostate, which is called a 'radical prostatectomy'. This option has many side-effects. As you see, each has its benefits and detriments…Mr. Webber, the decision is yours and yours alone to make. We discussed all three options in greater detail, the other pros and cons, which countries recommend each procedure, the hazards of the operations, etc. Within ten minutes, I had made up my mind…"Doctor, let's get rid of the entire thing. Let's schedule this operation."

Outside the doctor's office was again Sheikh Ahmed waiting…I sat next to him and told him of my decision. He was very happy with my decision as that was exactly the same decision he had made one year earlier.

So now one last step to what I thought was going to be: 'eternal happiness' ...the Radical Prostatectomy. I was well prepared and ready for the operation. It went very well even though it lasted for over four hours; the doctors said that was because my prostate was so enlarged. I remember I was just waking up from the anesthesia when they were wheeling me back into my room. Once I was transferred to my bed, I tried to relax, but I felt severe pain.

To my surprise, my first visitor was...Sheikh Ahmed. He was there before my wife, my two sons, or even the doctor. He was sympathetic to my pain and immediately called the nurse and virtually "ordered" her to give me some specific pain killers.

I stayed in the hospital for three days as there were a few 'complications' that followed, all not too serious. The very good news I received while recuperating was that they did a second biopsy on the removed prostates tumors, and indeed, they were completely benign. What a relief not just for me but for my entire family. Once I was discharged, I was driven back to the JW Marriott and remained there for another ten to fifteen days for recovery and recuperation.

I had suggested that my wife and sons enjoy Thailand and take some private and exclusive tours to see the immediate area around Bangkok. They enjoyed Pattaya on Koh Larn Island, and they swam and even enjoyed a Tiger Farm and a famous Zoo.

They both flew back to the Middle East with confidence in my recovery and the positive discovery that their dad did not have cancer. In addition, they both had a nice holiday away from work.

In total, we had spent 22 days at the JW Marriott for this entire prostrate narrative. Sheikh Ahmed came to visit me twice while I was at the Marriott, and then, one day, he finally announced that he needed to get back to Doha for some urgent business.

Unfortunately, I had seen Sheikh Ahmed only once since his last visit to my hotel. The last time I saw him in Doha, he was looking worse and sicker, yet he never complained of his intense pain and suffering. You see, Sheikh Ahmed had abdominal cancer and the cancer was eating away at all of his internal organs. I didn't realize that, as he never talked about it. I later learned that even during my visit to Bumrungrad American Hospital, he was seeing his cancer specialist also at Bumrungrad. I don't believe his friends ever knew the severity of his illness or the amount of pain he must have been suffering.

"The tender friendships one gives up, on parting, leave their bite on the heart, but also a curious feeling of a treasure somewhere buried." These were the beautiful words of the French aviator and writer: Antoine de Saint-Exupéry

To me, I will always remember his voice addressing me as: "Webber…" and his extreme kindness and generosity towards me. So this: "True Friend" was only in my life for a very, very short period of time, but he has left a long-lasting impression, not just on me, but on my wife and two sons. I still miss him immensely.

Chapter Eighteen

Final Chapter: My Epitaph

I have often thought of what people will think of me when I die, as well as what they would say about my life upon my death. I feel that Ernest Hemingway's famous saying sums up my views on my life and my adventures in life as follows: *"Every man's life ends the same way. It is only the details of how he lived and how he died that distinguish one man from another."*

I have always felt the following Lewis Howe's saying reflects my views on life exactly: *"Success in Life is not measured by the Amount of Money one makes, but by the Number of Lives you have touched."*

I feel that now after you have completed my book, you will agree that my life has been composed of many adventures, both positive as well as negative.